LIBREX —

WITHDRAWN

Addiction at Work

Addiction at Work

Tackling Drug Use and Misuse in the Workplace

Edited by
HAMID GHODSE

GOWER

Published by
Gower Publishing Limited
Gower House
Croft Road
Aldershot
Hants GU11 3HR
England

Gower Publishing Company
Suite 420
101 Cherry Street
Burlington,
VT 05401-4405
USA

Hamid Ghodse has asserted his right under the Copyright, Designs and Patents Act 1988 to be identified as the editor of this work.

British Library Cataloguing in Publication Data
Ghodse, Hamid
    Addiction at work: tackling drug use and misuse in the
    workplace
    1. Drugs and employment
    I. Title
    658.3'822

    ISBN 0 566 08619 0

Library of Congress Cataloging-in-Publication Data
Addiction at work: tackling drug use and misuse in the workplace / [edited] by Hamid Ghodse.
        p. cm.
    Includes index.
    ISBN: 0-566-08619-0
    1. Drugs and employment. I. Ghodse, Hamid.
    HF5549.5.D7A33 2004
    658.3'822--dc22

                                                                    2004023996

Typeset by Bournemouth Colour Press, Parktone, Poole, Dorset.
Printed and bound in Great Britain by TJ International Ltd, Padstow, Cornwall.

Contents

List of Figures

List of Tables

Foreword

Substance misuse affects all classes of society in all parts of the world, and those involved do not conform to any stereotype. Its extent is difficult to measure with any degree of accuracy, but there is no doubt that it is substantial and has grown dramatically in the last few decades. It is a complex, multifaceted and pervasive problem that destroys innumerable individual lives and undermines the health and safety of the community. The international response in recent years has focussed on demand-reduction activities, especially those aimed at the prevention of substance misuse.

In the workplace, problems related to drugs and alcohol may be manifested by the deterioration of workers' health, absenteeism, increased accident rates and, of course, lowered productivity. Their prevention is therefore a high priority for employers as well as being important for employees. Moreover the workplace offers unique opportunities for such interventions because individuals spend so much time there.

In the market economy of today, all firms must utilize all their human resources as effectively as possible if they are to remain competitive. Substance misuse undermines competitiveness and taking action against it can therefore be seen as sound business practice. Logically, such actions should be framed as a business case focusing on the health and safety of the employees, the work environment and productivity.

Accurate information and a better understanding of the problem are essential pre-requisites for making progress in this complex area. *Addiction at Work* contains information from many sources and offers a detailed analysis of the issues related to substance abuse in the workplace. It is hoped that it will help employers establish policies to minimize substance abuse and will encourage employees with substance abuse problems to come forward for treatment.

The authors are all experts in their respective fields and bring their scholarship to bear on practical measures to tackle substance misuse. The book provides evidence and experience-based knowledge on many aspects of the problem. I am confident that it will be of immense value to chief executives, directors of human resources, policy makers, employers and employees. Their increased knowledge of the problem and confidence in dealing with it will ensure that employees who are substance misusers will receive more help and support than formerly. This will benefit not just business but the whole community.

Baroness Cumberlege

Baroness Cumberlege was Parliamentary Under-Secretary of State for Health between 1992 and 1997, and a member of the NHS Policy Boards between 1989 and 1997. She is the Chair of Council of St. George's Hospital Medical School and also Chair of the International Centre for Drug Policy's Advisory Board.

Preface

Drug abuse and a whole range of associated problems have increased dramatically over the last 30 years and, as a significant number of drug abusers are in employment, the workplace has not escaped the consequences of these increases. However, until now, it has not been possible to access an authoritative source of information on these issues because a comprehensive text has not been available. This book attempts to fill that gap, bringing together the best contemporary thinking on all aspects of the field.

It has three parts, the first of which puts the subject of misuse into context, explaining for example that this problem includes the use of socially acceptable drugs, such as alcohol, as well as illicit substances, and identifying the risks and side effects of legitimately prescribed psychoactive substances. Clear definitions are provided of commonly used terms and the extent and nature of substance abuse is explored, both generally and in the workplace. The effects of different drugs are described including their potential impact on attendance at work, performance, accident rates and so on. Conversely, the ways in which different organisational cultures encourage, discourage or conceal substance misuse are also examined.

The second part is about companies' drug policies, explaining the need for a policy and the legal aspects of drug abuse at work, including employers' responsibilities. There is a detailed explanation of what should be covered by such a policy and how to implement it, including advice on how to communicate the policy to employees and other stakeholders and how to enforce it via employees' contracts.

The final part focuses on the tools that are available for managing substance abuse in the workplace including educational programmes, drug screening and specialised interventions. The ethical issues associated with testing for drugs and screening are examined, employee assistance programmes are described and the important points of employment law in relation to substance abuse are elucidated.

The appendices include examples of established policies and programmes.

As editor, I will be satisfied if managers across a wide range of organisations, public and private, large and small, can turn to this book as a useful and practical resource when they are faced with problems related to substance abuse that they don't know how to handle. It would be very gratifying if it stimulated an interest in this important area so that, instead of avoiding some of these admittedly complex issues and reacting only when they become unavoidable, managers feel sufficiently competent and confident that they can tackle them comprehensively within their organisations.

I would like to take this opportunity to record my gratitude to the publisher for their support in the preparation of this book and particularly to Jonathan Norman for his insight into the problems of substance misuse in the workplace; he provided helpful support throughout and managed the details of production with great care. I would also like to thank Marlene Nolan and Norma White who skilfully coordinated inputs from all contributors. Finally, I must emphasise that the authors of individual chapters, all well known and well respected in their field, have generously shared their knowledge and made it accessible to a wide audience. I am deeply grateful to them for their authoritative contributions.

HAMID GHODSE
EDITOR

List of Contributors

Jill Bachman, MSN, RN, CEAP, is the Outreach Manager at Peer Assistance Services, Inc. Jill works to raise awareness about substance abuse prevention, and intervention, especially as it affects health care workers in Colorado. Jill is responsible for the quarterly agency newsletter, the websites, and other marketing media. Jill provides EAP services to employee and organizational clients, develops resource materials and offers educational programs about workplace wellness. Jill is a member of the Employee Assistance Professionals Association (EAPA), and the International Nurses Society on Addictions (IntNSA). Jill is a Certified Trainer of TEAM Awareness, a SAMHSA (US Substance Abuse and Mental Health Services Administration) approved, evidence-based model workplace prevention program. Jill can be contacted via e-mail at: jbachman@peerassist.org.

Alexander Baldacchino is Clinical Senior Lecturer in the Psychiatry of Addictive Behaviour at Ninewells Hospital Medical School, Dundee, responsible for initiating clinically oriented addiction-related research throughout Scotland, management of research grants and development of undergraduate/postgraduate modules/lectures in addictions to medical students, nurses and psychiatric trainees. He is founding member and director of the Centre for Addiction Research & Education Scotland (CARES) – www.dundee.ac.uk/psychiatry/res_addictions/research_addictions.htm. He has instigated several research ideas and supported successful grants in the field of addiction (biological or clinically oriented) in the United Kingdom and Europe.

In addiction to this Dr Baldacchino is Consultant Psychiatrist in Addictions with Fife NHS Addiction Services and has been responsible for the strategic development of a rapidly expanding new service providing a Fife-wide equitable service for people with drug and alcohol dependence. This includes involvement in the clinical governance and effectiveness drive to provide the necessary clinical and educational support to all general practitioners, community pharmacists and addiction/mental health specialists in the field of addiction as well as the ability to work in partnership with other disciplines and agencies (voluntary and statutory). Dr Baldacchino has also been instrumental in setting up the East Central Scotland Managed Care Network in Addictions involving services from Fife, Forth Valley and Tayside. As an executive member of the Fife Drugs and Alcohol Team he is actively involved in monitoring and responding to NHS-related issues.

Joannah Caborn is an expert on psychosocial issues at the International Labour Office in Geneva, Switzerland. She coordinates and implements SafeWork's SOLVE training programme addressing interrelated psychosocial problems at work using an integrated policy and action approach. She is also responsible for research capacity, material development and web-based outreach.

William Cheng LLM MD FRCP FFOM is Honorary Consultant in Occupational Medicine at Medway Hospital, Gillingham, Kent.

John Christofides MSc, Dip. CB, MRSC, CChem. has worked in the NHS since 1976. He is Principal Biochemist at the Regional Toxicology and Endocrinology Laboratory at West Park, Epsom. His particular areas of interest include drugs of abuse, therapeutic drugs, the porphyrias, biogenic amines, vitamins and fatty acids. He has developed new assays using chromatographic or immunoassay techniques and introduced them into the laboratory repertoire in order to facilitate and expand services to clinicians. Some of the methods have been published as original techniques, others have been developed and adapted for collaborative publications with clinical colleagues. He lectures to various groups including medical undergraduates, clinical staff and students on the MSc in Addictive Behaviour at St George's. John can be contacted via e-mail at: John.christofides@epsom.sthelier.nhs.uk.

Martyn Egerton BSc MCB FRCPath is Consultant Biochemist at Epsom and St Helier University Hospitals NHS Trust. He has long standing clinical and research interests in toxicology, steroids, immunoassays, mass spectrometry, and all forms of chromatography. He has regular commitments in postgraduate teaching on analysis of drugs of abuse, the use for near patient tests to detect drugs and the role of drug analysis in the context of addiction services.

Michael Forbes embarked on a varied career which took him to many parts of the globe, working in both clinical and latterly business settings, after qualifying from Cambridge University and Guys Hospital in London. His interest in stress, and drugs and alcohol, was sparked off when he was working for Shell in the offshore oil industry in the North Sea. This was soon after the Piper Alpha tragedy and when the spin-off from the Exxon Valdez was concentrating the minds of those in HSE management. He gained considerable experience in the management of drugs and alcohol programmes both in the UK and abroad, where differing cultural and legal issues continue to be a real challenge. Michael can be contacted via e-mail at: drmichael.forbes@shell.com.

Raj Gakhal is the Programme Manager who worked on the successful implementation of an alcohol and drug testing policy for British Airways. This included working with the trade unions on the content of the policy, in areas such as support and referral, training and processes to help individuals return to normal full-time working. He has worked in the HR arena for over 14 years providing advice on specialist and generalist policy including drugs and alcohol testing.

Susanna Galea, MD, MRCPsych, MSc (Addictive Behaviour), Dip. (Forensic Mental Health), is a Clinical Lecturer and Specialist registrar in Addictive Behaviour at St. George's Hospital Medical School. Susanna started her career in Malta and moved to the UK in 1995 to initiate her training in psychiatry. Susanna is currently in her second year of training as a Specialist Registrar and is pursuing an academic career. She is involved in research activities at St. George's Hospital Medical School, with her main research interests being comorbidity and use of substances in special populations.

Hamid Ghodse CBE, MD, PhD, DSc, DPM, FFPH, FRCP, FRCPE, FRCPsych, Professor of Psychiatry and International Drug Policy, University of London, has worked for more than 30 years in the field of addictions, advancing clinical and academic understanding and policy, and working towards national and international drug control. His contribution to various aspects of university, Royal Colleges, National Health Service and voluntary agencies has been exemplary and for this he was awarded the CBE. His definitive textbook on addiction, *Drugs and Addictive Behaviour: A guide to treatment*, is in its third edition, as is his textbook on legal aspects of drugs and criminal justice, *Misuse of Drugs*. His book on the rational use of controlled drugs has been translated into eight languages. He is Editor of *Substance Misuse Bulletin, International Journal of Psychiatry* and editorial board member of *Addiction*, the International Journal of Social Psychiatry, and other journals. He is a member of the Expert Advisory Panel of WHO on Drug Abuse. He has been President of the International Narcotics Board: 1993–94, 1997–98, 2000–01, and 2004–present.

Christine Godfrey is a Professor of Health Economics at the Department of Health Sciences and Centre for Health Economics at the University of York. She has been researching into the economics of alcohol, tobacco and illicit drugs at the University of York since 1984. She is a past president of the Society for Study of Addiction and is currently a member of the WHO Expert Committee on Drug Dependence, Tobacco Advisory Group of the Royal College of Physicians and the Scientific Committee on Tobacco and Health at the Department of Health. Current research includes work into economic determinants of behaviour, the social costs of different substances and the cost effectiveness of interventions. Further details can be found at www.york.ac.uk/healthsciences/gsp/staff/christine.htm. Christine can be contacted via e-mail at: cg2@york.ac.uk.

David Gold PhD MOEd BA is the Senior Adviser, Psychosocial Problems, for the SafeWork Programme of the International Labour Office (ILO) (a specialized agency of the United Nations). Based on determined educational and training needs, Dr Gold develops, implements and evaluates training and educational programs in occupational safety, occupational health and psychosocial factors. The focus of his work is to educate a cadre of national facilitators and instructors to be able carry out training at a national level. To date he has worked in many countries in Asia, Africa, the Caribbean and Europe. As the ILO is a fully tripartite organization, Dr Gold continually works with governments, employers' and workers' organizations. He has also done considerable work in improving occupational safety and health in small- and medium-sized enterprises in developing countries.

Dr Gold is the co-author of the *ILO Training Manual on Safety and Health in the Use of Chemicals at Work* and the *ILO's Managing Emerging Health Related Problems at Work*. He authored the *Fire Brigade Training Manual* for the National Fire Protection Association. He is a professional member of the American Society of Safety Engineers and the International Commission on Occupational Health.

John Harrison BSc. MB.ChB. MD. FRCP FRCP(Edin) FFOM, is a consultant in occupational medicine and clinical director for occupational health for Hammersmith Hospitals NHS Trust. He joined the Trust in September 2003, having been Senior Lecturer in Occupational Medicine at the University of Newcastle upon Tyne. He is Academic Dean in the Faculty of Occupational Medicine, part of the Royal College of Physicians of London and Chairman of EASOM (European Association of Schools of Occupational Medicine).

His research interests involve the healthcare industry and rehabilitation. He is involved in a large multicentre pilot to evaluate the role of healthcare and workplace interventions in job retention and rehabilitation back to work and in a pilot study assessing 'work ability' in a healthcare population. John is co-editor of the newly published book *Atlas of Occupational Health and Disease* (Arnold Health Sciences, 2004).

John Henry FRCP FFAEM is Professor of Accident and Emergency Medicine at Imperial College, London.

Ian Hindmarch is Professor of Human Psychopharmacology and Head of the HPRU Medical Research Centre in the University of Surrey. His research for over more than 30 years has concentrated on defining the psychopharmacological profile of activity of psychoactive drugs, both licit and illicit. He developed the concept of 'behavioural toxicity' as a measure of the extent to which any particular drug would not only raise the user's predisposition to cognitive failure at home, on the road or at work, but also produce counter-therapeutic effects which would increase non-compliance via under- or over-dosing. Other things being equal (comparable clinical efficacy of available medications, concomitant medication, co-existing clinical conditions, known patient allergies and so on), these behavioural toxicity indices provide useful indicators of the 'risk' associated with the use of a particular drug in performing the activities of everyday living, particularly in those patients at work where the compromise of psychological function may place themselves or others at increased risk of accident. Ian can be contacted via e-mail at: i.hindmarch@surrey.ac.uk.

Gillian Howard is an employment lawyer, specialising in employment law, personal injury, medical negligence and defamation. She acts for both corporate and individual clients and has over 20 retained corporate clients. She has acted for Nomura in several high profile sex discrimination claims and most recently against Carina Coleman, successfully defending the Bank and its Chief Executive, Lansdowne Capital and Alan Dargan from a sex discrimination and breach of contract claim. She has recently settled two major sex discrimination claims in the City acting for Ann Iveson against BNP Paribas and Elizabeth Weston against Merrill Lynch. She has a wide-ranging practice in both contentious and non-contentious work. She represents clients at tribunals and in the High Court as well as advising and drafting on company policies and procedures.

Gillian is the author of many books and articles, including *Drafting Contracts of Employment* (The Law Society, 2004); *Vetting and Monitoring Employees at Work* (Gower, forthcoming), and contributing to four editions of *Fitness for Work – Medical Aspects* published by Oxford University Press.

She is an Honorary Fellow of the Faculty of Occupational Medicine, Royal College of Physicians, Lay Observer on the Board of the Faculty of Pharmaceutical Medicine, an Honorary Senior Lecturer at the Institute of Occupational Medicine at the University of Birmingham and is on the editorial board of Butterworth's *Occupational Health Review*.

Graham Lucas MB FRCP FRCPsych FFOM RCP D(Obst) RCOG. Current appointments include Consultant Psychiatrist to the Foreign and Commonwealth Office; Visiting Professor Postgraduate Medical School, University of Surrey; Health Supervisor to the General Medical Council; Emeritus Consultant Psychiatrist, Maudsley Hospital; Consultant in Occupational Mental Health to Priory Healthcare Services; Second Opinion Appointed Doctor to the Mental Health Act Commission, and a member of the International Association of Physicians for the Overseas Services.

He was formerly Secretary, Inter-Departmental Advisory Committee on Drug Dependence, Consultant Psychiatrist at King's College and Maudsley Hospitals and to the Civil Aviation Authority; Adviser in Mental Health to the Health and Safety Executive; Chair of HSE Working Parties on mental health and drug abuse at work; a member of the Faculty of Occupational Medicine Working Party on testing for drugs of abuse in the workplace; Chief Consultant Psychiatrist to the Ex-Services Mental Welfare Society/Combat Stress; Medical Member of the Appeals Service; Mental Health Review Tribunal, Major and Senior Specialist in Psychiatry in the Royal Army Medical Corps.

Special interests include occupational mental health and stress, alcohol and drug abuse, aviation psychiatry, post-traumatic stress disorder, anxiety and depression, and his publications include these subjects.

Elizabeth M. Pace, MSM, RN, CEAP, is the Chief Executive Officer and one of the founders of Peer Assistance Services, Inc. (1984), a non-profit, statewide, peer EAP. Elizabeth is responsible for the administration of prevention, EAP and case management programs focused on substance abuse and related issues. Elizabeth directs Peer Assistance Services, Inc. in providing services to a wide variety of people, including healthcare workers, small businesses throughout Colorado, parolees with substance-use disorders, and at-risk families. Elizabeth is a member of the Employee Assistance Professionals Association (EAPA), the International Nurses Society on Addictions (IntNSA), and the Colorado Nurses' Association (CNA). Elizabeth can be contacted via e-mail at: epace@peerassist.org.

Steve Parrott has worked as a research fellow on the Addiction and Health Promotion Programme at the Centre for Health Economics since 1995. He has a first class degree in Economics from the University of York, and an MSc in Health Economics. Steve's current research interests centre around the economics of addiction. Recent projects have included estimates of the cost of smoking to the NHS and industry, the cost effectiveness of smoking cessation programmes and economic evaluation of alcohol treatment services.

Steve also runs courses in economics for graduates in the Department of Social Policy and Social Work, and teaches in the Department of Health Sciences, the Department of Economics and Related Studies and also lectures on courses with the University of Leeds and University of London. Steve can be contacted via e-mail at: sjp22@york.ac.uk.

Dipti Patel, MRCGP MFOM LLM Dip Trav Med, is Consultant Occupational Health Physician for the British Broadcasting Corporation. She completed her specialist training in occupational medicine at Guy's, King's and St Thomas' School of Medicine and Dentistry in 2002, and has been working as a consultant occupational physician at the BBC for just over two years. Prior to her specialist training, she was a medical adviser to the Foreign and Commonwealth Office.

In addition to providing occupational health support to the BBC, she is responsible for managing the medical support to BBC staff working abroad. Particular work interests include medical law, travel medicine and teaching. Dipti teaches on occupational medicine courses at both Manchester and Kent University, and is one of the co-editors of the *ABC of Occupational and Environmental Medicine* which was published in September 2003.

Fabrizio Schifano is Senior Lecturer and Consultant Psychiatrist in the Department of Mental Health – Addictive Behaviour at St George's Hospital Medical School, University of London.

Andy Siegle, LPC, CRC, CAC II is the Workplace Programs Specialist at Peer Assistance Services,

Inc. Andy is responsible for organizing and implementing workplace prevention training programs, providing traditional EAP services to individual clients as well as their respective organizations. Andy has worked in the mental health services field, providing oversight of adults with chronic mental illness at a residential facility, case management and therapeutic counseling services. Andy is a member of Employee Assistance Professionals Association (EAPA), the Professional Association of Rehabilitation Counselors (PARC), and the Association for Addiction Professionals (NAADAC). Andy is a Certified Trainer of TEAM Awareness, a SAMHSA (US Substance Abuse and Mental Health Services Administration) approved, evidence-based model workplace prevention program. Andy can be contacted via e-mail at asiegle@peerassist.org.

David Snashall is Senior Lecturer in Occupational Medicine, Guy's Kings and St Thomas' School of Medicine and Head of Occupational Health Services, Guy's and St Thomas' NHS Foundation Trust. He has also held posts as Chief Medical Adviser, Health and Safety Executive (HSE) and Chief Medical Adviser, Foreign and Commonwealth Office. From 2005 he is President of the Faculty of Occupational Medicine of the Royal College of Physicians.

He has worked as an occupational physician for 27 years in the UK and abroad, with particular interests in the health of construction workers, expatriates and those working in the health care sector. He trained in medicine at Edinburgh University Medical School and in occupational medicine at the London School of Hygiene and Tropical Medicine. He also holds a medical law degree from the University of Wales.

David remains a consultant adviser to the HSE, is a member of the International Commission on Occupational Health, and an associate of the General Medical Council of the United Kingdom, acting as a fitness to practise panellist. He is a co-author, with Dipti Patel, of *ABC of Occupational and Environmental Medicine*.

Ian Stone is an adviser to the Chief Medical Officer (England) and HR Adviser to the National Clinical Assessment Authority – a NHS organisation focussed on supporting NHS organisations and clinicians in situations where there are serious professional concerns. He has worked in HR in the NHS for over 30 years and for most of that time as an HR Director of organisations of more than 6000 staff. He has also been national President of the NHS HR association (AHHRM) and Chairman of NHSP, an internal HR consultancy for the NHS. He has been an external examiner for HR postgraduate studies at the University of the West of England from 2001–2004. He is a corporate member of IPD and holds a masters degree in industrial relations as well as teaching qualifications. He is a frequent lecturer and tutor at national conferences.

Understanding the Problem

1 Drugs and Alcohol in the Workplace

Hamid Ghodse

Introduction

The Political Declaration adopted at the Special Session of the United Nations General Assembly in June 1998 called upon business and union leadership among others to actively promote a society free of drugs[1]. The inclusion of these social partners in this call to action was significant because it tacitly acknowledged that, outside the family, work is the most significant social system in most people's lives and that more focused efforts on prevention in special populations or the workplace are more effective than general prevention campaigns. It also reflected recognition of the growing societal importance of private firms and industry as well as public service employers in this endeavour.

Such programmes are particularly important because a significant number of people who use drugs and misuse alcohol are in employment and the workplace therefore provides opportunities for detection of substance misuse and the provision of help. There is also a shared interest in providing that help: employers and industry want productivity, growth and usually profits for their shareholders; workers want job security and opportunities for advancement; and the public want good products, adequate and competent services and value. All of these are threatened by substance misuse in the workplace, particularly if it is taking place on a significant scale.

Although it is difficult to estimate the scale of substance abuse with any degree of accuracy, it is generally recognised that in the twenty-first century it represents a global challenge, affecting human societies everywhere. It destroys the lives of young people and damages their families and communities. Traditional drug-related problems have been compounded by AIDs, hepatitis and other communicable diseases. As about 70 per cent of people with alcohol-related problems and more than 60 per cent of drug users hold some form of employment[2], it is essential that the workplace plays its full role in combating all forms of substance misuse. The point to emphasise here is that the workplace mirrors the surrounding community very closely and that just as no country is immune to the substance-misuse problem, no workplace is immune either.

History

The use of alcohol in the workplace is not a new phenomenon and until comparatively recently was often not perceived as a problem. Indeed, some employers positively encouraged its use in a way that now seems extraordinary. For example, during the seventeenth century, the Royal Navy introduced the rum ration by which the sailors were given a pint of rum a day with a ration of beer and a double ration of rum before battle[3, 4] and, in the United States, a 1790 statute authorised every soldier to be given a daily ration of a quarter pint of rum whisky or brandy[5, 6].

Outside the armed forces, the harsh conditions associated with the introduction of industrialisation drove many workers to take refuge in the consumption of alcohol and even of drugs, with nineteenth-century labourers in London fortifying themselves with stout beer to gain their strength whilst their Spanish counterparts had a glass of aguardiente in the morning[4, 7]. A recognised perk for workers in distilleries was to receive daily rations of the product that they were making and it is interesting to note that in the brewery workers' union of Germany in 1886, part of their demands for better living and working conditions included the allocation of free beer[4]. Indeed, in parts of Germany beer consumption by workers on the job has long been guarded[6].

On a more sinister note, in South Africa, the practice of wine in return for labour, the so-called 'dope' system created marginalised alcohol-dependent farm labourers and became a symbol of oppression such that the International Labour Organisation (ILO) introduced a ruling forbidding the payment of wages in the form of liquor of high-alcohol content[4, 8, 9].

Gradually however, in different places and at different times, there was a definite shift in attitude away from the use of alcohol in the workplace. For example in the nineteenth century farmers in the United States were distressed by the manner in which excessive drinking by employees impaired their work performance and this concern was the driving force behind the emergence of the Temperance Movement[6, 10]. Along with a recognition that alcohol and drugs abuse in the workplace may lead to harmful outcomes, came a greater sense of corporate and social responsibility. Employers felt a greater willingness to embrace responsibility which led to the rise of policies and efforts intended to prevent harm with an emphasis not just on alcohol abuse but also on illicit drugs. This evolved not only because of concern about performance, productivity and the cost to the business, but also because of issues of workplace security and public confidence. Such was the scale of this concern that some manufacturers and employers in the United States employed 'welfare secretaries' to shape a new and contented workforce that would not disturb factory life[6]. Out of such small beginnings grew modern approaches to substance misuse in the workplace.

Impact of substance misuse in the workplace

Substance abuse affects the workplace in many different ways although it can be difficult to pinpoint these effects in individual companies primarily because of the covert nature of much of this activity. Although there is more openness about alcohol and perhaps even some boasting about excessive consumption, employees until fairly recently kept any problems related to other substances to themselves, not least because dismissal has been the usual response of the employer.

Such decisions may relate to poor attendance and poor performance because heavy-drinking and drug-using workers are absent from work more often than other workers. In addition, they are more likely to arrive at work late and leave early which can put additional pressures on co-workers who have to carry an increased workload. Both intoxication and hangover (withdrawal) associated with a wide range of substances can lead to poor performance at work. For example, there may be observable mental changes such as slow reaction time, loss of concentration and poor memory, sometimes accompanied by depressive or aggressive mood changes. There may be visible physical effects too such as clumsiness and it is obvious how all of these impairments contribute to increased rates of accidents. In addition, substance misusers are more likely to be involved in disputes and grievances; they change jobs more frequently (and have been fired more often) than non-drug-using colleagues and may sometimes be involved in intimidation and trafficking in illicit drugs in the workplace, and sometimes in violence and theft.

Dealing with such problems takes up valuable managerial time, not least because they are often quite complex, involving a wide range of substances, both licit and illicit, which are taken with varying degrees of control by the individual concerned. Some substance abusers may shift in and out of periods of loss of control with varying degrees of duration and frequency whereas others may be more or less in control for a very long time. Thus performance, attendance and behaviour at work may be unimpaired some of the time while substance misuse is under control, only to be affected when control is lost, making this even more difficult to manage.

It is essential therefore that employers are aware of, and pay sufficient attention to, substance abuse in the workplace and particularly when it is associated with a significantly increased risk, not only to the substance misuser but also to his or her co-workers and the public. In addition, it must be acknowledged that certain working situations and conditions are associated with increased alcohol- and substance-use problems such that it appears that they may have a causal role. These include factors such as shift or night work, travel away from home, working in remote locations, unsatisfactory communications and job stress which in turn may result from unequal rewards, role conflict, excessive workload, job insecurity and so on. Many groups of workers, such as law enforcement and security officers, fire fighters, health service personnel, those working in transport (air, rail or road) and those dealing with hazardous substances can be perceived as at risk from these factors and do indeed suffer from substance-misuse problems. However, no group is immune and social pressure and the easy availability of substances of abuse also lead to some occupations, such as managers, sales staff, lawyers, bartenders and entertainers, being at higher-than-average risk of becoming dependent. Here too, the employer has specific and identifiable responsibilities.

It is clear that substance misusers may damage companies in a variety of different ways, both directly and indirectly. Loss of productivity is of immediate importance but the legal and financial liabilities related to breaches of safety and security in the workplace may also result in great expense to companies particularly in areas such as the maritime industry, energy (nuclear power, oil, gas) and public transport[1].

There can be no doubt that these serious financial implications have had a powerful influence on employers' perception of the need to take action. In recognition of these concerns, the seventy-third session of the International Labour Conference in 1987 adopted a resolution reconfirming the role of the social partners in addressing workplace drug and alcohol problems[2]. In support of this, the ILO has been extensively engaged in promoting policy formulation, improving working conditions, promulgating awareness and creating and supporting supervisory training assistance programmes in many countries around the world. These are particularly important because they have the potential to reach the entire working population from youth to mature adults.

Substance-misuse policies

DISCIPLINARY APPROACH

Employers' policies for substance abuse reflect changes of attitude and knowledge over the last decades. Awareness that alcohol addiction was a treatable disease antedated widespread experience of abuse of other substances and a punitive approach to the latter was all too common with some companies considering disciplinary action including dismissal to be the appropriate response for substance abuse. However, this type of punitive approach, although apparently simple, is associated with a number of serious problems. Dismissal has direct costs to the employer in terms of the loss of valuable workers and the consequent need to recruit and train replacement staff. In addition, if the work environment has been a contributing factor for substance misuse, dismissal does not deal with the underlying problem.

Furthermore, removing a particular individual from the workplace does not solve the problem of substance misuse in the wider community. Indeed, it may make it worse, leading to higher rates of crime and disorder in the surrounding environment which in turn impact upon businesses within that community. Dismissal may also be perceived by other workers as extreme and inappropriate and this encourages them to cover up for their colleagues; this may lead to a far bigger 'underground' problem for the organisation in the long term. Finally it is worth noting that if dismissal is challenged, industrial tribunals are increasingly demanding more constructive responses from employers.

To be fair, negative attitudes in the past were based on the belief that users would spread the habit rapidly among other employees and become involved in illicit trafficking to sustain their own habit. Thus, the response was mostly aimed at protecting other employees and preventing theft and other related social and health consequences of drug abuse.

PREVENTION AND TREATMENT

More recently, there has been a radical change of emphasis with substance-misuse policies focusing more on assistance and help and including preventive activities. In practical terms, it is generally accepted that policies should be non-punitive and constructive with provision for treatment, rehabilitation and follow-up, and maintain due respect for confidentiality.

The drivers for this change include[6, 12, 13]:

- true altruism – concern about the well-being of employees and the promotion of the common good;
- selfish altruism – a belief that in the long term firms will save money by assisting workers;
- pressure to comply with legal regulations and mandates;
- concern about legal liabilities;
- public relations – a desire to promote the corporate image;
- safety and security concerns;
- the wish to improve productivity and profitability.

DEVELOPING A POLICY

The modern approach therefore is that the policy should be set in the context of the need to focus on and improve the health, safety and productivity of all employees. As such it can be put forward as a business case and part of the company's core business development strategy. Writing the policy is, of course, only the first stage and what really counts is its successful implementation, which is much more difficult. To ensure widespread commitment throughout the company at this latter stage, it is essential that there should be a genuine sense of ownership of the policy which can be gained only with the active involvement from the start of a good cross-section of staff and employee representatives. It is fair to say that without this cooperation and ownership by the workforce, substance-abuse policies and programmes are unlikely to succeed. However, these days, many employees have witnessed the impact of substance abuse on their own family and friends, including their children. The emotional impact of this personal experience tends to make them more open to discussion about a substance-abuse policy and more sympathetic than they might have been in the past. Nevertheless, whatever the good will towards its objectives, it must also be emphasised that developing a policy with input from a large and disparate group is a complicated dynamic process which cannot be rushed through. There must therefore be genuine senior management commitment to the process and recognition of the time that it will undoubtedly take to develop the policy and related programmes. There can be no short cuts.

COMPONENTS OF THE POLICY

Any sound policy should include an explanation as to why the company has developed and implemented it, its objectives and the goals, roles and responsibilities of different individuals and departments. A substance-misuse policy should identify at the start the types of substance covered by the policy and the implications of their possession and use. Because of the nature of substance misuse, due attention should be paid to issues of confidentiality, testing for drugs and related therapeutic programmes and counselling services. Before developing specific programmes to help those with substance-abuse problems, a comprehensive needs assessment must be carried out. Managers and supervisors will require awareness training and there should also be education for workers with arrangements for self-assessment of personal substance use. Different treatment options should be set out (for example counselling, detoxification, treatment of associated problems and rehabilitation) and the mechanisms for seeking assistance must all be clear[14, 15].

PREVENTION

Substance abuse is a preventable health problem and preventative measures are an important part of any policy including the need to improve working conditions which have been identified as risk factors. Highlighting prevention in this way emphasises the importance of workers' health, well-being and safety. This is a positive approach which makes the policy much less threatening to all involved parties. In addition, successful prevention benefits the enterprise as a whole because the reduced productivity associated with entrenched substance abuse is avoided.

IMPLEMENTATION

The policy should be circulated to all employees, publicised and periodically reviewed and reaffirmed, with particular emphasis on its constructive rather than punitive approach. The most important factor for its long-term success is continuing and long-term management commitment to sustaining the policy. Dealing with substance abuse is never, and can never be, a quick, 'one-off' activity. However much effort is put in, there is unlikely to be an immediate change; but with continued commitment from the Chief Executive and all strata of management, there will be integration of the policy into all aspects of the company's work that will bear fruit in the longer term in terms of lower rates of substance misuse and all the consequent benefits.

The size of the company may affect which parts of the programmes for substance misusers are available 'in-house' and which are provided externally. However, the fundamental point is that successful programmes require experienced and well-trained counsellors with special expertise in dealing with people with substance-abuse problems. Although these may be available from within the company via the occupational health department, some companies may choose to use facilities provided within the local community – and some employees may prefer the greater anonymity associated with external agencies. It goes without saying that wherever help is provided, total confidentiality must be maintained.

Although small businesses tend to have their own unique characteristics and may appear to be very different from larger organisations, the fundamentals of a substance-misuse policy are the same for both types of organisation. As they are unlikely to have their own support structures such as HR and occupational health departments, they are more likely to link with the resources of the local community with which they usually have close links anyway.

Summary

The workplace is such an important part of life for so many people that it offers unique opportunities for the effective management of substance misuse. If these opportunities are seized and acted on, they can make a major contribution to the management of this serious problem in the wider community. Success in the work arena is dependent on the development of comprehensive and thoughtful policies which have been developed by and with the whole workforce. It requires whole-hearted commitment from senior management so that the organisation develops into one with healthy attitudes towards alcohol and other substances.

References

1.   United Nations, *Special Session of the General Assembly, Guiding Principles of Drug Demand Reduction.* IV. E. 15. New York, 8–10 June, 1998.
2.   International Labour Organisation, *Mobilising Small Business to Prevent Substance Abuse.* Report of the ILO Workshop, 12–16 May 1997 (Oslo). Geneva, ILO, 1998.
3.   Ranft, B., and Hill, J. R. (Eds), *The Oxford Illustrated History of the Royal Navy.* Oxford, Oxford University Press, 2002.
4.   International Centre for Alcohol Policies, *Alcohol and the Workplace.* Washington, DC, ICAP, 2003.

5. Ray, O., *Drugs, Society and Human Behaviour*, 2nd edn. St Louis, Missouri, C. V. Mosby, 1978.
6. Hanson, M., 'Overview on Drugs and Alcohol Testing in the Workplace', *Bulletin on Narcotics*. Vol. XLV, No. 2. pp 3–44, 1993.
7. Gamella, J. F., 'Spain', in: D. B. Heath (ed.), *International Handbook on Alcohol and Culture*. Westport, CT, Greenwood, 1995.
8. La Hausse, P., *Brewers, Beerhalls and Boycotts; a history of liquor in South Africa*. Johannesburg, Raven Press, 1988.
9. International Labour Organisation, *Convention on the Protection of Wages*. Article 4, No. 95, 1949.
10. Metzger, L., *From Denial to Recovery*. San Francisco, Jossey-Bass, 1988.
11. International Labour Organisation, *Drug and Alcohol Prevention Programmes in the Maritime Industry*. Geneva, ILO, 2001.
12. McClellan, K. and Miller, R. E., 'EAPs in Transition: Purpose and Scope of Services', *Employee Assistance Quarterly*. Binghampton, New York 3: 3/4 , pp 25–42, 1988.
13. Scanlon, W. F., *Alcoholism and Drug Abuse in the Workplace*, 2nd edn. New York, Praeger, 1991.
14. International Labour Organisation, *Management of Alcohol and Drug Related Issues in the Workplace*. Geneva, ILO, 1996.
15. Health and Safety Executive, *Drug Abuse at Work*. London, HSE, 1992.

2 Extent and Nature of Substance Abuse

Hamid Ghodse

Introduction

The use, in various forms, of mind-altering drugs has occurred throughout the history of humankind for both medical and religious purposes. Enhancement of physical well-being and heightened religious and mystical experiences were considered appropriate and legitimate reasons for the use of drugs; the relief of psychic pain, anxiety and emotional problems by means of drugs has always appeared to be more attainable than actually solving the underlying problems; drugs have also been used purely for hedonistic recreational intoxication.

Although concern about the non-medical use of drugs is not a new phenomenon, there is no doubt that this has become heightened in recent years. This probably relates to our greater understanding and awareness of the adverse health and social consequences that have followed the ever-increasing availability and use of drugs. These can now be found far from the communities where they were originally available and where they were used by the local population in a socially controlled and socially sanctioned manner.

Such developments should be seen in the context of the technological advances of the twentieth century: the ability to produce very pure and potent forms of drugs; the availability of syringes and needles; and modern methods of transportation and communication. It is easy to understand how drug use, which has been going on for thousands of years without causing too many problems, has become a global catastrophe in the twentieth century. Undoubtedly, however, human greed for the acquisition of power and profit is an old motive for the production, distribution and marketing of drugs for non-medical use, without concern for the adverse consequences[1].

Epidemiology

Practical planning for problems related to drug abuse requires knowledge of the number of people involved and the nature of their problems. Unfortunately, this information is not readily available: those involved may not perceive that they have a problem and, even if they do, they may choose to conceal it, sometimes because their drug use is illegal. The wide range and number of drugs that are abused compound these problems.

In this environment, no single epidemiological method will ever provide a simple estimate of the number within a population with a drug-related problem. Therefore, to assess this, it is necessary to use a variety of methods, each of which contributes partial information that may or may not blend or interconnect with the information from other enquiries, so that gradually a picture of drug abuse within the community, and the problems consequent upon this, emerges.

One way of finding out about patterns of drug use is to investigate the supply situation by obtaining information on production, importation, exportation and distribution. In practice, reliable data can only be obtained about licit sources of supply as no figures are kept on illicit practices. However, some information can be obtained about drug seizures and purchases made on the black market for investigation purposes. This data gives an idea of the availability, purity and costs of different drugs and further information can be obtained from sampling surveys of the general and drug-using populations, although this has problems of consistency and validity. Another way of investigating patterns of drug use is to assess the demand for and the actual consumption of particular (licit) drugs. Although such methods of inquiry are indirect, and the data obtained is unlikely to be absolutely accurate, its regular collection will show up changes in the supply of and demand for drugs and may, on occasion, give an indication of a developing abuse problem[2]. For example, epidemiological studies have demonstrated that 28 per cent of young people aged 16–24 have taken an illegal drug within the last year[3] and that 69 per cent of arrestees tested positive for one or more illegal drugs with 36 per cent testing positive for two or more drugs[4].

According to UNODC estimates, there are 185 million illicit drug users in the world, equivalent to about 3 per cent of the world population and about 4.7 per cent of those aged 15–64, although this does not include those who are using prescribed psychotropic drugs. Cannabis remains the most widely used substance involving about 150 million people, followed by amphetamine-type stimulants taken by 30 million, of whom 8 million use ecstasy. Heroin accounts for 9 million of the 15 million people who use opioids while 13 million people use cocaine[5].

Although all classes of drugs cause their own particular problems, the most serious problem drug for which people seek treatment according to the UN is opiates, accounting for 67 per cent of treatment demand in Asia and 61 per cent in Europe. In Europe there are about 4 million opioid users, a third of whom are in Western Europe with the highest level in the UK, Luxembourg, Portugal, Italy and Switzerland, equivalent to 0.6–1 per cent of the population aged 15–64[5, 6].

However, other continents have different drug problems. In Africa, for example, cannabis accounts for 65 per cent of treatment demand. Worldwide, it is estimated that about 3.7 per cent of the world population aged 15–64 years consumed cannabis in 2001–2003 and, although the number of people treated for cannabis abuse is smaller than for opiates or cocaine and definitely for alcohol, the proportion has shown upward trends in several parts of the world in recent years, reflecting growing consumption and more potent varieties. It is the most widely consumed drug in almost all countries in Western Europe where its use has increased throughout the last decade. In the UK, Europe's largest cannabis market, there was strong increase in cannabis use in the early 1990s and since then it has been relatively stable, albeit at a high level. Altogether, about 10.9 per cent of 16–59-year-olds in England and Wales admitted having consumed cannabis in 2002–2003. School surveys in England confirmed cannabis use to be widespread with an annual prevalence of 13 per cent among 11–15-year-olds in 2003[5].

There were increases in cocaine use throughout the 1990s, which continued in subsequent years, particularly in Europe, with the emergence of crack cocaine compounding the problem. However, in 2002, use was reported to be relatively steady with most increase occurring in south-west Europe[5].

Amphetamines account for some 10 per cent of treatment demand at global level, and up to 17 per cent in Asia. They are also very popular in Western Europe, with a prevalence of 0.6 per cent of population aged 15–64 years, mostly from the UK (1.6 per cent in 2003), Ireland (1.6 per cent in 2002) and Denmark (1.3 per cent in 2000). There has been some decline in the use of amphetamines in the UK over the last few years but there has been no significant change in the use of ecstasy there, with 2 per cent of 16–59-year-olds in England taking ecstasy in 2003. Worldwide there are more than 8 million ecstasy users (0.2 per cent global population aged 15–64), with significantly more in Oceania, Western Europe and North America[5].

The examples above show that there have been some shifts in the prevalence of different substances in different parts of the world with reductions in some places and increases in others. In other words, the pattern has been changing but, as yet, there are no convincing signs of overall reduction, let alone containment. For drug abuse therefore, the global picture is gloomy, and it appears that most of the drugs controlled by the international conventions are abused in most parts of the world. Although different patterns of abuse have been highlighted, the similarities between different parts of the world are more striking than the differences: the abuse of heroin by injection is becoming more widespread; cocaine abuse is becoming more international in the true sense of the word; and cannabis appears to be everywhere. Within this global picture, it is worth remembering that, numerically, alcohol is by far the greatest problem 'drug' making a major contribution to the number of individuals with substance-misuse problems, of whom a significant number can be identified within the workforce.

The production, distribution and use of social, psychotropic and illegal drugs are so intermingled and complex that, more than ever, multi-disciplinary, inter-agency and international cooperation and collaboration are required. Without this there is no way to combat this endemic public health and social problem and, in the absence of such commitment, all the evidence points to the fact that it will persist into the foreseeable future.

Definitions

DRUG

Establishing the epidemiology of drug abuse requires clarity about what constitutes a 'drug'. There are several possible definitions, as the examples below will show, but all have their limitations.

For many people a drug is a substance used to treat mental or physical illness. Although this may seem a practical approach it is based on a permanently changing understanding of therapeutic efficacy; coffee, cannabis and tobacco were used in times gone by for their medicinal properties and, accordingly, would then have been classified as drugs. Until recently, none of them has been used therapeutically and therefore none would have been classified as drugs, a decision that would make most people uneasy. Interestingly, cannabis has recently been the subject of therapeutic research and there is a possibility that it may move back within this surprisingly fluid definition.

Another definition of a drug is 'any chemical substance, other than a food that affects the structure of a living thing'. This definition is also unsatisfactory because there are a few substances generally considered to be drugs, but which are also consumed as foods. Alcohol is the obvious example, but there are others: some mushrooms would be food, while others would be drugs; caffeine, obtained in coffee jars from the supermarket, is perceived as a food, whereas in tablet form from the chemist, it is perceived as a drug[2].

An alternative approach is to limit the use of the term 'drug' to psychoactive substances (any substance that affects the central nervous system and alters mood, perception or consciousness). In practical terms, this is quite sensible: most concern about drugs and most of the epidemiology and management efforts focus on just these classes of drugs. However, this definition ignores the fact that non-psychoactive substances may, on occasion, give rise to very similar problems. This is of theoretical, if not numerical, importance because it emphasises the point that the drug-related problems are not solely due to the particular properties of psychoactive drugs, but are also due to qualities of the individual concerned and of society[2].

In light of these practical and theoretical difficulties, the chosen definition of a drug is deliberately broad. It has the added advantage that, having been developed by the World Health Organisation (WHO), it is used and understood internationally. According to this definition, a drug is 'any substance that, when taken into the living organism, may modify one or more of its functions'[7].

MISUSE, ABUSE AND DEPENDENCE

These terms too require clarification. 'Misuse', according to the Shorter Oxford English Dictionary, 'is to use or employ wrongly or improperly'. However, when misuse refers to drug misuse, definitions again become elusive. The term carries implications, according to the drug concerned, of social unacceptability, of illegality or of harmfulness. Sometimes it seems to mean that the drug is being used without medical approval; sometimes that it is being used excessively. Because of such ambiguities, and because of the associated value judgements, it is often avoided altogether. The term 'drug use' is then substituted, qualified by an appropriate adjective, such as illegal drug use, non-medical drug use and so on. Obviously this format begs the question of what constitutes misuse, but it can give a more precise picture of the way in which a particular drug is taken[2].

'Drug abuse' is an alternative phrase, although it too is often used imprecisely and is considered by many to be value laden. However, it has the advantage of an international (WHO) definition: 'Persistent or sporadic excessive use inconsistent with or unrelated to acceptable medical practice.'[7] This is an uncomfortable definition for those who smoke tobacco and for many of those who drink alcohol, forcing them to face up to the nature of their own drug-taking behaviour. It also emphasises the close relationship between socially acceptable drug-taking behaviour and what is generally perceived as problematic drug-taking behaviour[8,9].

The definition of 'drug dependence' is even more complex because of the wide range of substances that cause dependence and the very different characteristics of the associated dependent state. For example, some drugs cause marked physical dependence with a correspondingly severe withdrawal syndrome; others cause less physical dependence but profound psychological dependence. The extent to which tolerance develops also varies with different classes of drugs. Caffeine, consumed as it is by most people in tea or coffee, produces a limited degree of psychological dependence sometimes manifested as 'I can't get going in the morning without my cup of tea', and a mild state of physical dependence with headaches on drug withdrawal. This degree of dependence is not particularly harmful either to the individual or to society, although it should be noted that a more severe degree of dependence on caffeine (often in cola-type drinks) may sometimes arise[2].

Classification of drugs

Several classes of dependence-producing drugs affect the central nervous system profoundly, producing stimulation or depression, and disturbances in perception, mood, thinking, behaviour or motor function. The use of these drugs may produce individual, public health and social problems and is, therefore, a justifiable cause for concern.

There is no wholly satisfactory way of classifying drugs of abuse and dependence because drugs with very similar pharmacological effects may produce quite different types of dependence[2, 10]. Cannabis, for example, has both sedative and hallucinogenic effects but the pattern of its abuse, by millions of people worldwide, is quite different to the abuse of barbiturates which are sedatives, and LSD which is a hallucinogen. A pragmatic approach has therefore been adopted to take into account the drugs' most important pharmacological effects and the pattern of their abuse. Although hallucinogenic drugs do not cause dependence, they are included in this classification because of the serious dangers consequent to their abuse:

- Opiate analgesics
  - naturally occurring opiates, such as opium, morphine, codeine
  - synthetic or semisynthetic opiates, such as methadone, pethidine, dipipanone, dextromoramide
  - opiate agonist-antagonists, such as pentazocine, buprenorphine.
- Sedative-hypnotics
  - alcohol
  - barbiturates
  - non-barbiturate sedatives, such as chloral, methaqualone, glutethimide, meprobamate
  - benzodiazepines.
- Stimulants
  - amphetamines and similar stimulants, such as methylphenidate, phenmetrazine
  - anorectic agents, such as diethylpropion, phentermine
  - cocaine and coca leaves
  - khat – preparations of *Catha edulis*.
- Hallucinogens
  - lysergide (LSD), mescaline, psilocybin.
- Cannabis
  - preparations of *Cannabis sativa*, such as marijuana, ganja, hashish.
- Volatile solvent (inhalants)
  - toluene, acetone, carbon tetrachloride.

This list is not comprehensive, but includes the commonly abused psychoactive drugs. The most notable omission is tobacco, excluded because, although it causes psychological dependence and serious physical harm, and undoubtedly leads to public health problems, it produces little in the way of psychoactive effects.

Abuse and dependence on a wide range of other drugs also occurs. For example abuse of minor analgesics, such as aspirin, is widespread in many countries. This problem is frequently ignored in studies of drug abuse and dependence, firstly because it involves drugs over which there are no legal controls (or only very limited ones) and which may be easily obtained from outlets such as newsagents, supermarkets and even slot-machines, as well as from pharmacists. Secondly, it is easy to dismiss it as uninformed self-medication by a group ignorant of the dangers of excessive use of these drugs. In many ways, however, those who abuse minor analgesics (and other drugs not included on the above list) resemble those who abuse illicit or restricted drugs: they often deny their drug-taking and may go to considerable lengths to conceal it; they often admit that they take the drugs for the feeling of well-being that they induce and, in the case of aspirin, specifically to experience the dangerous state of salicylism (aspirin intoxication) that they find pleasurable. Above all, they are psychologically dependent on these drugs – showing craving, drug-seeking behaviour and an inability to stop taking them.

In addition to the drugs already discussed, there are many other drugs each of which are abused by just a few people who may then become dependent on them[2, 10]. Some, for example the antiparkinsonian anticholinergic drugs, may be taken for their psychic effects. Others, such as purgatives or anticoagulants, may be taken to produce fictitious disease, those who abuse them often concealing this fact, and seeking and apparently enjoying repeated, intensive medical investigation and care. Finally, some drugs prescribed for somatic disease may be taken excessively, primarily to avoid unpleasant withdrawal symptoms although eventually a true dependent state may develop. For example, increasing doses of ergotamine, prescribed for migraine, may be consumed to avoid withdrawal headaches, and increasing doses of steroids may be taken to avoid unpleasant psychological effects on drug withdrawal. The family, friends and colleagues of doctors as well as doctors themselves may be vulnerable to this type of drug abuse if their powers of persuasion overcome normal professional prescribing practices.

These much less common types of drug dependences are important because they demonstrate that abuse and dependence do not only occur with 'dangerous' psychoactive drugs. In other words, dependence is not just a manifestation of a specific drug effect, but is a behaviour profoundly influenced by the individual personality and the environment, as well as by the specific drugs that are available. As a behaviour, drug dependence is similar to compulsive gambling and compulsive eating, and what all have in common is an overwhelming psychic drive to behave in a certain way. A better understanding of this compulsion enhances our understanding of drug dependence and a whole range of similar human behaviours.

Causes of drug-related behaviour

The causes of drug dependence are not known. For example it is not clear why some people take drugs or experiment with them while others, in very similar situations, do not; nor why some, but not all, of those who experiment, persist in drug use and then become dependent. Despite these very obvious gaps in basic understanding, it is generally accepted that drug-related behaviour, including drug dependence, results from the interaction of three factors

– the drug, the individual and the environment – and that there is no single cause for drug dependence. This fits with the observation that, worldwide, there is vast range of dependence behaviour for which it would be very difficult to devise a single explanation. The availability of the drug is obviously a prerequisite for dependence, and although a few people become dependent on unusual substances (for instance laxatives), most drug dependence is concerned with a few classes of drugs only[2].

The obvious question therefore is how these types of drugs produce dependence. Although the avoidance of the unpleasant symptoms of the abstinence syndrome may be an important reason why a drug-dependent individual continues taking a drug (if it is one that causes physical dependence), this is not the only reason. Many opiate addicts, for example, continue to seek illicit heroin while receiving sufficient supplies of methadone (another opiate), to prevent withdrawal symptoms. In the laboratory too, animals can exhibit drug-seeking behaviour. For example, animals taught to press a lever to obtain a drug will do so repeatedly, even if they are not physically dependent on the drug. Not all drugs induce this behaviour; those that do are said to have 'reinforcing' properties because they reinforce or increase the behaviour resulting in drug administration[11-13]. Drugs shown to be powerful reinforcers in animals are opiates and cocaine and, to a lesser extent, some sedatives-hypnotics and alcohol. These drugs are the ones with a high dependence liability in people, but it is not known why they are reinforcers while other drugs of abuse and dependence (for example cannabis and LSD) are not. Nor is it known why drugs with such different chemical and pharmacological properties should share this ill-understood property of increasing drug-taking behaviour.

As well as studying the drugs of dependence, there have been many attempts to describe a 'dependence-prone' personality. Most studies have compared drug-dependent with non-dependent individuals. This is clearly an unsatisfactory approach because any difference may be the result of drug dependence rather than its cause. Often too, the drug-dependent individuals chosen for the study are from hospital or prison, where the process of institutionalisation may also affect observations on personality. Retrospective attempts to assess what the personality was like before dependence are difficult and unreliable.

It is quite understandable that environmental factors should be blamed for drug dependence, particularly when its prevalence starts to rise sharply; and poverty and unemployment are the usual candidates for blame. They may indeed be relevant, although it should always be remembered that not everyone in a particular environment becomes dependent on drugs, and that, ultimately, environmental factors are local and inapplicable to general and global theories of drug dependence. However, the immediate situation in which drug taking occurs, in other words the setting, may influence the effect of the drug and whether drug taking is a pleasurable experience likely to be repeated on another occasion.

In conclusion, when putting forward ideas and theories about drug dependence, it is important to remember that there is no single cause and that many factors may play a part, assuming different importance in different cases. A way of unifying the wide range of theories is to hypothesise that ultimately the different factors may share common or communicating pathways in the brain, the malfunctioning of which, for whatever reason(s), may lead to drug dependence[2, 14].

Criminality and drug abuse

Because the possession of controlled drugs is itself a criminal offence, there is an inbuilt statistical relationship between drug abuse and criminality: many offenders against drug legislation receive custodial sentences. A study of drug offenders in prison might therefore appear to be a good starting point for finding out about the relationship between criminality and drug abuse. However, it can be misleading: firstly, because some prisoners who are on remand may be acquitted, or may not receive a custodial sentence; secondly, not all offenders against drug legislation are themselves drug abusers or dependent on drugs; and thirdly, the majority of prisoners with drug problems have committed non-drug offences[1].

A common assumption is that this criminal activity is somehow caused by drug abuse. There is no pharmacological basis for this assumption as no drug has inherent criminogenic properties, although intoxication with drugs such as amphetamine or barbiturates may sometimes produce aggressive feelings, verbal abuse and, occasionally, physical aggression. However, as abuse of these drugs is rare in comparison with the frequency of violent crimes, no statistically significant relationship can be established. In practice, drug-related serious crime, including violent crime, is much less common than crimes against property, theft and burglary. In relation to the latter, it is often suggested that drug abusers steal to get money to buy their drugs and although this may be true, there is little evidence to support the hypothesis[1].

There is, on the other hand, some evidence that criminality often precedes drug abuse. For example, between a quarter and a third of male addicts are convicted of an offence before drug abuse starts. It is perhaps not surprising that most research has concentrated on those dependent on opiates and follow-up studies have shown that crime and continued drug use go hand-in-hand, and that when drug use stops, so do illegal activities. It is interesting, and somewhat disappointing, that attendance at a clinic and receipt of a prescription for opiates does not bring about a halt in criminal activities, although these tend to become restricted to drug, rather than non-drug, offences. Frugal prescribing policies of the drug clinics have been blamed for continued drug-related offences by their patients, but more liberal prescriptions do not seem to lead to reduced use of illicit drugs[1].

Because so many addicts commit crimes and receive custodial sentences, it is interesting to examine the effect of a prison sentence on their drug dependence. It is a widely held belief, particularly by those ignorant of the complexities of drug dependence, that a period of compulsory abstinence from drugs could be a turning point for many addicts. However, in the UK, the Mental Health Act excludes drug dependence as a reason for compulsory admission to hospital – prison is the only situation in which drug withdrawal can be enforced. In fact, the chances of remaining abstinent after a prison sentence are similar to those after treatment in hospital, and evidence from other countries also suggests that compulsory treatment is no more successful than voluntary treatment. Those findings are unsurprising – they reinforce the belief that drug withdrawal is merely the first stage of treatment and ineffective, unless followed by the all-important process of rehabilitation.

Consequences of drug abuse

Many of the complications of drug dependence are due not to the direct effects of the drugs themselves but to the life-style of the addict and to the method of drug administration. Self-injection of illicit drugs is particularly hazardous. Drugs may be injected intramuscularly, subcutaneously ('skin-popping') or intravenously ('mainlining') when the total dose is delivered straight into the bloodstream. Dirty injection techniques, using contaminated water and/or non-sterile syringes and needles introduce infection, causing septic injection sites and abscesses. The infection may spread through the bloodstream and affect other organs such as the lungs and the heart.

When syringes and needles are shared, there is considerable risk of transmitting viral infections such as hepatitis and AIDS (Acquired Immune Deficiency Syndrome). Linear scar marks ('tracks') develop over veins, usually in the forearms, used repeatedly for injection and the veins themselves become swollen and blocked (thrombosed). Other veins may then be used instead – in the foot, groin or even the neck – and it may eventually become difficult or impossible to find an unoccluded vein. Decorative tattoos may be placed to conceal evidence of drug injection[2].

Other complications of injection are due not to infection but to the contamination of illicit drugs with adulterants. Heroin, for example, is often 'cut' with substances such as talc, which, if injected into a vein, is eventually filtered out of the blood in the lungs where the particles of talc may cause serious complications later. The injection of drugs that were originally intended for oral consumption (for example the contents of capsules and crushed tablets) may cause serious problems. Barbiturates were often administered in this way and because of the progressive difficulty of intravenous injection, were sometimes injected into an artery instead of a vein. They have an acutely irritant effect and can cause arterial spasm, which if severe and prolonged, may lead to gangrene. This occurred most often when an attempt was made to inject barbiturates into small vessels in the hand; amputation of one or more fingers was sometimes necessary[2].

Summary

As the prevalence of substance abuse is increasing, the extent and nature of the problems associated with it are becoming increasingly varied. Some of these problems are old and familiar; others are starkly new. For example, TB and cirrhosis of the liver have been with us for many years; HIV and hepatitis C have emerged as major public health threats only in the last couple of decades. Because of their widespread nature, substance abuse and related problems cannot fail to impact on the workplace where they have become a major cause of concern in relation to health and safety, both for the substance abuser themself and for other employees. Better knowledge and understanding of the extent and nature of these problems is pivotal if they are to be adequately addressed. However, these are complex problems, multifactorial in their genesis, prevention, treatment and rehabilitation. This chapter, together with others in the book, provides a comprehensive knowledge base to increase understanding of this complex phenomenon in the workplace.

References

1.   Bucknell, P and Ghodse, A H (1977) *Misuse of Drugs, 3rd edition*. London, Sweet and Maxwell
2.   Ghodse, H (2002) *Drugs and Addictive Behaviour: A guide to treatment*. London, Cambridge University Press
3.   Condon, J and Smith, N (2003) Prevalence of drug use: Key findings from the 2002/03 British

Crime Survey, findings 229. *Research, Development and Statistics Directorate Report*. London, Home Office

4. Bennett, T and Holloway, K (2004) Drug use and offending: Summary results of the first two years of the New-ADAM Programme, findings 179. *Research, Development and Statistics Directorate Report*. London, Home Office
5. UNODC (2004) *World Drug Report 2004*. Vienna, United Nations. Office on Drugs and Crime
6. UNODC (2002) *Global Illicit Drug Trends 2002*. Vienna, United Nations. Office on Drugs and Crime
7. World Health Organisation (1969) *WHO Expert Committee on Drug Dependence. Sixteenth Report*. Technical Report Series 407. Geneva, WHO
8. World Health Organisation (1994) *Lexicon of Alcohol and Drug Terms*. Geneva, WHO
9. World Health Organisation (1993) *WHO Expert Committee on Drug Dependence. Twenty-eighth Report*. Technical Report Series 836. Geneva, WHO
10. World Health Organisation (1992) *The ICD-10 Classification of Mental and Behavioural Disorders Clinical Descriptions and Diagnostic Guidelines*. Geneva, WHO
11. Marrow, L P, Overton, P G, Bronn, P F and Clark, D (1999) Encounters with aggressive conspecifics enhance the locomotor activating effect of cocaine in the rat. *Addiction Biology*, 4, 437–41
12. Miczek, K and Mutsifler, N H (1996) Activational effects of social stress on IV cocaine self-administration. *Psychopharmacology*, 128, 256–64
13. Koob, G F (1992) Neural mechanisms of drug reinforcement. *Annals of the New York Academy of Science*, 654, 171–191
14. Crome, I, Ghodse, H, Gilvary, E and McArdle, P (eds) (2004) *Young People and Substance Misuse*. London, Gaskell

3 *Extent of the Problem and Cost to the Employer*

Christine Godfrey and Steve Parrott

Introduction

Drugs have played a part in recreational activity in many communities throughout history. However, it has also long been recognised that the use and misuse of some drugs can impair performance and that in turn affects the ability of individuals to perform productive tasks at work. The effects in the workplace can arise from drug use in leisure time, at the workplace itself and in the 'grey' area between work and leisure such as after-work activities, Christmas parties or other work-related events. How much do these problems in the workplace cost and who has to pay – the employee, the employer or the state? Most available data suggests that employers are bearing significant costs although they rarely have data specific to their company. If these costs are significant, are there cost-effective ways of reducing this burden and what responsibility should employers take on to reduce the costs either to themselves or to the rest of society?

The aim of this chapter is to set out what is known and what is not known about the costs of drug use that are associated with the workplace. There are three major steps in attempting to quantify the costs. First the different types of impacts have to be identified and listed. The next step is to find ways of measuring these impacts in some sort of units, for example, the number of days taken off sick associated with substance misuse. Finally the measured impacts have to be valued in some common currency terms. The structure of this chapter will follow these three steps with the focus on the use of alcohol, tobacco and illicit drugs to illustrate the issues. This is not to suggest that the inappropriate use of prescribed drugs can also involve costs and problems but reflects the even more scarce research data on these substances. The final section reviews briefly some of the evidence on the value for money of different strategies to reduce these costs from the employers' perspective.

The costs of drugs in the workplace and who pays

Costs of drugs in the workplace have mainly been considered in terms of productivity: how drug use influences the productive worth of any employee or potential employee. This concept can be further subdivided into the impact of drug use on the availability or supply of labour and the actual productivity of labour while at work. There are also different impacts depending on the type of drug misuse. For recreational drug users problems at work can arise from binge use in leisure time spilling over into work activities or the inappropriate use of drugs in work time. Increased and heavier consumption of drugs is associated with more health and behavioural problems that may have an impact on productivity whether or not the use extends into worktime.

Continued and chronic use of alcohol or tobacco is associated with higher rates of long-term sickness and therefore additional absences from work. The cost of such longer-term absences may fall on the individual, through spells of unemployment or reduced wages, or the employer, partly depending on the employment law in place in individual countries. For example there are different rules about the level and length of payment of statutory sick pay by employers or the right of employers to terminate employment of those with a long-standing illness. In some countries benefit payments may be available for some illnesses but not others and this may alter incentives for individuals to disclose substance problems.

An associated cost is the cost of health care. In some countries health insurance schemes are costs in part borne by employers through health insurance premiums. Preventing sickness absence may have direct implications for the health care costs falling on the company. These differences between and within companies on who bears the burden of sickness absence clearly impact on the incentives of individuals and their employers to attempt to change behaviour.

Both alcohol and tobacco use are also associated with high rates of premature death among working-age individuals. Often the costs of these deaths are included in estimates of the costs of drug use as part of the workplace costs. The argument being that such premature death means that productive worth is lost to the economy. The cost to employers is however likely to vary enormously by type of employee. For some firms the loss of key experienced personnel to premature death could be considerable. Such individuals may have accumulated considerable skills specific to the company's performance. Others, with fewer skills, may however be much easier to replace and therefore from the employers' perspective less of a loss.

Far less is known about the chronic use of illicit drugs on workplace performance compared to the impact of alcohol and tobacco use. Illicit drug use has been highest among the youngest adult age groups. Problem use is associated with very poor health but also in some countries the majority of such users are not in the legitimate labour force. For example, in the UK National Treatment Outcome Research Survey of drug misusers in treatment, only 12 per cent of the sample had a legitimate employment at the beginning of the survey, and even two years after the initial treatment episode this proportion had only risen slightly to 17 per cent (Godfrey et al., 2004). Hence in specific areas of high drug use, employers could have concerns about the recruitment of sufficient labour for their enterprises. Figures from US treatment studies suggest that drug misusers can be retrained to re-enter the workforce.

While chronic use of drugs can be associated with longer-term absences from work, other use can be associated with shorter-term sickness or more casual absenteeism. Indeed in cultures with common patterns of heavy weekend drinking (or now potentially recreational illicit drug use) some workplaces, particularly those involving manual work, expect more absences on certain days, typically Monday, and may arrange production schedules to account for this pattern of attendance. However, not all workplaces can have flexible patterns of work, and shorter-term absences in the UK account for 80 per cent of absence cases although the total proportion of lost days is somewhat lower at 60 per cent (Barham and Leonard, 2002). The relationship between recreational, acute or binge episodes and chronic use of alcohol or illicit drugs to these type of shorter absences remains under-researched. While some data is often available for the smaller number of chronic users, less is often known about more casual use among a much larger sector of the population. However, one survey in the UK suggested that even 12 per cent of male light drinkers and 9 per cent of female light drinkers admitted to feeling the effects of drinking at work in the past year (Goddard, 1991). Given the high rates of recreational illicit drug use among young people in many countries, a large number of employers overall may have experienced some dip in productivity associated with alcohol or drug use in any year.

The cost to employers of shorter notified absences and absenteeism can again vary. In some occupations, the cost of any short-term absence may be covered by increased productivity by colleagues. In other cases expensive alternative labour may be needed to cover the tasks due to be undertaken by the missing employee.

Sickness absence, premature death, excess unemployment and absenteeism all impact on productivity through the supply of labour available at any point in time. Drug use can also impact on the productivity of those who are present at work. This may be in the form of below-par performance. This can be directly related to drug use in the workplace, for instance lunchtime drinking, or again through recreational use impacting on workplace activity. For smokers the loss of productivity in work arises from the additional smoking breaks. The actual time lost will depend on the smoking policy of the workplace.

Other productivity impacts work through the mechanisms of enhancing the skills, or value of human capital, of individuals. For example, drug use may impede the training of workers. Misuse of drugs or alcohol by young people in school-age years has been shown to impact on educational attainment. This in turn reduces the potential future value of individuals to employers, although most of the cost of this may be borne by the individual in terms of lower lifetime earnings. As with the arguments about the cost of unemployment, however, the success of some enterprises does depend on the pool of labour in a community.

Finally, there is evidence that problematic alcohol or drug users are associated with higher turnover rate of jobs than non-drug users. There are four potential components of such turnover costs. First, there are the administrative costs involved with the leaver, and second, the costs of finding a replacement worker. Third, there is the cost of training for the new employee, and finally, there may be some impact on the customer satisfaction while a new employee is in training. Obviously the extent of such costs vary with the type of employee.

Productivity costs can fall on the individual through lower lifetime earnings, and on the employer in the cost of replacement labour and workmates who may have to work at higher productivity rates to cover for absent colleagues. However, some of the other impacts of drugs in the workplace have more direct impacts on colleagues: impaired performance from drug use in the workplace can result in increased accidents. There is clear evidence of the impact of alcohol use on accidents, particularly those involving road or other forms of transport and machinery. The costs of such accidents especially when they involve loss of life of innocent victims are considerable. The impact of drugs other than alcohol on accidents is still under-researched but in countries where prevalence of use is high, this could be a considerable current hidden cost.

One of the major harms to other workers arising from drug use in the workplace arises from the harmful impact of passive smoking. This is a particular issue in the hospitality industry. The effects are considerable and now well documented causing premature death as well as exacerbating illnesses such as asthma. The costs of additional ill health fall on the non-smokers but obviously the productivity loss through increased sickness absence will also cost the employer.

There are ranges of other effects that may be more specific to different drugs of misuse. Smoking is associated with an increase risk of fires and additional cleaning costs. Illicit drugs, especially where people are problematic users, may be associated with increased theft in the workplace. Alcohol and some other drugs may be associated with violent or other inappropriate behaviour, a problem that may particularly manifest itself in social activities associated with the workplace. These problems can have indirect effects especially if the morale in a workplace is affected and if such individuals are in customer services this may impact on the reputation of the company.

Table 3.1 shows a summary of the types of potential costs, their link with different drugs and the group, individual drug users, colleague or employer who may be bearing the costs.

Table 3.1   Types of costs and who bears them

Type of effect	Type of drug use	Who bears the cost
Availability or supply of labour		
Sickness absence	Potentially all drugs especially chronic use	Employer, State through benefits, individual
Absenteeism	Particularly associated with binge drinking	Employer and work colleagues
Unemployment	Alcohol and illicit drug use	State but may have macro economic effects
Premature death	Smoking, chronic drug and alcohol use	Employer for key individuals
Productivity of labour		
Reduce productivity at work	Use of alcohol and illicit drugs at work, chronic use	Individuals through lost earnings, colleagues and employers
Lower occupation attainment	Early use of illicit drugs and alcohol impacting on education, heavy drinking on career patterns	Mainly individuals through lost earnings, employers potentially through fewer benefits from training
Other impacts		
Accidents	Alcohol, illicit drug use at work, smoking through fires	Victims include colleagues or (through RTAs/other transport) members of the public
Passive use	Use at work, mainly smoking, but also violence with alcohol and some illicit drugs	Victims' health and death risks, State/employers for health care costs, employers for sickness absences.
Company reputation	Use at work and misuse	Employer
Workplace relationships	Use at work and misuse covering nuisance and fairness issues such as smoking breaks	Colleagues but potentially employers if morale affected
Other, e.g. excess cleaning cost	Use at work	Employer

Measuring the impacts of drugs in the workplace

While the list of potential problems outlined in Table 2.1 are recognised it has proven more difficult to find reliable estimates of the size of these impacts across workplaces. There are problems of causation, separating out the specific effect of the drug use from other factors that may impact on productivity or sickness absence. Also it may be thought the impact may well vary across time and across countries as labour markets, economic conditions and labour market law change. One source of data is studies in specific workplaces. However, few individual companies keep detailed records and even where these are in place, employees are unlikely to admit absences are related to their drug-use behaviour. Many individuals with a chronic problem also may still be in denial of the link between their smoking, drinking or illicit drug use and a specific health problem. In general therefore the extent of the problem has to be estimated using data from more detailed research studies and with a number of assumptions to give local estimates for a specific workforce or country.

EXCESS SICKNESS ABSENCES

A number of studies have looked at the relationship between sickness absences and drug consumption. The data has come from a variety of sources. Some are studies of large workforces, such as large companies or UK civil servants. Other studies have used data from problem users who have sought treatment. A number of studies of the cost of substance misuse in the workplace have compiled these estimates to estimate the excess sickness absences related to different drugs.

Parrott et al. (2000) estimated that smokers had 0.9 extra days of sickness than non-smokers, an excess of 32.2 per cent. Similarly Rannia (2003) estimated that between 11 million and 17 million days per year were lost due to alcohol-related sickness absence in England. The excess rates of sickness absences among dependent drinkers are in the range of 25 to 30 per cent. Other work also suggest that alcohol induces excess risks of absences due to injury among moderate and heavy drinkers equivalent to two additional days of sickness a year compared to light drinkers.

Far less evidence is available for the impact of other drug use. Most studies have been based in the US and have compared absenteeism rates based on drug screening tests. Other studies have explored the link between illicit drug use and young people's involvement with the labour market. However, results from research have been very mixed: some studies finding significant impact of illicit drug use while others have found little impact. For example, MacDonald and Pudney (2000) using data from the British Crime Survey suggested that there was little evidence that any illicit drug use impacted on the occupational attainment of young people, but there was evidence that any use of opiates, cocaine and crack cocaine was associated with an increased risk of unemployment.

REDUCED PRODUCTIVITY AT WORK

A more specific measurement problem occurs with determining the impact of substance use and productivity at work. A number of studies have examined the relationship between earnings and alcohol consumption levels. Earnings should be a signal of individual productivity: the more productive a worker, the higher their reward. However, employment practices especially in professions with set scales or workplaces where earnings are more linked to group rather than individual productivity can mean that individual earnings at any point of time may not reflect the current productivity of the individual. Also, income is one of the main determinants of the consumption of alcohol and therefore it is difficult to disentangle the impact of substance misuse on productivity using simple correlations between earnings and drug-use data. More recent research has attempted to explore this data with more sophisticated statistical techniques and use more detailed measures of consumption measures.

MacDonald and Shields (2001) for example, explored the relationship between alcohol consumption and occupational attainment in England. They found that moderate drinking was associated with a higher wage premium in each occupational group compared to non-drinkers. After applying appropriate statistical techniques to the data, it revealed that this premium dropped off sharply as consumption increased. While there was some imprecision in the estimates, the empirical work suggests that adverse effect of drinking occurred just above the current drinking limits. Similar U-shaped relationships have been found using US data, see the review in Rannia (2003).

OTHER IMPACTS

As with sickness absence, the measurement of the range of other impacts comes from individual studies. Some, such as major accidents, are hard to measure directly because they are rare events; also the link is not always made to workplace behaviour. There is no data in the UK, for example, that breaks down drink-driving deaths between people driving because of work-related activities compared to those driving in leisure time. The risks of such events are only measurable at the population level or observable through specific case studies. Much more is known about the impact of passive smoking on health and premature death. It has been estimated, for example, that about 700 premature deaths a year can be attributed to passive smoking in the workplace in the UK (Jamrozik, 2004). There is limited research linking illicit drug use and accidents at work: see for example Zwerling et al. (1993) and Kaestner and Grossman (1998). Also some cases are coming to light linking illicit drug use and road traffic accidents. However, it is difficult to generalise from this limited data to estimate the cost of drug use in other workplaces.

Drug use can also cause concern and nuisance for workmates, although such effects are difficult to measure. Employee theft from workmates or the employer is a major problem in some industries and a few studies have looked at the drug and alcohol use of those apprehended and concluded that illicit drug use or alcohol is associated in a high number of cases.

Valuing the different effects of substance misuse

By valuing effects in money terms the different impacts can be summed to give an overall estimate. This step involves taking some of the measured impacts, such as excess sickness absence rates, combined with the estimate drug use patterns in the particular workplace and country to give an overall estimate of the effect, for example, on total number of working days lost. This effect then requires a value applied. However, the paucity of measurement of many of the effects set out in Table 2.1 suggests most available figures are underestimates of the true costs.

Two main values have been used in available estimates – value of lost time and value of the loss of life. How these items should be valued has been subject to considerable discussion. Loss of working time has generally been estimated in terms of the value of loss earnings, including employers' costs. As discussed earlier the cost to employees and workmates from sickness absences or absenteeism will depend on the job circumstances. In some cases, where the productivity can be made up in the short term by existing staff, the loss may be smaller than the value of lost earnings but in cases where expensive cover staff are required, the cost may be greater than this value. More controversial however is to assume that excessive unemployment among alcohol and drug misusers can be valued in the same way. It could be argued that while there is still some structural unemployment in an economy, such excess unemployment is not a cost. Obviously when there is full employment and a shortage of skills, the loss of productive people can impact on the macro economy. Also, these arguments fail to account for the loss to particular employers of skilled workers and the cost of dismissing and replacing staff. It was estimated in 1995, for example, that the cost of replacing staff in England ranged from £4665 for routine unskilled labour to £23 333 for professional workers, with an average of £12 435 (IPD, 1995).

The value of premature loss of life is often included in workplace costs. As with unemployment this is seen as a loss of productive resource, more of a cost to the economy than to individual employers. Loss of life has generally been valued by estimating the lifetime loss of earnings discounted to a present value. However, this valuation method gives considerable lower values on the loss of life than other economic methods, such as willingness-to-pay methodology. Indeed the value put on the loss of life from alcohol-related premature mortality was valued at £147 187 in the recent England study from Rannia (2003). This is only a tenth of the value used by the Department of Transport (£1 144 890) in valuing the loss of life from traffic accidents. Clearly the impact of loss of life from accidents in the workplace or passive smoking should be given these higher valuations.

Workplace costs have made up significant proportions of the total costs of alcohol and drug misuse in some of the major empirical costing studies. For two countries estimates on productivity costs are available for alcohol, tobacco and illicit drugs are shown in Table 3.2. The figures seem to vary significantly between the two studies, with cigarette smoking being a much more sizeable cost in Australia than in Canada. However, these differences are much more likely to reflect the different ways the effects have been measured than a true difference. In the Canadian study the productivity costs were estimated using only an

Table 3.2 Sickness absence costs in the workplace in Australia and Canada, 2002

Drug/country	Australia £m	Canada £m
Tobacco	452	50
Alcohol	15	834
Illicit drugs	125	163

Note: Figures uprated by inflation and converted to UK currency

Source: Single et al., 1998; Collins and Lapsley, 2002

indirect measure reflecting the time spent in hospitals by smokers for smoking-related diseases, not other absences which did not result in hospital treatment. In the Australian study figures were used from observational studies of both smokers and excess smokers which gave estimates of the excess days taken in sickness absence. In both studies the figures for illicit drugs were included but based on very weak assumptions. For the Australian study it was assumed that drug users would have similar excess sickness absences to smokers although some allowance was made for excess unemployment rates among illicit drug users. For the Canadian study an estimate was based on the difference in mean annual earnings of those dependent on drugs compared to that of the general population.

All these studies indicate that many effects have been omitted because of the lack of data and therefore it is important not to draw too many conclusions about the relative importance of different substances. However, the impacts can be seen as sizeable across these economies as a whole, especially in terms of lost productivity through sickness absence.

This is further illustrated by considering data available for England. No data was found to estimate the costs of illicit drugs in the workplace. For alcohol, Rannia (2003) estimated a cost of between £1.2 billion to £1.8 billion from sickness absence and absenteeism and a further £1.7 billion to £2.2 billion from excessive unemployment among drinkers. For smoking, using the methodology from Parrott et al. (2000) the cost of active smoking in terms of sickness absence is calculated to be £588 million in 2002, with passive smoking accounting for between £61 million and £122 million. However, if the loss of productivity arising from smoking breaks is considered, this accounts for a much more substantial sum of £5.2 billion. The impact of drinking on productivity at work was not estimated by Rannia (2003) but previous estimates were well below the figure quoted here for smoking but still a cause for concern for employers.

The other impact for smoking is the cost of workplace-related passive smoking deaths. Using the Department of Transport figure for the value of premature deaths and the estimate of some 608 deaths in England from Jamrozik (2004) gives a value of £760 million. This is currently just a monetary value of an important consequence rather than a financial burden that employers have to bear. However, if employers are found to be legally liable for such harm caused by passive smoking, there could be a financial liability for employers from such deaths in the future.

Other impacts that have been valued tend to be of smaller sums but still significant. For example, the cost of fires and excess cleaning related to smoking in the workplace is between £400 million and £600 million a year. Also there are additional health costs of about £7 million from passive smoking-related problems in the workplace.

To conclude, more is known about the cost due to both smoking and drinking on the workplace than the cost due to illicit drugs. Not all effects have been costed but available estimates suggest both alcohol and smoking impose considerable costs on employers. Most of the estimated alcohol costs arise from heavy and chronic, problematic use, but there are also likely to be some costs from inappropriate drinking among light and moderate drinkers. For smoking there are also major costs in terms of lost productivity arising from both active and passive smoking. In terms of liability of employers the impact of passive smoking is considerable. The lack of estimates of the cost of illicit drug use does not mean there are not problems in the workplace.

Employers' costs to respond to the problems

The data currently available does not allow employers to separate out the costs of substances taken in the workplaces from recreational use or use in the grey areas of work-related activities. To some extent employers may have to react to societal problems and seek to minimise costs to themselves. This could be done by pre-employment screening and other techniques to select out those workers who may have substance-related problems. Workplace bans of substance use, including smoking, have also been put in place by a number of employers. Testing for substance use in the workplace is a way of enforcing such policies. However, the development of problems can be related to workplace stresses and indeed in some occupations the culture towards different substance use, especially alcohol. Another policy is therefore to provide assistance to employees to change their substance use. What is the evidence of the value for money of these different approaches?

Value for money is determined by comparing the costs against the benefits of the different policies. Also for the employers, it depends on the desired outcomes required and how far they are prepared to bear the costs from substance misuse.

It is costly to recruit new staff but it is very unclear what methods can be used to successfully screen out those who may have potential problems. Technology has advanced and there is a number of less invasive and also cheaper testing equipments available. However, it is unclear what information pre-employment tests may be picking up in terms of recreational drug use but not necessarily problematic use.

Three US-based cost–benefit analyses of employee drug screening were identified by the authors in a review conducted in 1997. Major methodological criticisms of available studies were also found in the literature. In particular, if drug using is correlated with other characteristics, for example risk taking, any workplace outcomes could be correlated with these characteristics not the drug use per se. Also if prospective employees know about the screening test they can abstain for the required period. Drug tests also are more likely to detect drugs such as cannabis than harder and potentially more problematic drugs such as cocaine and heroin. Two of the studies found cost savings, but these were dependent on the assumptions made and the best quality study found that a positive return from pre-employment screening came only when the prevalence of drug use was above 10 per cent.

It should also be noted that most evaluations have been based on pre-employment screening rather than in-work screening. About 80 per cent of large employers in the US use some form of testing. A more recent study used medical records of a large manufacturing firm to estimate the impact of drug testing on medical expenditures and injury rates (Ozminkowski et al., 2003). The study suggested that in order to yield positive results not only should a large percentage of the population be tested in any year (42 per cent) but that on average an employee needed to be tested 1.68 times per year. But these results were based on minimising medical expenditures, a cost not all employers bear. A recent UK inquiry concluded that there is less testing for illicit drugs in the UK, currently about 4 per cent of employers, and that it was costly both in direct terms and indirectly in potentially excluding productive workers (Joseph Rowntree Foundation, 2004). This report concluded that alcohol was more likely to be a problem than illicit drug use in the UK. Less work has been done to investigate the potential to screen for alcohol misuse in the workplace other than in safety-critical industries.

Most workplaces have some sort of substance-use policy. These do, however, vary in form. Some employers are concerned primarily with the avoidance of legal liability while others are more directed towards reducing problems. Many workplaces have introduced restrictions on use in the workplace, although there are still a sizeable number of workplaces allowing smoking, especially the hospitality industry. Bans can be cost-effective: using the data on the costs of passive smoking in the workplaces in England, for example, it can be estimated that a ban on smoking in the workplace could save £1.4 billion a year and potentially a further £2–3 billion if less time is taken by smokers on smoking breaks.

Some positive results have also been found from the economic evaluation of employment assistance programmes or other schemes to provide treatment to employees found to have problems. However, these cost–benefit analyses have focused on savings in health care costs associated with such programmes, relevant to US workplaces but less relevant to many other countries with mainly tax-based health care financing or social insurance systems. In these systems these savings would accrue to the State rather than the employer, but the workplace remains a place potentially to intervene to help direct problem users to helping agencies. Even when problems are recognised, employers do not always have good access to the evidence base of which treatments are the most cost-effective. Employing unproven and often expensive treatments can lead to an expensive waste of employers' money (Parrott et al., 2000).

Conclusions

Drugs in the workplace have the potential to be a considerable cost to employers. However, the data to make estimates is remarkably limited. Where estimates are available, the figures suggest employers could take a number of measures to improve the productivity of their workforce, hence profitability, and reduce potential legal liability. However, some solutions are costly and may not bring the desired savings. Indeed overt disciplinary programmes may lower staff morale and hinder recruitment of the best workers. In contrast neglect of the issues can not only hit the pocket of employers but also directly impact on work colleagues and cause costs more widely for society.

There are a number of challenges to researchers to improve the body of evidence on how different patterns of drug use impact on workplaces. The evidence base needs to be both stronger and capable of translation into specific types of workplace and situations. How much easier is it to take these problems seriously if some estimate can be made of the potential problem in a particular office or factory in a particular town. Measuring the size of the problem is only one step, however, and further research is needed to provide evidence on the costs and effectiveness of different workplace policies.

References

Barham, C. and Leonard, J. (2002) Trends and sources of data on sickness absence, *Labour Market Trends*, August, 177–185.

Collins, D. J. and Lapsley, H. M. (2002) *Counting the Cost: estimates of the social costs of drug abuse in Australia in 1998–9*. Commonwealth Department of Health and Ageing: Canberra, Australia.

Goddard, E. (1991) *Drinking in England and Wales in the Late 1990s*. H.M.S.O.: London.

Godfrey, C., Stewart, D. and Gossop, M. (2004) Economic analysis of costs and consequences of the treatment of drug misuse: two year outcome data from the National Treatment Outcome Research Study (NTORS), *Addiction*, 99(6): 697–707.

Institute of Personnel and Development (1995) *IPD Labour Turnover: Survey Results*. Institute of Personnel and Development: London.

Kaestner, R. and Grossman M. (1998) The effect of drug use on workplace accidents, *Labour Economics*, 5: 267–295.

Jamrozik, J. (2004) Estimates of the deaths from second-hand smoke in the workplace. Paper presented at the Royal College of Physicians, Environmental Tobacco Smoke and the Hospitality Industry, 17 May, London.

Joseph Rowntree Foundation (2004) *Drug Testing in the Workplace: The Independent Inquiry into Drug Testing at Work*. Joseph Rowntree Foundation: York.

MacDonald, Z. and Pudney, S. (2000) Illicit drug use, unemployment and educational attainment, *Journal of Health Economics*, 19: 1087–113.

MacDonald, Z. and Shields, M. (2001) The impact of alcohol consumption on occupational attainment in England, *Economica*, 68: 427–453.

Ozminkowski, R., Mark, T., Goetzel, R., Blank, D., Walsh, M. and Cangianelli, L. (2003) Relationships between urinalysis testing for substance use, medical expenditures and the occurrence of injuries at a large manufacturing firms, *American Journal of Drug and Alcohol Abuse*, 29(1): 151–167.

Parrott, S., Godfrey, C. and Raw, M. (2000) Costs of employee smoking in the workplace in Scotland, *Tobacco Control*, 9: 187–192.

Rannia, L. (2003) *Alcohol Misuse: How much does it cost?* London: Strategy Unit Cabinet Office.

Single, E., Robson, L., Xie, X. and Rehm, J. (1998) The economic costs of alcohol, tobacco and illicit drugs in Canada, 1992, *Addiction*, 93: 991–1005.

Zweling, C. (1993) Current practice and experience in drug and alcohol testing in the workplace, *Bulletin on Narcotics*, 14(2): 155–196.

4 Drug Misuse and the Work Culture

Susanna Galea and Hamid Ghodse

Problems related to the use of drugs and alcohol by individuals in employment translate into an economic burden, raising socio-political interest and concern. Societal trends and beliefs, employee characteristics, employer and organizational attitudes, as well as occupational characteristics, contribute to the shaping of a workplace culture that may enable or discourage substance-related work problems.

Job performance, worker productivity and health and safety costs resulting from use of drugs and/or alcohol, during or outside work times, have received much media attention, raising the profile of the problem. Despite the fact that global use of substances is on the increase, problems in the workplace due to use of substances may be overestimated due to the extensive political and media coverage received. The prevalence of drug abusers in the late 1990s is estimated at 180 million of the global population, with those aged 15 and above forming 4.2 per cent of the global population[1]. It is no easy task to estimate what proportion of this global percentage is engaged in employment; however, data from the *United States National Household Survey on Drug Abuse* indicate that around 70 per cent of drug users are employed, one-fifth as part-time and four-fifths as full-time. The survey also reports that 7.7 per cent of full-time workers admitted to current illicit drug use and 7.6 per cent to excessive alcohol use[2]. Such figures indicate that a crude estimate of 10–15 per cent of the workforce in the United States are likely to present with substance-related difficulties at work.

Organizations operate within their unique cultural context in relation to substance-misuse problems. Norms and expectations of each organization may serve the purpose of promoting, maintaining and/or initiating substance-related problems or, on the other hand, may effectively discourage such problems. This chapter will explore the links between the work culture and substance-related problems. It will discuss the various possible components of a work culture. Cultures which tend to have increased susceptibility to such problems and cultures with high-risk substance-related effects are discussed in more detail in the next chapter. Consideration will also be given to how work cultures are generated and maintained, and to what systems contribute to underlying cultural aspects.

The growth of a work culture

The culture within a workplace environment is usually evident by the way individuals within the organization behave from day to day. Their behaviour is shaped by underlying beliefs, attitudes and assumptions held by the organization, and is many times adhered to without much effort – that is, individuals usually take it for granted. Hence, exploring how the work culture influences substance-related behaviour, and how this, in turn, influences existing culture, is not easy to determine.

The culture within the work environment, in relation to the use of drugs and alcohol, is dependent upon several characteristics (see Figure 4.1) which, for the purpose of this chapter, have been classified into four broad headings:

- social trends and beliefs
- employer/organizational factors
- occupational factors
- employee factors.

These factors are the components/building blocks of a work culture and provide a useful framework to understand culture, in relation to the use of drugs and alcohol, within specific places of work.

Social trends and beliefs

Trends, norms and attitudes within the broader society influence work culture. For example, increased permissiveness for the use of cannabis within the western world increases the likelihood of cannabis use by the workforce. Impairment in cognition and psychomotor performance[3], associated with use of cannabis, may trigger accidents at work, which may be detrimental for occupations such as pilots, bus or train drivers and those operating heavy

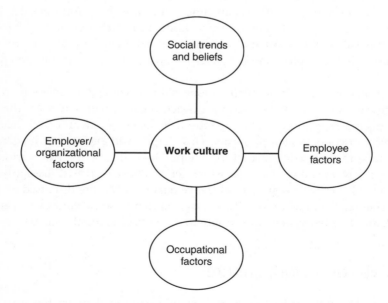

Figure 4.1 Components of work culture

machinery. Studies have shown that cannabis impairs driving performance, and in fact cannabis has been implicated in a large proportion of road traffic accidents[4, 5]. Studies have also shown that aircraft piloting skills are also significantly impaired with use of cannabis[6]. An additional concern with pilots and bus or train drivers is that the impact of risk is potentially high due to the associated risk to other members of society.

Alcohol is another substance extensively used and easily available within western society. Organizations within such societies are likely to hold a work culture that includes permissiveness for use of alcohol. Alcohol-related work performance problems are likely to be understood both by work colleagues as well as managers and/or supervisors. Figures from the UK General Household Survey[7] indicate that in 2002, one in five men and one in eight women drank on five days of the preceding week. Also, 38 per cent of men and 23 per cent of women drank excessively (more than four units for men; more than three units for women) on at least one day of the preceding week. Those who, according to the national socio-economic classification, occupied 'managerial and professional' positions drank more than those in 'intermediate' or 'routine and manual' positions. Similarly, those with higher earnings drank more. Such figures indicate that alcohol-related work performance problems are likely to be experienced within all tiers of the hierarchy of the organisation, contributing to a work culture of permissiveness for alcohol-related problems.

Within other societies, permissiveness to other substances may be evident, for example the chewing of khat leaves in Yemen and Ethiopia. A survey[8] carried out within rural Ethiopia, involving 10 486 adults, reported daily khat use by 17.4 per cent of the sample, with the majority of these being males. Such data indicates that use of khat is likely to impinge on work-related issues.

Employer/organizational factors

Organizational functioning also contributes significantly to the work culture in relation to use of drugs and alcohol. Policies on substance abuse, levels of supervision, support and cohesiveness within the workforce, and several other organizational characteristics, determine the organization's behaviour and work culture. In this section, the *cultural web*[9] will be applied as a framework to describe how organizational aspects may influence the work culture.

The cultural web is a representation of the norms, attitudes and beliefs of an organization. It consists of six distinct elements which outline the various functions within an organization:

1 power structures
2 organizational structures
3 control systems
4 rituals and routines
5 stories
6 symbols.

The cultural web facilitates the understanding of aspects of the organization that influence its standing in relation to substance-related work problems.

POWER STRUCTURES

This refers to the organization's core workers and its core values and beliefs. For example, a small car repair firm has the mechanics as its core workers and may hold the core values of team cohesiveness and collaboration, manifested by going out for a drink after work. Workgroup cohesion has a buffer effect on negative work consequences related to substance use[10]. Hence, sharing a drink together may be protective within such a work culture. However, a larger organisation holding a similar core belief may share the same protective effect. Larger companies are likely to employ individuals from different geographical areas and more diverse backgrounds with the consequence that not all workers can join in the team-building behaviour, or that workers who join in suffer the risk of associated logistical problems, such as drinking and driving.

ORGANIZATIONAL STRUCTURES

This refers to whether the organization functions within a hierarchical and/or formal system and whether it encourages competition or collaboration. Hierarchical and formal systems tend to follow 'work to rule' trends with clear boundaries on work productivity. Absenteeism, sickness days and decreased work output are easily recognized and may be addressed quickly. Areas within the National Health Service may operate within such hierarchical systems. Such a system operates on a risk management approach, given that the risk of substance use by National Health Service employees may have a detrimental effect on patient care.

A characteristic feature of such systems is that problems due to use of drugs and alcohol are usually perceived as a burden to the workforce, and consequently stigmatizing to the employee with the problem. Hence employees may fail to seek help, making efforts to hide the problem in order not to feel marginalized[11] or risk losing their job.

In general, hierarchical, formal systems are reported to generate workplace stress. Stress has a strong association with use of substances and hence such systems may be indirectly promoting substance use[10].

On the other hand, an organizational structure based on collaboration, tends to promote workplace cohesion. Such structures have the potential to indirectly promote early detection of problems related to use of substances, due to the underlying supportive and informal structure.

CONTROL SYSTEMS

What an organization monitors and rewards reflects what is important for that organization. For example, organizations may have drug policies and employ regular testing for use of drugs to give a clear message that the organization holds a value that its employers should not have their work performance affected by use of substances. Such an approach tends to be adopted by, for example, football clubs, with the expectation that footballers' performance must not be influenced by use of drugs. Other organizations operating similar control systems include railway and airline companies, where the risk of impaired performance due to use of substances is substantially high. Similarly, the medical profession has systems of regular appraisal to monitor malpractice, including that related to use of substances.

Other organizations may not apply such sanctions and may not have explicit drug and alcohol policies, but may encourage employees with difficulties to engage in treatment through their employee assistance programmes. Their monitoring may involve ensuring that the employee remains in treatment, implying that the company perceives its employees as valuable assets for the company's survival and is thus willing to support the individual through treatment. Such monitoring can be observed in the entertainment industry, with actors and models for example. Small companies and companies with recruitment difficulties may also employ such control systems.

RITUALS AND ROUTINES

This refers to 'the way things are done' within the organization, including both formal and informal processes. For example, a company favouring training may readily adopt employee education programmes to increase the awareness of substance-related work problems, decrease the stigma around them and increase the possibility of employees with difficulties seeking help. Such programmes are also likely to increase the knowledge and confidence at the managerial level to deal with such problems sensitively and effectively.

More informal 'routines and rituals' of an organization also contribute significantly to the work culture. Some examples include: What goes on at the organization's Christmas party. Does the company provide free drinks? Do people normally get drunk? Do people talk favourably about getting drunk? Other examples include: drinks in the pub after work; the dress culture of employees (wearing t-shirts with cannabis symbols or beer adverts); and drinking tea out of 'no smoking' mugs.

STORIES

This refers to which experiences or jokes members of the organization remind or relate to one another. Stories related tend to be around highly approved or highly disapproved behaviour. New employees hearing approval stories around occasional binge drinking are indirectly encouraged to follow suit to be more accepted in the organization.

SYMBOLS

Logos, material assets and terminology used within the organization represent the beliefs of the organization. An organization with 'no smoking' signs, posters on the negative effects of passive smoking on its walls and with designated smoke-free areas gives a message that it does not favour cigarette smoking within the workplace and wishes its employees to respect the possible harm related to passive smoking by the non-smoking employees.

The cultural web provides a useful framework to explore how employer/organization's characteristics contribute to the culture within the work environment around the use and effects of drugs and alcohol.

Occupational factors

Some occupations/vocations may be at high risk to the use of drugs and alcohol. One clear example is working behind the bar in a pub. Easy access to alcohol makes employees in this occupation highly susceptible to workplace alcohol-related problems. The same applies to other workers within the entertainment industry, such as those working in clubs, and actors, where both drugs and alcohol are potentially easy to obtain.

An earlier study by the Royal College of Psychiatrists reported on high-risk occupations for alcohol problems, such as deaths from liver cirrhosis and alcohol dependence. High-risk occupations included jobs within the drinking trade, caterers, the armed forces, the merchant navy, fishermen, medical doctors and journalists[12]. It is difficult to ascertain why such occupations present as high risk but some of the reasons identified in the study were: easy access to alcohol; difficulties in engaging in relationships due to occupational demands; lack of support and supervision; and stresses and strains of the occupation. The more recent General Household Survey in Britain identified that occupations of professional and/or managerial status, tend to drink more heavily than other occupations[7]. Possible reasons for such increased drinking could be the high level of work-related stress associated with such occupations, or a higher income making it more financially feasible to spend money on drink.

Other occupations which appear to carry higher risk for use of substances include occupations with unsociable working hours, such as that of postmen. In the UK, postmen start working in the early hours of the morning, and tend to finish in the late morning. Several empirical reports by patients attending drug and alcohol services indicate that finishing at such times increases the risk of use of substances as a result of having time on their hands, when other people would be working.

The occupational characteristics mentioned are by no means exhaustive. However they provide an indication on what factors might contribute to a high- or low-risk work culture.

Employee factors

Employees bring in their own beliefs and attitudes to an organization. Their choice of occupation is also to some extent dependent on such beliefs and attitudes. Similarly, the recruitment selection by the organization is partially based on whether the individual's beliefs and attitudes fit in with those of the organization's.

Employee characteristics contribute significantly to the culture around substance use and its effects within the workplace. Studies have shown that employees exhibiting work problems due to use of substances, in general tend to lead a deviant style of behaviour[13, 14]. In these studies, the most likely profile of such employees was being young, male, having low self-esteem, having a family history of use of substances and also a significant forensic history. Individuals also frequently mixed with other substance users in their social time[15]. However, general deviance indicators are thought to be the strongest predictors of substance use[16].

Employees with work problems due to use of substances are also more likely to be employed in jobs carrying a potential physical risk of harm to self and/or others[13, 15], for example, working in labouring jobs in the building industry. Employees using substances also tend to be involved in more accidents at work than other employees[14, 16]. Research on the link between personality attributes, choice of employment, use of substances and accidents at work is sparse. Risk-taking behaviour may be the common attribute linking all issues together, or the increased accidents may simply be the result of the nature of the job being of high risk within itself.

Individual employee characteristics are not the only aspects contributing to the work culture. The diversity within the workforce as a whole is also contributory. Organizations having an appropriate balance of diverse beliefs and attributes are less likely to be overburdened by substance-related work problems, and are more likely to deal with such problems effectively. On the other hand, organizations with less diversity may generate undue stigma, hindering detection and help-seeking.

Summary

Workplace culture in relation to the use of substances develops through a complex interaction of various components with resultant effects on work performance and productivity. Social trends and beliefs influence the development of a workplace culture. Also, occupational characteristics, factors directly related to the employee, employer factors and organizational attitudes contribute to the development of a unique culture, which may, directly or indirectly, either discourage or promote substance-related work problems. The culture within the work environment related to the use of substances also tends to be substance specific. The permissiveness of a society to the use of specific substances – for example, the use of alcohol and cannabis within the western world – tends to be reflected within a work environment. Specific jobs also function within their specific cultures, making some environments more supportive than others. The application of the cultural web to a workplace environment is a useful approach to the exploration of the existing culture within that workplace. It provides a framework which allows analysis of change in culture within an environment, as well as comparison between one workplace culture and another.

References

1. United Nations Office for Drug Control and Crime Prevention (2000) *World Drug Report 2000*, Oxford University Press, Oxford.
2. Zhang, Z., Huang, L. X. and Brittingham, A. M. (2003) *Worker Drug Use and Workplace Policies and Programs: Results From the 1994 and 1997 National Household Survey on Drug Abuse*, US Department of Health and Human Services, Substance Abuse and Mental Health Services Administration (SAMHSA), from www.oas.samhsa.gov.
3. Ashton, C. H. (2001) Pharmacology and Effects of Cannabis: A Brief Review, *British Journal of Psychiatry*, 178, pp. 101–106.
4. Department of Transport (2004) *Cannabis and Driving: A Review of the Literature and Commentary*, from www.dft.gov.uk.
5. World Health Organization (1997) Programme on Substance Abuse. *Cannabis: A Health Perspective and Research Agenda*, WHO, Geneva.
6. Bandolier (2004) *Cannabis and Flying*, from www.jr2.ox.ac.uk/bandolier/bandopubs/cannfly/cannfly.html.
7. Rikards, L., Fox, K., Roberts, C., Fletcher, L. and GODDARD, E. (2004) *Living in Britain: Results From the 2002 General Household Survey, No. 31*, Office of National Statistics, London, TSO, from www.statistics.gov.uk.
8. Alem, A., Kebede, D. and Kullgren, G. (1999) The Prevalence and Socio-Demographic Correlates of Khat Chewing in Butajira, Ethiopia, *Acta Psychiatr Scand Suppl.*, 100, pp. 84–91.
9. Johnson, G. and Scholes, K. (2002) *Exploring Corporate Strategy*, 6th Edn, Prentice Hall, London.
10. Bennett, J. B. and Lehman, W. E. K. (1998) Workplace Drinking Climate, Stress and Problem Indicators: Assessing the Influence of Team Work (Group Cohesion), *Journal of Studies on Alcohol*, 59 (5), pp. 608–618.
11. Bennett, J. B. and Lehman, W. E. K. (2001) Workplace Substance Abuse Prevention and Help

Seeking: Comparing Team-Orientated and Informational Training, *Journal of Occupational Health Psychology*, 6 (3), pp. 243–254.

12. Royal College of Psychiatrists (1986) *Alcohol: Our Favourite Drug. New Report on Alcohol and Alcohol-Related Problems*, Royal College of Psychiatrists Special Committee on Alcoholism, Tavistock Publications Ltd, London.

13. Lehman, W. E. K. and Bennett, J. B. (2002) Job Risk and Employee Substance Use: The Influence of Personal Background and Work Environment Factors, *American Journal of Drug and Alcohol Abuse*, 28 (2), pp. 263–286.

14. Holcom, M. L., Lehman, W. E. K. and Simpson, D. D. (1993) Employee Accidents: Influences of Personal Characteristics, Job Characteristics, and Substance Use in Jobs Differing in Accident Potential, *Journal of Safety Research*, 24, pp. 205–221.

15. Lehman, W. E. K., Farabee, D. J., Holcom, M. L. and Simpson, D. D. (1995) Prediction of Substance Use in the Workplace: Unique Contributions of Personal Background and Work Environment Variables, *Journal of Drug Issues*, 25 (2), pp. 253–274.

16. Lehman, W. E. K., Simpson, D. D. and Bennett, J. B. (2003) Drugs in the Workplace: Employee Surveys on Drug Use: Project Summary, from www.ibr.tcu.edu/projects/workplac/surveys.html.

5 *Effects and Risks of Workplace Culture*

Graham Lucas

The workplace culture implies modus operandi – it varies with the nature of the operation, and the size of the organisation, be it a small- or medium-sized enterprise or a global plc. It is dependent on how management and workforce interact amongst themselves, within the organisation, and with contractors, clients and the public. Each workplace has its own culture; no two organisations or industries being identical. Thus the culture of a high-street organisation in New York will differ from a similar outlet in London. There is also considerable overlap between the culture of the workplace and the culture within domestic and community environments, all of which impact on the individual employee and the workforce as a whole. Hence, the importance of the local community supplying the workforce. This is of special relevance in the case of alcohol and drugs where they form part of local culture and custom.

Both alcohol and drugs are substances which can rapidly alter the mental state. They also alter behaviour, level of consciousness, cognitive function, judgement and hand-eye coordination resulting in adverse effects on work performance and safety. Whatever the culture of the organisation, it is in the best interests of itself, the employee with the drug misuse or alcohol problem, co-workers, and productivity to achieve early identification, appropriate intervention and ongoing rehabilitation. Moreover this may be mandatory if the nature of the work is safety critical. Awareness, sensitivity in the process of intervention, access to treatment facilities, reassurance regarding sickness absence and job security are all vital aspects of such a process. This necessitates recognition and acceptance of the problem as an illness, as indeed do the Confederation of British Industry, Trade Union Congress, Health and Safety Executive, the Departments of Health, Trade and Industry and private medical insurance companies.

Apart from impaired productivity, the Health and Safety at Work Act (1974) requires any organisation employing more than five people to avoid all possible risks and to prevent accidents, especially those that could have been the consequence of problem drinking or the misuse of drugs. Hence, whatever the culture of the organisation, the size of its workforce or its working practices, it has to be capable of addressing risk avoidance in the most effective way.

The culture and structure of the organisation determines whether identification and intervention are feasible regarding problem drinking and misuse of drugs. Whatever the culture of an organisation, it is in the best interests of the health and safety of the workforce, contractors, clients and the local community to eliminate problem drinking and the misuse of drugs.

Quoted statistics vary, but according to Smith et al. (2004) about 25 per cent of workers under the age of 30 have used drugs during the previous year. Also one in ten employees is a problem drinker. The misuse of prescription and illicit drugs is also increasing, although it is still of significantly less importance than that of the increase in problem drinking, including hazardous binge drinking in social or occupational settings. Hemmed in by fashionable sexual mores, the male image seems to have enhanced the habit of problem drinking, regarding it as macho, albeit inappropriately. Peer pressure, originally among males but now increasingly among females, drives the need to demonstrate camaraderie and to follow the crowd in the pursuit of enjoyment. While overt sexism has declined, men still use pubs, golf and other clubs to discuss career moves. Over a third of women managers feel excluded by such informal, alcohol facilitated 'old boy networks' (McCarthy, 2004).

In considering employee problem drinking and the misuse of drugs, cultural trends are key. For instance, working practices (Frith, 2004) designed to help female employees, such as flexitime, may actually be counter-productive for networking by causing them to miss out on after-hours drinking. Paradoxically, such loss of opportunity could be advantageous: quick after-work but occupationally orientated conviviality, fuelled by alcohol and or drugs, is perhaps too easy and ultimately becomes a self-destructive habit.

Minor psychiatric morbidity such as anxiety and depression occurs in up to a third of the general population, and sometimes predisposes to the quick relief achieved through alcohol or drugs. Similarly, psychosocial aspects of the working environment can predispose to occupational stress, which may result in resorting to alcohol (Head et al., 2004) and also to the misuse of drugs. However, such temporary psychological stress relief, is transient and counter-productive with adverse effects on sleep, mood and cognitive function. It can also result in aggression and violence, such as the tribal behaviour of a football mob or street fighting as night clubs empty, or of equal or even greater importance to dangerous and irresponsible behaviour in the workplace.

Moderation with alcohol is essential, and in the workplace appropriate regulations must be enforced (Frone, 1999) regarding the timing of alcohol consumption prior to any safety-critical work. Whatever the culture, problem drinking and the misuse of drugs is usually considered as unacceptable in any workplace.

Definitions

Drug misuse is the taking of any illegal drugs, or the deliberate or unintentional use of prescribed drugs and substances such as solvents. The practice is not confined to any specific occupation or social class. There is no stereotype of a problem drinker or of those who misuse drugs. Anyone who takes drugs or alcohol can be harmed physically, mentally and socially. Performance can be impaired and accidents can occur, endangering co-workers and impairing productivity. Depending on its location, the perceived culture of an organisation can impact on a community. For instance, noise in the vicinity of airports or toxic substances from nuclear installations can be offensive, frightening and potentially dangerous, and can cause hostility to the workforce, which can itself be a significant stressor.

Here, *problem drinking* is used to cover the whole spectrum of alcohol dependence, both physical and psychological. 'Problem drinking' (*The Problem Drinker at Work*, HSE, 1981) is a practical term and more appropriate to the workplace, where functional effectiveness for the job in question is the crucial factor. It covers interpersonal relationships, performance and productivity. Problem drinking is said to occur when the pattern of alcohol use is such that it adversely affects any of the following: mental and/or physical health, occupational, domestic or community life. It may impair work performance, cause dangerous accidents, serious economic consequences, relationship or family break-up, or a drink-driving charge. Four out of five cases seen in accident and emergency departments on a Friday night are said to be alcohol related, as are eight out of ten domestic assaults. Some afflicted workers then take sickness absence on the following Monday morning. In some UK working cultures it seems that a 'good night out', end-of-project celebratory bonding implies getting drunk, and this applies with varying degrees of sophistication throughout the occupational spectrum. Although not supported by statistics, there is a suggestion that the continuation of problem drinking and the misuse of drugs is more prevalent among the affluent 'City types'. However, other groups must be considered, such as those with anxiety and depression, the bored, the spiritually empty, the aimless and those with low self-esteem. Alcohol, by its ability to release dopamine, can make the world look rosier again, albeit very transiently. What is not understood, or is ignored, is the fact that alcohol is a depressant, heightens anxiety and impairs sleep, quickly reversing its fleeting improvement in these areas (Gossop et al., 2001).

The following section discusses factors, external and internal to the workplace, that predispose to problem drinking or misuse of drugs.

Cultural factors predisposing to problem drinking or misuse of drugs

EXTERNAL TO THE WORKPLACE BUT INTRINSIC TO THE EMPLOYEE

A family history of alcohol abuse carries increased vulnerability to alcohol-related problems. Personality encompasses life-long traits dictating how an individual responds to a given situation, interacts and is themselves perceived. Interpersonal tension in any domain of life can predispose to resentment and, fuelled by alcohol or drugs, can erupt into anger or even rage which is extremely dangerous in any occupational setting, but particularly in those which are safety critical such as transportation: road or air rage being examples, not to mention trolley rage in the supermarket. When any personality trait significantly impairs an individual's functional effectiveness, it can result in neurotic behaviour. Anxiety, depression and the obsessional states are common psychiatric conditions, all of which can predispose to problem drinking or to the misuse of drugs or substances. Personality is key to interpersonal relationships and the culture of an organisation depends on each individual in that organisation, from the boardroom to the shop floor. The addictive personality predisposes to the whole range of impulsive behaviours. In addition to resorting to alcohol, drugs, tobacco smoking and abnormal eating patterns, gambling and inappropriate spending may occur in those with low self-esteem, poor self-confidence, and lack of control and assertive skills. These lead to unresolved resentment, anger the comfort-seeking effects of centrally acting agents. In this context, the culture of the employee, their background and socio-economic group, as well as family, may all contribute to their basic social anxiety and vulnerability, upon which the workplace culture impacts. Additionally, there is peer-group pressure from friends who themselves drink heavily or misuse drugs.

It is recognised that up to a third of all patients who consult their GP have some form of psychiatric morbidity (Jenkins, 1992). Of those in employment some may not warrant or may refuse sickness absence. However, their physical complaints include musculo-skeletal pain, impaired sleep, indigestion, irritable bowel or psoriasis, which may all be the symptoms of underlying stress, anxiety or depression. Such individuals may resort to problem drinking or to the misuse of drugs or substances including over-the-counter analgesics, hypnotics, anxiolytics (anxiety-reducing drugs) or anti-depressant medication prescribed by their GP. These 'working wounded' may decline the recommended sickness absence and psychiatric referral or even counselling within the Primary Care setting. This applies to employees of whatever seniority in both public and private sectors of employment, whatever the culture of the organisation.

Epidemiological studies confirm that anxiety and depression, are common in the general population and, therefore, also in the workplace. Those so affected are more vulnerable to inevitable workplace stressors (Jenkins, 1992). Around 15–30 per cent of the population experience anxiety, including phobic and obsessional disorders and depression at some time during adult life. Inevitably these conditions predispose to problem drinking and drug misuse in the workplace. Anxiety is even more common than depression, and social anxiety is the commonest form. This predisposes to the seductively quick – albeit transient – relief gained from alcohol or drugs.

Global business travel can be stressful. This can present problems due to increasing in-flight alcohol, sometimes together with that of drug misuse. The consequences of champagne and cocaine use in first class and of less exotic mixes in club or economy are presented to the cabin crew. Hence the importance of the appropriately strict regulations regarding alcohol consumption imposed by the UK Civil Aviation Authority and corresponding safety regulators throughout the air industry internationally (JAR-FCL3, 2000). Apart from operating safely, aircrews must be capable of dealing with aberrant passenger behaviour. The prime duty of a flight attendant being that of safety regulation.

Certain personality characteristics – poor behavioural self-control and lack of self-discipline – predispose to alcohol excess, especially when subject to social peer-group pressures. The rigid perfectionist is prone to making unreasonable internal demands on themselves, just as fierce and uncompromising as those of a bullying line manager. These create feelings of guilt, worthlessness and inadequacy – all fertile ground for alcohol- and drug-generated relief. Also marital, family or extended family problems, bereavement, house move, medical investigations, neighbour disputes and other community stressors can all compound the situation. Hence the baggage and vulnerability brought to work, and increased susceptibility to inevitable work-related stress.

INTERNAL/INTRINSIC TO THE WORKING ENVIRONMENT

These factors can be categorised into various paradigms:

- **Social control:** Low level of supervision and lack of monitoring of performance during the working day, result in lack of regulation by job routine and integration into the organisation, with increased alcohol intake (Frone, 1999).
- **Social availability** of alcohol at work permits a degree of freedom, and co-workers may either exert peer-group pressure to drink or misguidedly cover up for another's

problem drinking or even misuse of drugs. The old justification for bars in the workplace was that visible on-site drinking was preferable to going out to pubs at lunchtime. However, now the majority of organisations are increasingly stringent whether in the boardroom or canteen.

- **Cultural availability:** The employee may take advantage of the situation when they are serving members of the public with alcoholic drinks, especially at work-related events. Applicants for such jobs may be attracted by the certainty of this availability if they have a need for alcohol themselves. Bar and catering staff are the prime example of such a self-selected group.
- **Difficulties in adapting to macro or micro workplace changes** constitute significant stressors which may predispose to problem drinking and misuse of drugs or substances and office politics may prevail.
- **Work-related stress** is common. The Health and Safety Executive defined stress as the reaction that people have to excessive pressure or other types of imposed demand with which they feel unable to cope (*Stress at Work*, HSE, 1995). Stress can result from an ultra-authoritarian culture of an organisation with unrealistic demands by the CEO or line manager, new job, change of boss, promotion, enforced sideways move or unexpected adverse job appraisal, job insecurity or the threat of redundancy. The uncertainty associated with pending mergers may generate anxiety. Other predisposing factors include boredom, fatigue, exclusion from decision making, interpersonal conflict with line manager, superiors, co-workers or subordinates, bullying, unenriched repetitive work, inadequate skill-set for the allocated job (poor person–job fit), little control over pace of work, inadequate pay and benefits together with a lack of promotion prospects, physically dangerous or adverse ergonomic aspects (temperature hot/cold, noise, dirt) or other working conditions which cause continuous anticipatory anxiety. Traumantic near-death experiences can cause post-traumatic stress and sometimes even post-traumatic stress disorder.

Effective management of change can best be achieved when employees feel personally and positively involved with the organisation. This depends on the individual's perception of what is required of them – their role. 'Role conflict' ensues from unclear definition and encompasses incompatibility, ambiguity, overload or underload. The job description should clearly define the organisation's expectations of the individual and his or her role. These should be clear and stimulating, as opposed to ambiguous or daunting. Role overload results in the individual having too many separate responsibilities. Conversely, while multi-tasking may have advantages for some, its imposition is counter-productive. Underload can make the employee feel undervalued.

During periods of re-organisation, uncertainty generates high levels of anxiety, as it does during mergers, or the threat of enforced redundancy. In such circumstances, the culture of the organisation should be capable of containing matters, sustaining good working relationships and quashing destructive rumours, which can result in the employee 'catastrophising'. Unfortunately, this is all too frequently the case. Again, when changes are announced, supportive strategies are essential in helping the individual employee and staff as a whole to work through the imposed difficulties and hopefully to positively accept them. However, clear, effective, truthful, factual and timely communication is vital.

Stressors can be generated by the employee's role in the organisation causing conflict of loyalties between work and family. Ideally there should be an acceptable work-life balance of time and interaction between the two. Uncontrollable levels of stress predispose employees to the risk of problem drinking or the misuse of drugs as a 'quick fix'.

Occupational specifics

Every organisation has its own specific culture, priorities and differing safety-critical requirements. Three cases are described in detail, to illustrate differing occupational cultures. Resorting to mind-altering chemicals is not confined to any specific trade or profession and, in the occupational context, the problem drinker or drug misuser may occur at any level of seniority and, as already explained, there is no stereotype. However, addictive personality characteristics are relevant.

RISKS TO HEALTH CARE PROFESSIONALS

Health care professionals work in an environment offering the easy availability of prescribed drugs and which is conducive to social drinking, particularly when tired. This can predispose to mental or physical health impairment. Medical students, junior doctors and nurses are particularly vulnerable. Alcohol consumption is said to exceed safe limits in some two-thirds of newly qualified doctors. Subsequently, doctors are distrustful as regards confidentiality, self-conscious at exposing perceived weakness to a colleague, and prone to suspicion. There is denial and unwillingness to adapt to the patient role. Prognosis is guarded in cases of poly-addiction as participation in the essential addictions treatment programme can be unreliable. Health care, social service and the emergency services are the occupations which are exposed to a demanding and potentially aggressive section of the community – a situation which creates maximum stress (Birch et al., 1998).

The British Doctors and Dentists Group (BDDG) is networked throughout the UK. It is a sensitive organisation and is capable of responding to its members' vulnerability and supporting those who have such problems. As stated, excessive and inappropriate alcohol consumption often dates from the student or junior doctor era, providing a swift though counter-productive method of achieving relaxation. On graduation, there is suddenly an availability of drugs through hospital supplies or self-prescription, obviating the necessity for blatant theft of money to support the habit experienced by those in other occupations. BDDG provides a safe place in a way that even Alcoholics or Narcotics Anonymous cannot achieve. This in no way detracts from the value of the latter. It merely clarifies the culture of these professions. Being used to clinical confidentiality and to the jealous guarding of personal privacy, doctors and dentists are understandably dedicated to its preservation for themselves. Also, they are appropriately apprehensive regarding the impact of their condition on their professional future. As with AA, the BDDG follows a 12-step programme, which is in keeping with evidence-based medicine. This is widely recognised as a vital component of maintaining recovery even following the most sophisticated of residential alcohol and addictions treatment programmes. Unfortunately, until recently the medical profession has been slow and ineffective in responding to the needs of colleagues. The previous cultural approach was counter-productive, albeit very sincere. However, with the current compassionate, highly effective lead from the General Medical Council, the well-being and safety of patients is recognised as key, while constructive support is provided to the vulnerable doctor without stigmatisation, problem drinking or the misuse of drugs being regarded as is any other health issue. Moreover, the majority of cases which result in GMC intervention could well have been prevented had the problem been addressed sooner. Perhaps the respective medical defence organisations should give even more prominence to this scenario in their routine advice. Historically, there is a legacy from the sincere and well-meaning 'Three Wise Men', perhaps more appropriately 'The Three Blind or Deaf Men' of yesteryear, when denial of one's own or a colleague's problem drinking was the norm, a form of benign but hazardous collusion. Doctors, dentists and nurses are particularly resistant to confronting themselves with such issues. Is this due to denial or to an inability to accept the patient role? It must be emphasised that the nursing and dental professions are now addressing the situation with similar and encouraging vigour.

There are various reasons why health care professionals are at risk from problem drinking and drug misuse, although prevalence statistics are scanty. Doctors in particular have long years of training during which there is intense competition and fear of examination failure. This is compounded by an enormous clinical workload, with savage and unrealistic time constraints, particularly as house officers and in primary care. There are ever increasing expectations of patients and their relatives. Obligatory documentation is increasing exponentially, unsocial hours and continuous medical responsibility whether or not on duty is the norm, and the threat of increasing litigation is constant. In addition, the entirely appropriate but time-consuming continuous professional development, appraisal, audit and preparation for proposed revalidation is required. In two-thirds of junior doctors alcohol consumption is said to exceed safe limits (Birch et al., 1998). Availability of drugs, the nature and subjective effects of which are well understood, allied to legitimate self-medication with prescribed drugs of whatever nature, is seductively enticing for the vulnerable. Hypnotics, anxiolytics, antidepressants and analgesics are commonly misused and their effects can be increased by alcohol excess and can result in confusion and a counter-productive and dangerous pattern of behaviour. The depressant effect of alcohol is not understood by people in general, and until recently, by some health care professionals. Nevertheless, despite all the proven health hazards caused by alcohol, it is known to be a most effective quick-acting anxiolytic. However, its use is counter-productive, the relief is extremely brief and can result in impaired sleep with distressing rebound nocturnal anxiety. Poly-drug misuse must always be considered.

OCCUPATIONAL CASE PRESENTATIONS

Armed services

Ex-military doctor aged 60, whose only child was brain-damaged at birth. A caring father, family man and highly thought of professionally, whose drinking pattern had not previously caused concern. Having left the service on compassionate grounds, he found adaptation to civilian life and to the NHS very difficult. The stress of general practice predisposed him to anxiety with depression and to an increase in alcohol consumption, leading to a drink-driving charge, an 18-month loss of licence and GMC involvement. Initially, there was typical denial and difficulty in accepting his illness and the patient role, although he had been recognised as highly effective in treating others with the same condition. Engagement with Alcoholics Anonymous locally was understandably unacceptable, as he was reluctant to risk meeting his own patients. In fact, this was illogical as already there had been enormous media publicity regarding his drink driving. Also he felt he was being 'regarded as a doctor' at Alcoholics Anonymous meetings, which made sharing and involvement predictably difficult. Despite his wife's support, progress was very slow, including lapses and secret drinking, prior to his accessing the BDDG and feeling that it was a safe place. He is now in his fifteenth year of recovery.

Airline pilot

Thirty and single; father, paternal grandfather and brother have had serious drink problems, hence the conducive family culture. He is gregarious, gained a BSc first class in physics and enjoys amateur dramatics. From the University Air Training Corps, he completed flying training and gained a commercial pilot's licence uneventfully. Simulator and route checks have never presented significant problems. He enjoyed long-haul duties and the social life involved. However, alcohol consumption increased both down the route and at home. Inexplicable short sickness absences and irritability led to concern on the part of his fleet manager, who appropriately advised involvement with the company's occupational health physician. He readily agreed to a residential addictions treatment programme to which he was highly motivated, and he engaged effectively with Alcoholics Anonymous. He regained his Class 1 medical certification, the prerequisite for a commercial pilot's licence. Fortunately, he has also been able to utilise the 'buddy system' whereby a colleague supports and reports on his condition. His basic self-confidence has allowed him to be comfortably up-front as to why he is no longer drinking, whether down the route or at home. Predictably, his supportive partner's worries have been relieved and she is now willing to consider marriage and starting a family, both of which are favourable prognostic features. The air industry has a macho self-sufficient culture, entirely in keeping considering the nature of duties.

IT recruitment consultant

Single male, 30, charismatic, achieving excellent appraisals and corresponding bonuses, a natural leader capable of motivating his team. However, the Chief Executive Officer became progressively concerned regarding his misuse of crack cocaine, combined with prodigious alcohol consumption. Reluctantly, the consultant agreed to referral from the occupational health physician and was admitted to an addictions treatment programme. However, he illogically assumed that his absence would be detrimental, despite the Chief Executive Officer's initiation of and strong support for such a treatment regime. He claimed that his clients would feel let down and discharged himself after a week, against medical advice, being convinced that he was indispensable. Predictably he resumed unacceptable levels of binge drinking and the use of cocaine, albeit no longer crack cocaine. This minor modification he unrealistically boasts of as an achievement! Unfortunately, it seems that a further catastrophe, in addition to his present three years' drink-driving ban, may have to ensue prior to his acceptance of the necessity to address his illness realistically, with the same respect and prioritisation that any other serious, life-threatening clinical condition demands. His supportive loving partner broke off their relationship in despair. The prognosis is very guarded. He exhibits serious denial, and a lack of insight and judgement regarding his health, occupation and personal life. The culture of the organisation predisposes to his attitude as his basic salary is very low and any sickness absence constitutes a financial hardship due to loss of commission. Nevertheless, the culture does include caring and sensitivity rarely seen in this occupation.

Financial services

A stockbroker, married, supportive wife, referred from a liver unit with severe alcoholic liver disease, responded well to a residential addictions treatment programme, being motivated to indefinite abstinence. However, he was very resistant to essential ongoing community-based Alcoholics Anonymous involvement, an essential intervention prognostically significant in recovery. 'My professional business credibility would end if it were known....' In due course, he did attend and later enthused 'half the people there were my clients, the other half were my competitors'.

Commercial driver

A long-distance lorry driver with HGV licence and impeccable occupational and private driving records, completed an extensive eight-day assignment uneventfully, although drinking heavily during night stops. He returned his lorry to the depot and collected his own car to return home – a journey of some ten miles. Due to his wife's longstanding objection to his level of drinking, and disliking confrontation, he stopped in a lay-by about a mile from his home to consume three-quarters of a bottle of duty-free whisky and went to sleep on the back seat. The police found him, suspected he was ill, but then smelt the alcohol. He was breathalysed and found to be over twice the legal limit. He was fined and lost his HGV and private driving licences for two years. Despite not being in the driving seat, he was judged to have been technically in charge of his car. The culture of this occupation is appropriately rigid and his occupational future was inevitably jeopardised.

Aeronautics fitter

Fifty-three and married. Wife (50), a civil servant, and daughter (20), a medical student, are supportive but distraught by his occasional unpredictable serious three-day binges. These have resulted in several warnings at work. He is now on his final one. He is a very sensitive, kindly man who is highly thought of by his employers for using his own time to teach apprentices. He has a recent two-year drink-driving ban. He enjoys competitive badminton and 'works out' regularly. His anxiety and depression date from his mother's terminal illness. However, his drinking pattern preceded her deterioration in health. Anything short of indefinite abstinence being unrealistic, he agreed to an addictions treatment programme and fortunately engaged well with Alcoholics Anonymous.

Cultural risk factors

The following section lists factors within the workplace culture that present an increased risk to the use of substances:

- availability of alcohol – licensed trade, catering, work entailing entertaining clients
- social pressures
- co-worker collusion – well-meaning but misguided covering up, when, in fact whistle-blowing is more effective for the organisation and for the individual
- time constraints – unrealistic deadlines
- peer group pressure macho ethos – seamen, service and airline personnel
- lack of supervision – lawyers, doctors, international business executives (global travelling with frequent zone changes), politicians (irregular hours and a plethora of bars)

- income – financial independence can predispose to use of substances. Paradoxically, so do economic constraints, predisposing to the seeking of solace and escape
- physical danger – seamen, miners, construction workers, oil-riggers, and many others
- separation from stabilising social/domestic/sexual relationships – some occupations self-select
- interfacing a demanding and potentially aggressive public – exemplified by police, traffic wardens, firemen, school teachers, social workers, and health care professionals.

Women at work

Although the proportion of successful women is increasing, the majority are still in repetitive or clerical jobs. There are progressively more women in employment, and their attitude is changing, perhaps due to the so-called 'ladette' culture which is represented across the spectrum of employment and socio-economic backgrounds.

Also, women who have resumed work during the year following childbirth are particularly vulnerable to stress. In keeping with current statutory maternity leave entitlement, during this time re-entry to employment is obligatory. Workplace stressors impact on a woman following the birth of the first child in particular as she is unfamiliar with the art of combining the respective roles of wife, mother and employee. Here for the first time, the true implications of maternal instinct are confronted.

The prevalence of post-natal depression is one in ten following an uneventful pregnancy and the uncomplicated delivery of a normal healthy baby at term. This group, as in any other of either sex with minor psychiatric morbidity, may be considered as the 'working wounded' – that is, sickness absence is not indicated but they are predictably more vulnerable to any stress. Thus, inappropriately but understandably, some resort to alcohol to switch off from the conflict of occupational and domestic demands. Fortunately, it is becoming increasingly recognised and accepted that childbirth impacts very significantly on the husband, partner and father who also has to adapt to an enormous change. Therefore, whatever the culture of a profession or occupation, from cabinet minister to labourer, paternity leave is indicated.

Summary

In summarising, cultural trends are key in the occupational context throughout the demographic spectrum, be they football supporters or students – the workforce of the future. Hence, the Royal Bank of Scotland's finding that students spend more on alcohol than on anything other than accommodation is significant (RBS, 2004).

Already 10 million workdays are lost through staff calling in sick. Fifty one per cent of the UK workforce consider that the proposed 24-hour drinking culture will cut productivity further, according to a recent survey by the recruitment website reed.co.uk (2004). Is it too late to re-think this legislation?

References

1. Health and Safety at Work, Act 1974. Elizabeth II 1974. Chapter 37. London: HMSO, 1974
2. The scale and impact of illegal drug use by workers. Andy Smith, Emma Wadsworth, Susanna Moss, Sharon Simpson. *Health and Safety Executive Research Report*, 193/2004
3. *Girlfriends in High Places* Helen McCarthy. London: Demos, 2004
4. Women held back at work by old boys' network. Maxine Frith. *Independent*, 23 April 2004
5. The psychosocial work environment and alcohol dependence: a prospective study. Head J, SA Stansfield and J Siegrist. *Occup Environ Med*. 2004 Mar; 61(3); 219–24
6. Work stress and alcohol use. MR. Frone. *Alcohol Res Health* 1999; 23(4):284–91
7. *The Problem Drinker at Work*. Health and Safety Executive. London: HMSO, 1991
8. Health care professionals referred for treatment of alcohol and drug problems M Gossop, S Stephens, D Stuart, J Marshall, J Bearn and J Strang. *Alcohol and Alcoholism*. 2001 Mar–April; 36(2): 160–4
9. Prevalence of mental illness in the workplace. R Jenkins. *In Prevention of Mental Ill Health at Work*. R Jenkins, N Coney, (eds). London: HMSO, 1992
10. Joint Aviation Authorities/Joint Aviation Requirements JAR-FCL3 Flight Crew Licensing (Medical). Global Engineering 1 December 2000 Documents
11. *Stress at Work: a guide for employers*. Health and Safety Executive. Sudbury: Health and Safety Executive, 1995
12. Alcohol, drinking, illicit drug use, and stress in junior house officers in north-east England. D Birch, H Ashton and F Kamali. *Lancet* 1998 5 September 352(9130): 785–6
13. Student Living Index 2004. Royal Bank of Scotland
14. 24-hour drinking will be bad for business, say UK workers. www.reed.co.uk/research.aspx 23 August 2004

Bibliography

Review of the literature on illegal drugs in the workplace. Johanna Beswick et al. Sheffield: Health and Safety Laboratory (an agency of the Health and Safety Executive) 2002 (*Health and Safety Laboratory series report WPS/01/02*)

Health aspects of well-being in working places; report on a WHO working group, Prague, 18–20 September 1979. World Health Organization. Copenhagen: WHO (*Euroreports & Studies 31*), 1980

6 Symptoms of Drug Abuse in the Workplace

Fabrizio Schifano

Introduction

Most users of illicit drugs are employed adults with rates of drug use which are especially high, up to 17 per cent, in specific workforce environments (for instance the construction industry).[1] On the other hand, heavy alcohol intake has been reported in 7–44 per cent of employees.[2, 3, 4] Symptoms of drug abuse are often more clearly identified where the consumers spend most of their time (for example at school, in the workplace). Recognition of these issues will help subjects in both breaking their denial attitude and in accessing the available employee assistance programmes, which will ultimately result in a safer work environment.

In this review, a description of symptoms and signs consequent to use, misuse and dependence of a number of psychoactive compounds will be given. In doing so, the single compounds will be individually commented first. Eventually, a comprehensive list of signs and symptoms possibly linked to a drug abuse situation will be tentatively attributed to single substances. In taking into account both different conditions of use and possible different implications for the workplace environment, the psychoactive substances here commented have been grouped as follows: a) classified drugs, most usually taken on a long-term basis (cannabis, opiates/opioids, cocaine); b) substances most usually linked to the 'recreational' drugs' scene (ecstasy and ecstasy-like drugs, methamphetamines, methylphenidate, phencyclidine and ketamine, LSD and DMT, GHB, dextromethorphan, cathinones, smart and ecological drugs); c) common psychoactive compounds (alcohol, benzodiazepines, nicotine, caffeine). Finally, a few diagnostic guidelines will be proposed to distinguish between social and problematic misuse.

Classified drugs

CANNABIS

Marijuana ('joint', 'hashish', 'cannabis', 'weed', 'skunk') is the illicit compound most used in the EU countries. The source of marijuana is the hemp plant (*Cannabis sativa*) and its most notorious active ingredient is THC (delta-9-tetrahydrocannabinol). Hashish is a resinous substance, taken from the tops of female plants, which contains the highest concentration of THC. The concentration of THC may vary considerably, the 'skunk' variety being one of the most powerful available. Popular use of marijuana has arisen from its effects of euphoria, sense of relaxation, increased visual, auditory and taste perceptions that may occur with low to moderate dosages of the drug. Most users report an increase in appetite as well. Unpleasant effects which may occur include depersonalization, changed body image, disorientation, acute panic reactions and severe paranoia. Occasionally, delusions and hallucinations may be observed. Marijuana has specific effects that may decrease one's ability to perform tasks requiring a great deal of coordination (such as driving a car). Visual tracking is impaired and sense of time is typically prolonged. Learning may be greatly affected because the drug decreases one's ability to concentrate and pay attention. Other marijuana effects may include bloodshot eyes, increased heart rate and blood pressure, bronchial irritation leading to bronchospasm, pharyngitis, sinusitis, bronchitis and asthma in heavy users. THC metabolites (substances formed when the body breaks marijuana down) are normally stored in body fat tissues. As a result of that, evidence of marijuana may be demonstrated in heavy users up to 4–6 weeks after discontinuing the drug. Between all of the classified drugs being searched in workplace urine testing programmes, THC is the most frequently reported compound. Occurrence of a clear withdrawal syndrome following cessation of heavy cannabis use has been described. Its symptoms include anger, anxiety, decreased appetite, decreased body weight, irritability, restlessness, shakiness, sleep problems and stomach pain. Onset typically occurs between days 1–3, peak effects are seen between days 2–6 and most effects last 4–14 days.[5]

OPIATES/OPIOIDS

Originally developed for the treatment of acute pain, opiates/opioids are still used for that purpose in clinical settings. The abuse potential of opiates/opioids is considerable, the most well-known illegally used opiate being heroin. The pleasurable subjective experience induced by these drugs makes them particularly popular as drugs of abuse.

Several sources indicate an increase in new, young users across Europe who may well be part of the active workforce population and who are attracted by high-purity heroin that can be sniffed or smoked instead of being injected.[6] Generally however, chronic heroin use is observed in individuals well familiar with the illicit drug scene and for this reason less likely to reach stable employment levels. On the other hand, consumption of opioid analgesics may be frequently represented in the actively working population. Some opioids (for example codeine) are found in over-the-counter medications, usually in combination with non-steroid anti-inflammatory agents (for example paracetamol).[7] There has been a significant controversy about appropriateness, efficacy, safety and wisdom of treating chronic pain patients with opioids. Arguments against their use have included concerns about tolerance, dependence, addiction, persistent side effects and interference with physical or psychosocial functioning. However, in appropriately selected patients, opioids have a low addiction potential. Moreover, in addition to their primary analgesic action, they can facilitate reduction in suffering, enhance functional activity level and improve quality of life without significant risks of addictive behaviours.[8]

Effects of heroin intoxication (which are largely determined by dose levels, route of administration and tolerance) may include euphoria, decreased anxiety, drowsiness, irritable mood, 'pinpoint pupils' (pupillary constriction), slurred speech and attention deficit. Tolerance and physical dependence may develop quickly. In regular abusers, withdrawal may occur as early as a few hours after last administration. Its symptoms include drug craving, restlessness, muscle and bone pain, insomnia, diarrhoea and vomiting, and cold sweats accompanied by goose bumps ('cold turkey'). Major withdrawal symptoms peak between 48 and 72 hours after the last dose and fade away in about a week.

COCAINE

Traditionally, cocaine is snorted. However, over the last few years a significant increase in the attitude of smoking the drug has been observed. In fact, since cocaine hydrochloride cannot be smoked (because it decomposes at high temperatures) consumers have invented a process through which the alkaloid part is freed from the base through the use of ether. The result of this process is known as 'free-basing'. Another product of the free-basing process is called crack, obtained by heating hydrochloride cocaine with baking soda and water. With baking soda, consumers are able to get rid of the impurities and pure cocaine crystals may be obtained.[6] With respect to hydrochloride cocaine, the free-base formulation gives the user both a quicker and a stronger 'high', although of a shorter duration. These characteristics can explain the huge potential of dependence liability of the free-base formulation. After the binge, the beginning of the withdrawal phase is observed. This is schematically divided into three different sub-phases: crash; withdrawal properly called; extinction. Crash begins 15–30 minutes after the binge and lasts for a period of nine hours to four days. It is characterised by dysphoria and by different levels of craving. The withdrawal properly called lasts approximately for one to ten weeks; in the last period of this phase the craving, anxiety and dysphoria levels may be very high and relapse risk is considerable. If the patient is then able to continue to abstain from cocaine use, the extinction phase begins and both patient's behaviour and mood level are gradually reverting back to normality. However, if the patient is exposed to environmental stimuli which reminds themself of cocaine (for example the sight of some white powder, like table salt), sudden peaks of craving are observed. Different modalities of cocaine administration have been observed in different social groups across different countries. Cocaine is snorted by social elite ('champagne style'), whilst both intravenous use and/or crack form consumption are usually seen in the groups of long-term, high-dosage, cocaine consumers. With a chronic use of the drug, paranoid ideation is commonly observed; with the free-base formulation, due to its higher frequency of consumption, risk is understandably higher.

Recreational drugs

Since abuse of these drugs is observed mostly in the dance scene, these compounds are also known as 'dance' or 'club' drugs. Clubbers are usually well integrated into society: they are employed or students and are able to build up and maintain relationships.[6] The different drugs are, to a certain extent, linked to different sounds: ecstasy and ketamine are frequently used in the techno scene; cocaine is more likely to be linked to the 'garage' version of techno music. On the other hand, alcohol is a sort of a 'trans-scene' compound, because it is widely used in different settings. An analytical description of the most important synthetic drugs now follows, their order of presentation being related to their different impact on the drug scene.

MDMA (ECSTASY OR XTC) AND MDMA-LIKE DRUGS

Ecstasy use, which started in Europe at the end of the 1980s, steadily increased throughout the 1990s. It is very popular in the club scene because users can dance frenetically for many hours. Apart from clubs, ecstasy may be used in bars and private parties as well. In the last few years, addiction treatment units have been approached by drug abusers who have been taking ecstasy together with opiates to reciprocally modulate effects of the two different compounds: heroin is self-administered to come down from the long-lasting untoward effects of ecstasy.

With chronic ecstasy consumption, a dependence syndrome can be observed, although this happens in only about 10 per cent of all cases. After acute self-administration, a number of different physical conditions have been described: tachycardia, increased blood pressure, cerebral haemorrhages, convulsions, coma, midriasis (increase of pupil size), vomiting, diarrhoea, thrombocytopenia (decreased platelet count), acute renal and liver failure.[9, 10] One of the most feared consequences is given by hyperthermia, when body temperature can rise up to 43°C. This may be due also to characteristics of the crowded environments and to the intense physical activity in which clubbers are involved. As a consequence, consumers tend to massively increase their water intake, so that a decreased concentration of sodium in brain tissue and cerebral oedema can be observed as a dramatic result. Moreover, MDMA ingestion can cause a series of behavioural disturbances after leaving the club: a few patients who showed bizarre, impulsive and dangerous behaviour when driving back home have been described.[9]

Long-term psychopathological consequences of a chronic MDMA exposure may be not easily recognised. Those who usually take ecstasy state that they do feel significantly more depressed, asocial, irritable and very angry. Possible untoward consequences of heavy and/or long-term use of ecstasy include depression, psychotic disturbances, cognitive disturbances, bulimic disorders, impulse control disorders, panic attacks and social phobias. Cognitive performances are significantly reduced in the MDMA-misusing subjects with respect to well-matched controls and memory recall is compromised even in previous consumers who are now drug-free. The data pertaining to possible reversibility of both psychiatric disturbances and neurobiological damage consequent to MDMA misuse in humans are worrying.

METHAMPHETAMINES AND OTHER AMPHETAMINE-LIKE STIMULANTS

These compounds are frequently nicknamed as 'speed', 'meth' and 'choke', whilst its smokable forms are known with names as 'ice', 'crystal', 'crank' and 'glass'.[6] Meth is found as a crystal white powder, easily soluble in water and alcohol. Meth can be snorted, smoked, ingested or injected intravenously. Soon after inhalation or intravenous administration, consumers feel a strong sensation of 'rush', which can last for several minutes. After snorting or ingesting the drug, effects are still euphoriant but both less intense (due to different bioavailability levels achieved) and more delayed (they do appear only after 15–20 minutes and can last for up to 12 hours). As happens with cocaine, the clinical picture ('tweaking') is characterized by a sort of a 'binge and crash' cycle. After 'meth' intake, hyperactivity, anorexia and arousal increase levels may be observed. Dependence is easily observed with chronic use of the drug. Most frequent psychopathological consequences include violent and bizarre behaviour, anxiety, confusion, sleep disorders, psychotic disorders (paranoid type), aggressive behaviour (both suicide and homicide episodes have been described) and tactile hallucinations (such as the sensation of parasites under the skin). Psychotic symptoms can last for a long time after drug intake has been stopped. Withdrawal symptoms include depression, anxiety, strong craving and tiredness. Dexamphetamine sulphate (also known as dexedrine, 'evans.db' or 'dexies') is found in tablets and its effects are very similar to those of methamphetamine. Lastly, ephedrine is a stimulant compound which may be found as the active ingredient of 'herbal ecstasy'; different varieties of this product are widely offered from different websites.[11]

METHYLPHENIDATE

This compound is a stimulant drug which is prescribed to children diagnosed with an attention deficit hyperactivity disorder and in some depressive forms who are resistant to traditional treatment. However, methylphenidate is also found on the black market.[6] Its effects include decreased appetite, increased arousal and attention, and euphoria. Tablets are ingested or crushed, reduced to powder and snorted. Powder can also be injected. Complications are consequent to blood vessel obstruction in both lung and retinal districts. Cardiovascular problems are also reported. With chronic use of this drug, dependence may occur.

PHENCYCLIDINE AND KETAMINE

Between the 1950s and 1980s, phencyclidine (also known as PCP, 'angel dust', 'super grass', 'killer weed', 'embalming fluid' or 'rocket fuel') was used in a number of countries as an anaesthetic drug for both humans and animals. In Europe, its misuse has only been occasionally reported. On the other hand, PCP-like drug ketamine (also known as 'special-K' or 'K') use has increased significantly over the last few years. Its clinical effects include derealization, slurred speech, motor incoordination, gait disturbances, sensations of strength and invulnerability. Visual and perceptual disturbances, affective disturbances, schizophrenia-like episodes, amnesia, serious episodes of violence and impulsivity have also been reported.[6] Effects last for about one hour but motor incoordination is particularly long-lasting (18–24 hours). Ketamine is usually diverted from veterinarian market, since the compound is still used for surgical intervention in small animals. For consumption, ketamine (which comes usually in liquid formulations) is heated and the resulting powder is snorted. Ketamine can be smoked as well, usually in combination with marijuana. The liquid formulation can be injected. Schizophrenia-like symptoms and cognitive disturbances can persist up to three days after consumption.

LSD AND DMT

Diethylamide of lysergic acid (LSD, 'acid' and at least other 80 nicknames) is probably the most famous hallucinogenic compound. LSD was first discovered and experimented with in 1938; it is found in tablets, small capsules ('microdots') and occasionally in its liquid form, which is odourless, colourless and with a slightly sour taste. Moreover, LSD can be found as a product adsorbed on tiny and coloured pieces of paper ('stamps' or 'windowpanes'). During the 1960s and the 1970s, LSD dosages were in a 130–300 micrograms dose range per tablet, but the typical concentration is now of 20–50 micrograms per unit. At this last dosage range, only euphoriant effects are usually reported.[6]

Effects appear 30–90 minutes after intake and symptoms include pupil dilation, temperature rise, tachycardia, hypertension, sweating, anorexia, insomnia, dry mouth and tremors. With higher dosages, delusions and vivid hallucinations (for instance consumers 'hear' colours and 'see' sounds) are reported. Panicky and extremely unpleasant sensations ('bad trips') are described as well. Hallucinatory experiences can last for up to 12 hours. Since consumers may not appreciate consequences of their at-risk behaviour, incidents and death may occur. Even weeks or months after last ingestion, LSD users may report flashbacks (re-occurrences of those hallucinatory experiences they had during intoxication). Long-lasting psychotic episodes have been reported in vulnerable individuals exposed to LSD. A tolerance to LSD effects can develop and it is not unusual to observe compulsive phenomena of LSD consumption in some individuals.

Dymethyltryptamine (DMT) powder can be snorted or injected intravenously. Although DMT is found in some lianas growing in the Mato Grosso, it is its synthetic version ('businessman special') which is of recreational use. DMT, in combination with other psychoactive compounds, is found in 'ayahuasca' beverages as well. DMT has strong psychedelic properties.

GHB

Gamma-hydroxybutyrate (or GHB) is also known as 'liquid ecstasy', 'Georgia Home Boy', 'Grievous Bodily Harm', 'somatomax' and 'scoop'. Because of its euphoriant, sedative and (much-appreciated by body-builders) anabolic properties, a widespread use of GHB has been observed in the USA and in the UK in the last 10 years or so.[10] GHB is usually found in the liquid form but it is also possible to find GHB as a powder or in tablets. Generally, its psychoactive properties appear 10–20 minutes after intake and last for about one to three hours; some hangover effects are observed thereafter. With GHB, both a tolerance and a physical dependence can develop. GHB withdrawal syndrome lasts for 3–12 days and usually fades away without any after-effects; its symptoms include insomnia, muscular cramps, tremor and anxiety. Acute intoxication is more profound if the drug is taken together with other sedatives; its symptoms include vomit, deep sedation, dreamy states, dizziness and respiratory distress. Since the compound is odourless, tasteless and colourless, it can easily be added to a drink. Due to this reason, GHB is also a well-known 'date rape drug' (administered to sexually take advantage of an unwilling partner).[6] Given that GHB can also induce amnesia, the rape victim might find it difficult to remember precisely what happened, and reporting to police forces may be more unlikely.

DEXTROMETHORPHAN

Dextromethorfan (also known as 'DXM' or 'Green Triangle') is usually prescribed as a cough suppressant. It is also found in some of the tablets sold in the illicit market as ecstasy. Symptoms of recreational intoxication include bizarre behaviour, hyperactivity, hallucinations and pupil size modifications. In chronic users, erection dysfunctions have been reported as well. If administered at low dosages, DXM can cause mild side effects, such as sedation, tiredness, dizziness, skin rashes. In case of overdose, symptoms include stupor, restlessness, coma, toxic psychosis, respiratory depression, tachycardia, nausea, vomiting and lowering of seizure threshold. Although infrequently reported, chronic use of DXM can lead to dependence. Symptoms of withdrawal include intense craving, overreaction to sensory stimuli, sensation of being able to fly or to float and visual or auditory hallucinations. One of its active metabolites (dextrorphan) has some PCP-like effects.

POPPERS AND OTHER INHALANTS

Amyl nitrite has been used in the medical field for about a century, mostly for treatment of chest pain from cardiovascular origin. In the last few years, poppers have been widely used in most of the European countries. Amyl, but also butyl and isobutyl, nitrite is able to induce blood vessel dilation. Other effects include higher perfusion of brain tissues and smooth muscles relaxation. Its effects start 7–10 seconds after inhalation and last for about 30–60 seconds. After intake, feelings of 'repletion' of the head, rush (similar to the one described with nitrous oxide) and mild euphoria are reported. These effects can be followed by tachycardia, headache, dizziness and sedation. Tolerance can develop very rapidly.[6] Consumers feel nitrites can increase their sexual performance; poppers are especially appreciated by homosexuals. Its long-term use can decrease competence of the immune system and susceptibility to HIV infection may be increased.

Known by such street names as 'huffing' or 'sniffing', the habit of getting high by inhaling the fumes of common household products (which can start as early as seven years of age) is estimated to claim the lives of a number of children in the UK each year. Death due to inhalants can occur as a consequence of several mechanisms, including sudden sniffing death syndrome, suffocation, dangerous behaviour and aspiration.

CATHINONES

Methcathinone is known with a number of different terms such as 'crystal meth', 'burn', 'cat', 'khat', 'miraa' and 'crank' (not to be confused with the smokable form of methamphetamine). In some parts of the USA, cat is found as a white powder with a characteristic taste.[6] Although in Somalia and Yemen there is a tradition of chewing the khat leaves in social environments, the formulation which is recreationally used by youths is a synthetic one. Cat is usually snorted, but can also be ingested or injected intravenously. Its effects are similar to those of cocaine, but cat powder is cheaper and its effects last longer. After intake, abdominal pain, flushing, sweating (alternating with chills), tachycardia, restlessness and anxiety may be observed. Affective disturbances and paranoid ideation are reported in chronic users. Although a few reports of consumption have already been suggested from the UK, widespread diffusion of recreational use is mostly limited to the USA.

SMART DRUGS, SMART DRINKS AND ECOLOGICAL DRUGS

These compounds are constituted by drugs, nutrients, drinks, vitamins, vegetable extracts and potions which are derived from herbs. Distributors and proponents of the use of these compounds emphasize their capacity to increase intelligence, to improve memory performances, to increase attention and concentration and to facilitate body detoxification, especially so after an alcohol/drugs binge.[6]

Most often, smart drinks are mixed with vitamins, amino-acids and other nutrients. Occasionally, some caffeine can be found as well. In the youth culture, a number of different herbal ('ecological') products are becoming increasingly popular. These compounds can be easily and conveniently purchased through dedicated websites.[11]

Common psychoactive compounds

ALCOHOL

Alcohol affects the central nervous system as a sedative/depressant, resulting in decrease of motor activity, anxiety, tension and inhibitions. Both concentration and judgement functions become impaired. Nutritional deficiencies and alcoholic hepatitis (which may also progress to a fatty liver condition and then cirrhosis) are also reported in long-term misusers. Heart, sexual function and nervous system may also be affected in chronic alcoholics. After an alcohol binge, consumers complain of hangover, whose symptoms include headache, nausea, diarrhoea, decreased appetite, shakiness, tiredness and an overall feeling of being unwell.

A six-year follow-up of a cohort of male and female white-collar workers revealed that even moderate alcohol consumption in this population was associated with social costs for both employer and employee, particularly in terms of sickness absence. Early intervention in a drinking situation may reduce alcohol consumption and consequently avoid years of morbidity and sickness absence, as well as having a favourable influence on promotion prospects and labour turnover.[12] For aircraft, trains and commercial vessels, operators are subject to sanctions for having 0.04 g% or higher blood alcohol concentration (BAC). A study examined the effects of alcohol (between 0.04 and 0.05 g% BAC) on simulated merchant ship handling. Participants (who were volunteer deck officer cadets) were randomized to receive alcohol or placebo and then completed a bridge simulator task. A main effect for alcohol was found, indicating that performance was significantly impaired by low doses of alcohol relative to performance in placebo condition.[13] Apart from impaired performance, the more significant the amount of alcohol intake, the higher the global levels of psychological suffering being reported. In a study carried out with graduates from all Scottish dental schools from the years 1991 and 1994, a total of 232 graduates were sent questionnaires. Measures included a wide range of conditions at work, including alcohol consumption, sickness-absence and mental health. Mental health and alcohol consumption were equivalent to age-matched junior doctors, but increased psychological symptoms in female dentists were significantly associated with number of units of alcohol consumed.[14] Moreover, alcohol consumption does increase aggression, especially in those persons who show baseline higher levels of irritability.[15] Absentee rate in alcoholics is 3.8 to 8.3 times greater than that for non-alcoholic workers.[16] Marmot et al[17] reported that alcoholics lost more days per year through sickness absence and spent considerably more days in hospitals than their control groups. Through absence due to illness or accidents, alcoholics lost 22.3 days annually compared with 7.0 days for controls. First notification of alcohol problems of an employee came from within the company in 80 per cent of cases. Striking features were mainly drinking before and during work and erratic time-keeping. As part of the Whitehall II study,[16] the relationship between different drinking patterns and sickness absence was examined. A total of 10 314 male and female civil servants completed a baseline questionnaire about their drinking habits. All sickness absence had been recorded prospectively. Alcohol consumption was strongly related to employment grade (that is the lower the grade the higher proportion of men and women reporting no alcohol consumption). For men, increased rates of absence were found only in frequent drinkers.

BENZODIAZEPINES

(For a more comprehensive review of this issue, please refer also to Chapter 7 in this book.)

Any prescription for benzodiazepines must be preceded by a careful risk-benefit analysis considering the issues of an individual particular life situation, personality style and psychiatric diagnosis. Risks of both abuse and cognitive/psychomotor impairments have to be balanced against therapeutic benefits.[18] On the other hand, the annual prevalence of benzodiazepine use in the general European population is quite significant. Factors significantly associated with benzodiazepine use include female gender and higher levels of self-reported pain and stress. Benzodiazepines' side effects include sedation, dizziness, motor incoordination, slurred speech, mental confusion and gastro-intestinal disorders. Concurrent administration of benzodiazepines together with alcohol increases the risk of excessive sedation and overdose. With chronic use, dependence, tolerance and withdrawal may be observed. Symptoms of benzodiazepine withdrawal include increased anxiety, panic attacks, insomnia, nightmares, increased depression, breathless feelings, nausea, aggressive outbursts, distortion of vision, shaking hands, increased sensitivity to light, sound, touch and smell, hyperactivity, sweating, palpitations, blurred vision and craving. In severe withdrawal states, both hallucinations and seizures have been reported. A benzodiazepine dependence condition is more easily observed if a high-dose, long-term (more than a few weeks/few months), high potency, compound prescription is made.

Data drawn from a study of a sample of working Swedes revealed that approximately 3 per cent reported taking prescribed psychoactive medications regularly. This was correlated with increases in long-term sick leave, periods of unemployment and frequent job changes by both sexes. These workers also scored high for neuroticism, and had high rates of in-patient psychiatric treatment and suicide.[19] Consumption of prescribed medications is higher in certain workplace environments. A sample of nurses was sent an anonymous survey and data were collected on three dimensions of access: perceived availability, frequency of administration, and degree of workplace control over storage and dispensing of substances. Each dimension was independently associated with increased use. When these dimensions were combined into an index, nurses with easy access were most likely to have misused prescription-type drugs.[20]

Flunitrazepam ('roofies') is one of the different benzodiazepines.[6] It is prescribed for treatment of insomnia and as a pre-anaesthetic medication in a large number of countries, but it is also self-administered as a drug of abuse. In fact, tablets may be crushed and powder is snorted or injected intravenously. In this way, consumers may be able to modulate the effects of stimulants or can boost the effects of sedatives like methadone, heroin or alcohol. Although flunitrazepam is a sedative compound, occasional paradoxical reactions (increased levels of aggression and impulsivity) may be observed with administration of high dosages. Temazepam ('jellies') is another benzodiazepine which is sought after by abusers.

NICOTINE

It has been noted that tobacco and alcohol constitute together the real 'gateway' drugs. Young people who smoke are three times more likely than non-smokers to use alcohol, eight times more likely to use marijuana and 22 times more likely to use cocaine.[21] Psychological problems are associated with heightened cigarette and alcohol consumption, which in turn increase sickness absence. In women, it seems that life events are associated with psychological problems and smoking but not with sickness absence.[22] An interactive effect between nicotine deprivation and trait irritability and physical aggression has been reported. Addictiveness of tobacco products is particularly detrimental to vulnerable groups, such as blue-collar workers.[23]

Effects of nicotine deprivation seem to affect work performances: Giannakoulas et al[24] subjected 20 healthy male aviators who were regular smokers to a 12-hour abstinence from cigarette smoking. Most frequent symptoms reported during nicotine deprivation were nervousness, craving for tobacco, tension-anxiety, fatigue, difficulty in concentration, decrease in alertness, disorders of fine adjustments, prolonged reaction times, anger-irritability, drowsiness, increase in appetite and impairment of judgement. All tests recorded an impairment of cognitive functions during abstinence. It was concluded that abrupt cessation of smoking may be detrimental to flight safety and that smoking withdrawal syndrome may influence flying parameters. Moreover, nicotine withdrawal may induce a decrease in job satisfaction together with an increase in depression, absenteeism, caloric intake, craving, aggressiveness, confusion and impulsivity.[25]

Cigarette smoking can be seen as a way of coping with a stressful work situation in order to get short-term relief. Negative emotional states associated with low-status jobs, combined with a lack of economic resources, are also likely to reduce the individual's motivation to seek proper medical treatment and thus increase the risk that transient symptoms develop into chronic illness.[26]

Far from acting as an aid for mood control, nicotine dependency seems to exacerbate stress. This is confirmed in the daily mood patterns described by smokers, with normal moods during smoking and worsening moods between cigarettes. Thus, the apparent relaxant effect of smoking only reflects the reversal of the tension and irritability that develop during nicotine depletion. In summary, dependent smokers need nicotine to remain feeling normal.[27]

CAFFEINE

Many people tend to think of coffee, tea and cola drinks as main sources of caffeine, but caffeine can be found in chocolate, pain relievers, cold remedies, weight-control aids and in a number of prescription medications as well. Caffeine content can vary in different sources from 25–35 mg (for an ounce of chocolate or cola-containing drinks) to 100–140 mg (a cup of coffee).

In some individuals, caffeine can cause sleeping troubles, mood changes and stomach pain. People who have a high caffeine intake (higher than 600 mg daily)[28] may experience a withdrawal syndrome characterized by headache, lack of concentration, drowsiness, nausea, vomiting and dysphoria. Because of its stimulant properties, caffeinated beverages are not recommended for replacing body fluids lost while sweating in hot weather or hot work environments. Caffeine use is highly prevalent; almost everybody regularly ingests caffeine. Signs and symptoms of caffeine intoxication include[29] heart racing/palpitations, arrhythmias, hyperactivity, restlessness, irritability, pressurised thought and speech, and dehydration (which may be the result of increased urinary frequency caused by caffeine intake). Coffee disrupts normal sleep architecture and, as a result of that, coffee drinkers crave for coffee to increase alertness.

Signs and symptoms of drug abuse in the workplace

GENERIC SIGNS

The three workplace areas which should be investigated in case of a substance misuse condition are performance, behaviour/appearance and safety hazards.

Performance[30]

Is a certain employee's quality of work inconsistent? Is the employee's work pace slow, slower than usual, or sporadic? Does the employee have trouble concentrating on their work? Are there signs of fatigue? Are there any records of increased mistakes, errors in judgement or a sudden inability to fulfil complex assignments or meet deadlines? These are the usual questions which supervisors should ask in observing a situation of possible substance misuse. Increased absenteeism or late arrival, both of which have a direct impact on performance of both the troubled employee and their co-workers who have to carry extra workload, also could indicate that a substance abuse problem exists. Other performance-related signs of substance abuse may include excessive sick leave, frequent early departures, extended coffee breaks, excessive time on the phone and patterns of absenteeism (Mondays, Fridays, before or after holidays, and following paydays).

Behaviour and appearance[30]

Sudden changes in behaviour, irritability, moodiness, arguing with co-workers, borrowing money from co-workers, stealing from company and co-workers and insubordination towards supervisors are not uncommon among substance abusers. Troubled workers will often show up to work looking unkempt or dressed inappropriately (long-sleeved shirts in the summer, sunglasses indoors, and so on). Also, employers may begin receiving complaints from customers and colleagues.

Safety hazards[30]

Substance-abusing employees are not safe employees. Depending on the type of work employees do, substance-abuse problems can begin manifesting themselves in employee safety records. Substance-abusing employees will be involved in more accidents than other workers, even though they are not necessarily those who are injured. They also tend to display carelessness in operation and maintenance of potentially hazardous materials or dangerous equipment. Other safety-related signs of substance abuse may include risky behaviour, increased involvement in off-the-job accidents and damaging equipment or property.

CHARACTERISTIC SIGNS[21, 31]

(In brackets are the substances that may cause the sign; please see note as well.)

Behaviour

- sleepiness, slurred speech, unsteady movements (recent use of sedatives)
- shaky hands, vomiting/sickness, fits (alcohol withdrawal)
- cold sweaty palms, unusual weight loss or gain (opiates/opioids, cocaine)
- accident-proneness (stimulants: cocaine, amphetamines, ecstasy)

- paranoia, suspicious attitudes, panic reactions (cannabis, stimulants)
- acute nudity, psychotic episode (LSD, PCP, ketamine, stimulants)
- blackouts, including complete amnesia (alcohol)
- emotional: personality modifications, sudden mood changes, irritability, bizarre behaviour, low self-esteem, poor judgment, depression and a general lack of interest (stimulants)
- frequent complaints of headache (alcohol hangover, caffeine withdrawal)
- social problems: new friends who are less interested in standard activities, problems with the law (opiates, cocaine, crack cocaine).

General appearance
- lack of cure of oneself: doesn't shave, doesn't shower (alcohol, heroin)
- smell of alcohol (alcohol recent intoxication)
- smell of solvents on clothes, paint stains on face and clothes, unusual chemical breath smell (inhalants)
- changes to less conventional styles in dress and music (recreational drugs).

Cardiorespiratory
- chest pain, tachycardia, arrhythmias (cocaine, amphetamines)
- cardiomyopathy (alcohol)
- bronchospasm (opiates/opioids, cannabis).

Hormonal problems
- irregular anovulatory periods (heroin, methadone).

Eyes
- constricted pupils (opiates/opioids recent use)
- dilated pupils (stimulants; opiates/opioids' withdrawal)
- reddened conjuntivae (THC recent use)
- red and runny eyes (inhalants).

Mouth/nose
- sores around the mouth, perioral infections, chemical burns around the mouth (inhalants)
- dental deterioration (alcohol, opiates/opioids)
- haemorrhages from nose, nasal septal perforation (cocaine, inhalants).

Gastroenteric
- reflux ulcer symptoms, diarrhoea, gastritis (alcohol)
- constipation (opiates/opioids).

Skin
- needle tracks, generalised pruritus (heroin and opiates).

(Note: Some warning signs listed in the table can also be signs of other problems. Consulting the GP to rule out physical causes of warning signs is a good first step. This should often be followed or accompanied by a comprehensive evaluation by an addiction psychiatrist.)

Social and problematic use

Kandel[32] has identified four stages that enable physicians to classify drug misusers based on their pattern of use:

- Stage 1   Experimentation
- Stage 2   Recreational use
- Stage 3   Problematic use
- Stage 4   Addiction

Some people may try substances once, have an unpleasant experience (negative reinforcement) and never progress beyond the stage of curiosity and *experimentation*. Others may be episodic, *recreational* users. They use drugs only in particular situations such as parties and patterns of use do not apparently lead to negative consequences in their functioning. *Problematic* users may be identified as those who have used substances with a negative consequence in three or more areas of life: home, school, peers/significant others, legal, work and changes in recreational activities. *Addiction* is the phase in which consumers display a compulsion to take the compound: they show lack of control on its use, a clear craving and a desire to cut down drug use.[33]

After diagnosing a substance-misuse condition, clinicians should investigate for the coexistence of a mental health problem (dual diagnosis).

Conclusions

The number of substance abusers who demonstrate performance deterioration in their early stages of misuse is relatively small. In addition, only a few members of the misusing population are responsible for costs to the organization resulting from poor job performance. The identification rate differs for alcoholics/drug addicts depending on their sex and level in the organization and on the supervisory style of their managers. Hiding symptoms and covering up for others adds to the proportion remaining unidentified. While identification through performance evaluation may be considered the only legitimate procedure in the workplace, it is not in fact identifying anywhere near the estimated number of substance abusers. Diagnostic value of urine toxicological checks carried out in the workplace have to be taken into account; do those employees who tested positive have significant substance-abuse problems or are they merely 'recreational users' who have got caught? Analysis using probability theory indicated that among workplace drug users who tested positive 52 per cent were daily users, 41 per cent monthly users and 7 per cent were annual users. At a 50 per cent testing rate, random drug tests may identify 40 per cent of daily users, 8 per cent of monthly users and only 1 per cent of annual users during the course of a year.[34] Estimated rate of illicit drug use among employees is approximately eight times the average random testing positive rate. Random drug tests in the workplace are effective in identifying near-daily users of illicit drugs, but they are less effective at identifying infrequent drug users.[34] The age factor is not to be overlooked when deciding which substances have to be chased in the biological samples: older workers tend to use more alcohol and prescription drugs; younger employees are more likely to use marijuana and cocaine.[35]

Health care supervisors interact daily with their employees and are responsible for work production and performance standards. Likewise, they are usually first to detect changes in these standards and changes in their personnel. Supervisors play a pivotal role in any drug abuse policy. With a non-judgemental approach, they should create an atmosphere of zero tolerance with regard to substance abuse consumption in the workplace.[36]

To avoid difficult personal confrontation, early intervention programmes accessible to employees over the internet have been proposed. A specially designed web site enabled employees to self-assess their stress levels, coping styles and risk for substance-related problems. It provided personalized feedback, recommendations, mini-workshops, links to other online resources and an interactive forum for direct participant-to-participant communication. These web sites provided resources for employees who were concerned about another individual's drinking as well.[37]

The workplace can be therapeutic as well: long-term therapeutic workplace effects were evaluated in heroin- and cocaine-dependent, unemployed, treatment-resistant young mothers. Participants were paid to work or to train in the 'therapeutic workplace' but had to provide drug-free urine samples to gain daily access. Participants were randomly assigned to a therapeutic workplace or a usual care control group. Therapeutic workplace participants could work for three years. Relative to controls, therapeutic workplace participants significantly increased cocaine and opiate abstinence on the basis of monthly urine samples collected until three years after intake.[38]

In the workplace, the greatest controversy centres on the use of medications during the different phases of recovery. Particularly controversial, despite considerable supporting scientific data, is the long-term use of agonists such as methadone. Occupational physicians and other non-prescribing staff can play a crucial role by supporting the responsible use of medications, maintaining contact with other medical and psychosocial treatment providers, enlisting support for medication compliance in patients' personal and professional support systems, advocating for comprehensive patient care, and being alert to signs of medication misuse.[39]

References

1.   Hersch RK, McPherson TL, Cook RF. Substance use in the construction industry: a comparison of assessment methods. *Subst Use Misuse* 2002:**37**:1331–58
2.   Chagas Silva M, Gaunekar G, Patel V, Kukalekar DS et al. The prevalence and correlates of hazardous drinking in industrial workers: a study from Goa, India. *Alcohol* 2003:**38**:79–83
3.   Medina-Mora E, Carreno S, De la Fuente JR. Experience with the alcohol use disorders identification test (AUDIT) in Mexico. *Recent Dev Alcohol* 1998:**14**:383–96
4.   Roberts S, Fallon LF Jr. Administrative issues related to addiction in the workplace. *Occup Med* 2001:**16**:509–15
5.   Kouri EM, Pope HG Jr. Abstinence symptoms during withdrawal from chronic marijuana use. *Exp Clin Psychopharmacol* 2000:**8**:483–92
6.   Schifano F. New trends in drug addiction: synthetic drugs. Epidemiological, clinical and preventive issues. *Epidemiol Psich Soc* 2001:**10**:63–70
7.   Ghodse AH, Schifano F, Oyefeso A, Jambert-Gray R, Cobain K, Corkery J. Drug-related deaths as reported by coroners in England, Wales, Scotland, N Ireland and Channel Islands. *Annual review* 2002 and np-SAD Report no. 11. European Centre for Addiction Studies, St George's Hospital Medical School, London (UK), 2003
8.   Aronoff GM. Opioids in chronic pain management: is there a significant risk of addiction? *Curr Rev Pain* 2000:**4**:112–21
9.   Schifano F. A bitter pill? Overview of ecstasy (MDMA; MDA) related fatalities. *Psychopharmacol* (Berl) 2004:**173**:242–248 (Epublication ahead of printing 13 December 2003)

10. Rodgers J, Ashton CH, Gilvarry E, Young AH. Liquid ecstasy: a new kid on the scene. *Br J Psychiatry* 2004:**184**:104–6

11. Schifano F, Leoni M, Martinotti G, Rawaf S, Rovetto F. Importance of cyberspace for the assessment of the drug abuse market: preliminary results from the Psychonaut 2002 Project. *CyberPsychol Behavior* 2003:**6**:405–410

12. Harvey S, Butler T, Thomas RL, Jenkins R. Patterns of alcohol consumption in white-collar workers – a cross-sectional and longitudinal study. *Br J Addict* 1992:**87**:91–102

13. Howland J, Rohsenow DJ, Cote J, Gomez B et al. Effects of low-dose alcohol exposure on simulated merchant ship piloting by maritime cadets. *Accid Anal Prev* 2001:**33**:257–65

14. Baldwin PJ, Dodd M, Rennie JS. Young dentists – work, wealth, health and happiness. *Br Dent J* 1999:**186**:30–6

15. Giancola PR. Irritability, acute alcohol consumption and aggressive behavior in men and women. *Drug Alcohol Depend* 2002:**68**:263–74

16. Watkins JP, Eisele GR, Matthews KO. Occupational medical program alcohol screening. Utility of the CAGE and BMAST. *J Subst Abuse Treat* 2000:**19**:51–7

17. Marmot MG, North F, Feeney A, Head J. Alcohol consumption and sickness absence: from the Whitehall II study. *Addiction* 1993:**88**:369–82

18. Roy-Byrne PP, Cowley DS. The use of benzodiazepines in the workplace. *J Psychoactive Drugs.* 1990:**22**:461–5

19. Allgulander C, Evanoff B. Psychiatric diagnoses and perceived health problems in a sample of working Swedes treated with psychoactive medications. *J Psychoactive Drugs* 1990:**22**:467–78

20. Trinkoff AM, Zhou Q, Storr CL, Soeken KL. Workplace access, negative proscriptions, job strain, and substance use in registered nurses. *Nurs Res* 2000:**49**:83–90

21. Schifano F, Zamparutti G, Zambello F. Substance misuse in adolescence: theoretical and clinical issues. *Progr Neurol Psychiatry* 2004:**8**:25–34

22. Kivimaki M, Vahtera J, Elovainio M, Lillrank B et al. Death or illness of a family member, violence, interpersonal conflict, and financial difficulties as predictors of sickness absence: longitudinal cohort study on psychological and behavioral links. *Psychosom Med* 2002:**64**:817–25

23. DeLucia AJ. Tobacco abuse and its treatment. Turning old and new issues into opportunities for the occupational health nurse. *AAOHN J* 2001:**49**:243–59

24. Giannakoulas G, Katramados A, Melas N, Diamantopoulos I et al. Acute effects of nicotine withdrawal syndrome in pilots during flight. *Aviat Space Environ Med* 2003:**74**:247–51

25. Sommese T, Patterson JC. Acute effects of cigarette smoking withdrawal: a review of the literature. *Aviat Space Environ Med* 1995:**66**:164–7

26. Lundberg U. Stress responses in low-status jobs and their relationship to health risks: musculoskeletal disorders. *Ann N Y Acad Sci* 1999:**896**:162–72

27. Parrott AC. Does cigarette smoking cause stress? *Am Psychol* 1999:**54**:817–20

28. Schifano F, Di Costanzo E: Caffeina e caffeinismo. *B Raz Ter* 1990:**20**:671–6

29. Dews PB, O'Brien CP, Bergman J. Caffeine: behavioral effects of withdrawal and related issues. *Food Chem Toxicol* 2002:**40**:1257–61

30. http://www.drugtestcenter.com/content1/employers/uncovering_hidden.htm (accessed on 12 January 2004)

31. Dias PJ. Adolescent substance abuse. Assessment in the office. *Ped Clin N Am* 2002:**49**:269–300

32. Kandel D. Stages in adolescence involvement in drug use. *Science* 1975:**190**:912–4

33. American Psychiatric Association. *Diagnostic and Statistical Manual of Mental Disorders*, 4th edition, revised. APA, Washington DC, 1994

34. DuPont RL, Griffin DW, Siskin BR, Shiraki S, Katze E. Random drug tests at work: the probability of identifying frequent and infrequent users of illicit drugs. *J Addict Dis* 1995:**14**:1–17

35. Tirrell CD. Psychoactive substance disorders among health care professionals. *Plast Surg Nurs* 1994:**14**:169–72

36. Mazzoni J. A supervisor's role in workplace drug abuse. *Health Care Superv* 1990:**8**:35–9

37. Matano RA, Futa KT, Wanat SF, Mussman LM et al. The Employee Stress and Alcohol Project: the development of a computer-based alcohol abuse prevention program for employees. *J Behav Health Serv Res* 2000:**27**:152–65

38. Silverman K, Svikis D, Wong CJ, Hampton J et al. A reinforcement-based therapeutic workplace for the treatment of drug abuse: three-year abstinence outcomes. *Exp Clin Psychopharmacol* 2002:**10**:228–40

39. Krejci J, Ziedonis D. Medications in the treatment of addiction: workplace issues. *Occup Med* 2002:**17**:91–104

7 Effects of Prescribed and Over-the-Counter Drugs on Workplace Performance

Ian Hindmarch

Medicines, those drugs properly prescribed by a physician and those substances legally bought over the counter (OTC) from a pharmacy, are treated differently by the courts from illegal drugs, when health and safety in the workplace issues are involved. The use, possession or trading in illicit drugs invokes prosecution of the individual for a criminal offence and a liability on behalf of the owner of the premises involved. However, such a separation of liability in law is not reflected in differences in the health and safety issues resulting from the use of illicit and licit drugs, as the impairment of performance and cognitive function are broadly similar for both legal and illegal drugs.

Any psychoactive medication has the potential to affect the safe performance of the habitual tasks in the workplace. Should performance be impaired by a prescribed medication to such an extent that an individual is involved in an accident then, it could be argued that the individual worker's employers had not exercised reasonable practical care in ensuring that no harm was visited on their employee.

Drugs and medicines involved in accident causation

Psychoactive drugs are, by definition, those substances which have a direct effect on the central nervous system (CNS) and include, though not exhaustively, medicines for the treatment of depression, anxiety, sleep disturbance, dementia, neurological disorders, psychoses and psychological disorders (for example post-traumatic stress disorder, obsessive compulsive disorder, panic and social phobia). In recent years it has become increasingly more likely that patients suffering from psychological disturbance will receive their pharmacotherapy at the hands of their general practitioner. Modern psychoactive drugs are significantly less toxic (fewer adverse effects on the heart, liver and metabolic systems) than their predecessors and are, therefore, more frequently prescribed to a wider population of patients than was possible with older medications.

It is outside the scope of this chapter to comment on the comparative clinical efficacy of individual compounds, but a cursory examination of the relevant clinical literature suggests that there is little to choose between the various psychoactive medications with respect to their overall clinical utility. However, there are considerable differences between drugs in the extent to which they cause side effects on a patient's cognitive (information processing, mental ability, memory and decision-making) skills and psychomotor (sensori-motor co-ordination or skilled activities) behaviour. The concern of this chapter is the extent to which modern psychopharmaceuticals have the potential to interfere with everyday decisions and the safe performance of everyday tasks of living in the home, on the road and, particularly, at work. The work context is naturally broad and encompasses not only the consequences of errors made following cognitive impairment in computer programmers, but also the increased risks of accident associated with psychomotor impairment in workers on an industrial shop floor.

The clinical activity of a psychoactive drug is beneficial for the patient in alleviating depression, lifting mood, reducing anxiety and perceived stress and so on. The side effects, a necessary consequence of action of a particular pharmacological agent, are unwanted and the cause of the detrimental impact of certain psychoactive agents on work performance.

It is perhaps useful to provide a short description of the pharmacology of the major psychoactive drug groups implicated in accidents, so as to identify the particular side effects which give rise to concern.

BENZODIAZEPINES AND OTHER SEDATIVE TRANQUILLISERS

The benzodiazepines are heterocyclic compounds discovered and developed in the late 1950s to early 1960s (Baenninger et al., 2004). They act on specific sub-units of the widely distributed gamma-aminobutyric acid chloride (GABA-Cl) ion receptor situated in the brain. In conjunction with GABA, the benzodiazepines have five major clinical utilities:

- anti-anxiety or anxiolytic agents
- sedative hypnotics
- anti-convulsants
- muscle relaxants
- amnestic agents.

This five-fold clinical activity is possessed, to a greater or lesser extent, by all benzodiazepines in current clinical use. To a certain extent it is possible to talk of these generic clinical properties, although in clinical use different galenic formulations and dose treatment regimens coupled with a particular drug's profile of clinical properties make some benzodiazepines more useful than others for particular conditions.

The properties of benzodiazepines make them ideally useful for managing anxiety (diazepam, chlordiazepoxide, lorazepam), insomnia (temazepam, nitrazepam, loprazolam, flurazepam, lormetazepam), epilepsy (clobazam, diazepam, lorazepam), sports injuries where muscle relaxation is required (diazepam) and as pre-medications prior to surgery (midazolam, lorazepam). The benzodiazepines have numerous other utilities for example in the management of alcoholism (chlordiazepoxide, diazepam) and restless legs (clonazepam). The widespread clinical utility of these drugs ensures their widespread prescription.

The basic problem with benzodiazepines, as far as accident risk is concerned, is the intrinsic pharmacological mode of action on the GABA-ergic system. GABA is an inhibitory neurotransmitter which causes a reduction in CNS arousal manifested as sedation (feelings of tiredness, sleepiness, lack of alertness and so on) which naturally causes impairment of the integrity of psychomotor performance and cognitive function.

When the drugs are used as daytime anxiolytics, such sedation might aid or produce a symptomatic relief of the psychological agitation associated with anxiety, but at the same time, the sedation will cause impairment of the safe performance of work-related behaviours. For those benzodiazepines given at bed-time for sleep induction and/or sleep maintenance in patients with insomnia, the problem arises when the clinically desired effect of nocturnal sedation carries over into the early part of the next day to cause impairment of daytime functioning (Hindmarch, 1990).

The duration of the sedative side effects of benzodiazepines have erroneously been thought to be due simply to the elimination half-life of the drug and its active metabolites. However, the issue is much more complex with long elimination half-life drugs like diazepam having a short duration of clinical action. The overriding feature which determines the severity of the drug's impact on safety in the work environment is the dose treatment regimen used; the higher the dose the greater the risk of increasing accident liability.

There are several other drugs which are also ligands of the GABA-chloride ion receptor complex, notably the barbiturates, chloral hydrate and the newer non-benzodiazepine hypnotics, zopiclone, zolpidem and zaleplon ('Z'-drugs). The barbiturates and chloral are perhaps only of historic interest as their use is curtailed to specialist neurological applications or in hospitalised patients where safety at work is not an issue.

The Z-drugs are demonstrably freer from residual next-day sequelae than clinically equivalent doses of most benzodiazepines. In spite of being a completely different chemical entity and of having specific, as opposed to the general effect of benzodiazepines, activity on discrete sub-units of the GABA-chloride ion receptor complex, the drug's principal action is of sedation. This leads to similar risk factors for psychomotor and cognitive impairment the day following nocturnal medication if too high a dose of any of these drugs is prescribed.

Alcohol also has the potential to attack the GABA-chloride ion receptor complex, which is of great importance where patient safety is an issue, as concurrent administration of benzodiazepines and alcohol will lead to an augmentation of the side effects of both drugs, that is patient reports of drowsiness, sleepiness and so on will increase and a demonstrable increase in impairment of essential skills will be evident. In many instances, the interaction of the benzodiazepines with alcohol will be synergistic and greater than the additive effects of the two drugs taken alone.

Patients beginning treatment with benzodiazepines, who work in any high accident risk environment, for example heavy machinery or iron foundries, as well as those where cognitive failure could cause accident to themselves or others, should be warned about possible interactions of benzodiazepines and alcohol. Even at social doses well beneath the blood alcohol concentration limit of 80 mg alcohol per 100 ml blood, used to define the legal limit for operating a motor vehicle, alcohol and benzodiazepine interactions have been linked to an increased accident risk.

ANTIHISTAMINES FOR ALLERGY, DERMATOLOGICAL DISORDERS AND NIGHT-TIME SEDATION

The sedative- and sleep-inducing effects of antihistaminic agents are important causal agents in augmenting accident risks. Many, especially the older compounds, are freely available over the counter (OTC) in pharmacies without the need for a prescription and, as such, can be used for self-medication on dose regimens which are incompatible with the safe performance of work-related tasks.

Histamine receptors in the brain are thought, alongside several other functions, to play a part in maintaining arousal and alertness. If an antihistamine which crosses the blood-brain barrier is administered and occupies the histamine receptor, then sedation and impairment of psychomotor function must necessarily follow. It is thought that antihistamines act as inverse agonists; that is they cancel out the effects of histamine at the receptor site and so cause sedation and feelings of tiredness which compromise the performance of tasks requiring attentiveness and alert behaviour.

Such sedation is profound enough for some antihistamines (for example promethazine, chlorpheniramine, triprolidine, diphenhydramine) to be marketed OTC as sleeping aids, yet the same substances are also to be found for use as daytime anti-allergy preparations. Often the warnings on the packs of OTC products are ambiguous and the impact of such drugs on safety at work is not made clear.

There are some OTC products (cetirizine and loratadine) which have a lower incidence of sedation and impaired performance than the so-called first generation antihistamines given above. However, loratadine in particular is not a particularly potent product at the packaged dose and patients have been shown to double the recommended dose regimen in order to obtain relief from the symptoms of hay fever. As with other groups of drugs, this increase in dose is associated with an increasing impairment of CNS function and, by virtue of that, an increase in accident liability.

Several newer antihistamines, available only via prescription (for example fexofenadine and levocetirizine) have no demonstrable effect on performance at appropriate clinical dose regimens. With fexofenadine, the lack of a measured effect on psychomotor and cognitive performance is due primarily to its inability to penetrate the brain, as demonstrated by PET scans and low lipophilicity. This antihistamine is unique in that its lack of effect on psychomotor and cognitive function is independent of dose administered even when three to four times the daily clinical dose is administered.

ANTIDEPRESSANTS

In recent years the use of antidepressants for disorders other than major depression has increased considerably. Many of the conditions conventionally classified as anxiety states, such as post-traumatic stress disorder, generalised anxiety disorder and social phobia, are now treated with antidepressants, licensed by medicine control agencies specifically for such clinical usage.

All antidepressants have equipotent clinical activity within their licensed applications as demonstrated by numerous clinical studies with controlled trials against placebo. In general, antidepressants exert their clinical effect by increasing the available concentrations in the brain of one or more of the neurotransmitters, noradrenaline, serotonin and dopamine. The neurochemical mechanisms by which this happens and the neural systems involved differ from compound to compound as does the extent to which a particular drug produces untoward side effects.

Side effects of cognitive and psychomotor impairment are not primarily due to the neurotransmitters underlying the drugs' clinical activity, but to other aspects of the drug's intrinsic pharmacology, namely the level of anticholinergic, antihistaminic and α_1-adrenergic activity of the various antidepressants.

The Defeat Depression campaign of the Royal College of Psychiatrists found that patients desired antidepressants that did not make them tired and drowsy. The clinical manifestation of depression is associated with tiredness and slowed motor function – in some cases to such an extent that patients appear psychomotorically retarded and slower in responding to stimuli. Clearly, drugs which increase tiredness and cause sedation are countertherapeutic, and many have been shown to cause an increased number of falls (Lord et al., 1995), hip fractures (Sobel & McCart, 1983) and road traffic accidents (Alvarez & Carmen del Rio, 1994; Ray et al., 1992). A study of emergency room admissions (Currie et al., 1995), showed the risk of accident was six times greater in a group of patients treated with tricyclic antidepressants than those not receiving medication.

Furthermore, sleepiness and feelings of tiredness associated with taking a medication are principal causes for non-compliance with drug treatment. This is especially true in ambulant outpatients and in those requiring unencumbered faculties to perform their daily activities safely and efficiently (Montgomery et al., 1994; Rudorfer et al., 1994).

The enhancement of cholinergic function has often been seen as the basis for improved memory and cognition. The pharmacological basis of many anti-dementia agents rests on their abilities to augment cholinergic activity and so delay or modify a patient's cognitive behaviour – especially memory. On the other hand, anticholinergic activity will necessarily impair or reduce cognitive and memory functions. Depressed patients often complain of poor or defective memory and increased cognitive failures. The added impairment due to anticholinergic activity can only be seen as further countertherapeutic action and side effect burden. Cognitive failures are well established as major causal factors in accidents. Lapses of attention, failure in executive memory, inappropriate decision making and mild confusion are all side effects associated with the anticholinergic activity of some antidepressants.

Clumsiness, disorders of balance and poor concentration are also countertherapeutic and antidepressants with pronounced α_1-adrenergic blockading activities not only increase the discomfort of pharmacotherapy, but also increase the potential risk of accident – especially falls.

Pharmacology of side effects of antidepressants

Tricyclic antidepressants (TCAs) (amitriptyline, dothiepin, imipramine and so on) have pronounced anticholinergic, antihistaminic and α_1-adrenergic blockading properties. As such, their side effects in clinical use include:

- *antihistaminic*: drowsiness, sedation, daytime tiredness, impaired psychomotor speed;
- *anticholinergic*: memory loss, confusion, poor judgement, cognitive failure;
- *α_1-adrenergic blockade*: loss of balance, poor co-ordination, psychomotor retardation.

Selective Serotonin Re-uptake Inhibitors (SSRIs) (for example fluoxetine, sertraline, paroxetine, citalopram, fluvoxamine) selectively raise synaptic levels of serotonin and have a much lower impact on antihistaminic, anticholinergic and α_1-adrenergic mechanisms, when compared to the TCAs. However, the SSRIs are not devoid of the potential to affect cognitive and psychomotor function. Furthermore, one of the principal side effects of SSRIs is sleep disturbance, the extent of which has a direct relationship with the integrity of subsequent daytime performance.

Other antidepressants include substances which operate to a greater or lesser extent on two transmitter systems namely noradrenaline and serotonin (venlafaxine, milnacipran, mirtazepine) or three, namely noradrenaline, serotonin and dopamine (moclobemide). Some of these and other drugs, including trazodone and mianserin possess sedative side effects to a greater extent than the SSRIs: mirtazapine is profoundly sedative due to its antihistaminic effect almost double that of the TCA amitriptyline, for example.

Evidence that psychoactive drugs affect performance

There is substantial literature to demonstrate that many prescribed and OTC medications alter behaviour to such an extent that an increased risk of accident accompanies their use (Oster et al., 1987, 1990). Although these surveys have not specifically investigated accidents happening in the workplace, it is evident that patients experiencing falls, fractures and an impairment of vehicle operating ability, would be compromised by the accident if it happened there. Again, of major concern for the employer is the possibility that their workplace health and safety practices might be brought into question, should the role of prescription medicine not be excluded as a possible causative factor.

One of the first attempts to investigate the relationship between psychoactive medicines and car driving accidents (Skegg et al., 1979) found the use of minor tranquillisers (primarily benzodiazepines) increased the relative risk of a road traffic accident. Honkanen et al., 1980 also found that diazepam was associated with an increased risk of car driving accidents and later studies (Barbone et al., 1998; Neutel 1995, 1998) also highlighted the increased risk of road traffic accidents following the use of a variety of hypnotics (sleep-inducing agents) such as flurazepam, flunitrazepam, loprazolam, lormetazepam, nitrazepam, temazepam, oxazepam, zopiclone and anxiolytics (minor tranquillisers) such as alprazolam, bromazepam, chlordiazepoxide, clorazepate, diazepam, lorazepam. Although the foregoing surveys were conducted in populations with a mean age of up to 35 years, similar results, though the range of medicines identified as increasing the risk of accident was much reduced, were obtained for older populations of patients, where the mean age was 65 years or more (Hemmelgarn et al., 1997; Leveille et al., 1994; Ray et al., 1992). The elderly have an increased risk of falls following the initial doses of therapy with benzodiazepines (lorazepam, oxazepam) and antipsychotics (thioridazine and haloperidol) (Neutel et al, 2002). Antidepressants, various hypnotic and anxiolytic benzodiazepines and polydrug use (the use of three or more drugs) have been associated with an increased risk of falls (Neutel et al., 2002; Tromp et al., 2001; Ray et al., 2000, 2002; Passaro et al., 2000; Mendelson, 1996; Lord et al., 1995; Campbell et al., 1989; Granek et al., 1987) both in the elderly aged 60 years or more and in younger users (Maxwell et al., 1997). In many instances (Wang et al., 2001, Sgadari et al., 2000; Ray et al., 1987) hip and leg fractures have been associated with the use of a variety of benzodiazepines. The increased risk of accidents in the elderly due to prescribed psychoactive medications is becoming increasingly important for health and safety managers as the average age of the workforce increases.

Although the relationship between alcohol and accidents is outside the scope of this paper, its role in causing impaired cognition and performance (Kerr and Hindmarch, 1991) and as a causative agent in accidents is well established (Cherpitel, 1993; McLellan et al., 1995). However, of relevance to the current discussion is the potential for many psychoactive drugs to interact (make worse than the combined effects of the two substances taken separately) with alcohol, even at low levels (Chan, 1984). Patients drinking modest amounts of alcohol could be compromised by the interaction of a prescribed medication with alcohol. This interaction is perhaps most evident with the concurrent use of alcohol and benzodiazepine type drugs, as both alcohol and benzodiazepines occupy similar receptor sites in the brain.

It would be wrong to assume either that the psychoactive drugs involved with increasing accident risk are always and only benzodiazepines or that accidents are restricted simply to those on the road or resulting from a fall. Currie et al. (1995) demonstrated that prescribed antidepressants as well as benzodiazepines were associated with increased risk of accidents in a study of consecutive admissions to an emergency operating theatre. Alcohol was associated with the greatest risk to the youngest victims whereas prescribed medicines, including antidepressants and minor tranquillisers, were more associated with older, though not necessarily elderly, victims.

Safe performance of work within an industrial context is also dependant on the individual patient's psychological/emotional stability. Benzodiazepines and antidepressant usage have been associated with an increased risk of attempted suicide and violence (Neutel and Patten, 1997; Mendelson and Rich, 1993) which in itself would exert an effect on the safe performance of industrial tasks. Psychoactive drugs have also been shown to increase the number and severity of accidents occurring in a recreational context (Barnas et al., 1992; MacDonald et al., 1998) and it is therefore likely that those less formal tasks in the work environment would be equally influenced by CNS active substances.

Behavioural toxicity of psychoactive drugs

In assessing the potential for a particular drug to raise safety concerns in the workplace, it is necessary to determine the extent to which a particular drug or class of substances disrupts the performance of skilled cognitive and psychomotor behaviour. The 'behavioural toxicity' (Hindmarch, 1999) of a drug is the extent to which that particular compound has effects on the psychological substrate of behaviour that are either countertherapeutic or liable to increase the risk of accident.

Ratings of behavioural toxicity are objective assessments of the impact of a drug's intrinsic pharmacology and a patient's behaviour will necessarily be changed in accordance with this pharmacological action. The extent to which an individual patient is affected will be dependant on many idiosyncratic variables, including the severity of the illness, the level of prior drug experience, the basic level of competence and behavioural skill, individual metabolic variables, the dose treatment regimen employed, the patient's gender and age and the numerous other psychological and physiological variables which modify an individual response to a drug. However, the complexity of the individual patient's reaction to a drug should not reduce the utility of the psychometric ratings of behavioural toxicity when identifying those medications likely to increase the frequency of risk of work-related accidents. The generalisation can be made that, even given the massive inter- and intra-individual variation in response to medication, those drugs with a high index of behavioural toxicity are less safe than those with a low index, especially values significantly beneath placebo treatment.

It is useful to remember that the same inter- and intra-individual variables operate regarding the magnitude and severity of the effects of alcohol, yet no one would doubt that the use of the drug is incompatible with the health and safety demands of the workplace. Similarly, with the behavioural toxicity ratings of other CNS active drugs there can be no doubt that the use of those substances with ratings of high behavioural toxicity is unnecessarily increasing the risk of behavioural failure within an industrial context.

Measurement of behavioural toxicity

The basis of measurement of behavioural toxicity is a valid and reliable psychometric assessment of relevant aspects of cognition and psychomotor performance. There are numerous tests by which the behavioural change brought about by drugs can be assessed. Behavioural skills in the workplace are complex patterns dependent upon experience, motivation, training and level of expertise. In order to assess performance it is necessary to break down the diffuse and heterogeneous aspects of skilled behaviour into simpler tasks for psychometric measurement. These simplified tasks are necessary for inter-subject variation to be reduced. With complex tasks, inter-subject differences in strategy due to learning and experience can mask drug-induced changes. Effective psychometric tests are simple enough to avoid the use of strategic behaviours and thus the variability of performance due to task-related features is minimised.

Compare, for example, an experienced machine operator to a beginner both of whom had taken a drug and were to be assessed on a test involving a lathe. Not only will the machine operator perform better at baseline compared to the novice, but also the drug will have less effect due to strategic behaviour and high skill level. The machinist's years of experience have resulted in a strategy to cope with the effects of stress or unusual situations. In other words, the effects of experience and the presence of learned schemata make for difficulties in assessing behavioural toxicity. The inter- and intra-subject variability using real-life behaviours is, therefore, too great and recourse has to be made to the basic elements from which all behaviours are derived.

All skilled behaviours are made up of basic psychological abilities which experience and familiarity conjoin. Skilled behaviour in the workplace can be parsimoniously reduced to its sensory, motor and central processing aspects. Psychoactive drugs have the potential to affect some or all sensory, motor and cognitive functions.

To illustrate the assessment of behavioural toxicity, two particularly reliable and valid psychometrics will be used, namely Choice Reaction Time (CRT) and Critical Flicker Fusion Threshold (CFFT). Choice reaction time requires the subject to move their index finger as quickly as possible following the illumination of a signal light to extinguish that light by touching a button adjacent to the light. The stimulus light is one of six identical ones arranged about the arc of a circle. Thus there is an element of attention demanded in determining which response button is needed to extinguish a particular stimulus. The variable used for assessment is the average speed of reaction to 50 consecutive stimuli. Any drug which significantly lengthens the reaction time will be seen as increasing its ratings of behavioural toxicity. The CRT measures do correlate with brake reaction times in an on-the-road car driving task and so possess some face validity as an indicator of accident risk. Although there is virtually no large database linking psychometrics with real-life behaviours and accidents, there is a substantial concordance between the impairment produced by, for example, tricyclic antidepressants, sedative antihistamines and many benzodiazepines on laboratory tests of performance both with impairment produced on analogues of daily activity and with drug-associated accident statistics.

Critical Flicker Fusion Threshold (CFFT) is a psychophysiological measure which relies on a subject's ability to perceive a set of flickering lights, flashing at a critical frequency, as a continuous stream of uninterrupted light. The higher the frequency of flicker at which a continuous light can be perceived, reflects an elevated level of CNS arousal and an intact information processing capacity. Conversely, subjects with lower thresholds will have a relatively impaired cognitive processing capacity and lower levels of arousal and attentiveness.

Taken together, CRT and CFFT present a basis for determining the behavioural toxicity indices for CNS drugs. The results from such tests can be augmented via information from other psychometrics regarding the impact of a medication on, for example, memory, vigilance, dynamic balance and visual acuity, for circumstances where specific work-related tasks involve such basic skills.

Behavioural toxicity is an index of the intrinsic pharmacodynamic activity of a psychoactive agent and so the measurement of the severity of the impairment produced by a particular drug will be made in asymptomatic volunteer subjects. Meaningful indices of behavioural toxicity can only be found from well-designed crossover studies where both placebo and positive internal controls are employed. The positive internal control (verum) is a psychoactive drug known to cause an evident and significant performance decrement (for example promethazine, lorazepam, dothiepin, mirtazapine, flurazepam) and is expected to establish the sensitivity and validity of the psychometric test battery used in a particular experiment by demonstrating impairment on the individual measures.

The results from individual trials are, even if well-controlled experiments, of limited value and in order to obtain more general measures various 'meta-analytical' techniques have been employed. Two ways of summarising behavioural toxicity will be illustrated.

The first uses the Cohen's 'd' statistic to compare the 'strength of effect', that is, the magnitude of the impairment of the function produced by a particular drug, from a series of placebo-controlled studies in which that particular drug has been evaluated. The strength of effect value is based on the standard deviation of a normal distribution curve, so a value of 1.00 would represent 1 standard deviation from the mean. The use of a standard distribution curve gives some indication of how seriously a particular index of behavioural toxicity needs to be to have some clinical significance. Values of 0.7 are seen as clinically relevant, whereas 1.0 or greater can be regarded as significant levels of risk.

Tables 7.1 and 7.2 represent a meta-analysis of the effects of antidepressants using the same psychometric assessments of performance impairment (CFFT and CRT) from a range of published studies in patient and volunteer populations. The 'strength of effect' measures give an indication of the likelihood of a particular antidepressant impairing behaviour intrinsic to everyday industrial skills: placebo is represented by a score of zero; excess sedation or impairment of cognition is given by a negative score; and excitation or arousal by a positive score. The effects of alcohol at a dose to give a blood alcohol concentration (BAC) of approximately 80 mg per cent (the legal limit for operating a motor vehicle) provides a further reference point for estimating the potential impact of antidepressants likely to be associated with increasing risk of accident. It should also be noted that those antidepressants which disrupt performance are all at sub-clinical dose levels, whereas those newer drugs without impairment are at least equivalent to usual daily dose levels and in some cases are without effect at supra-clinical regimens.

Such measures of the impact of antidepressants on important aspects of skilled behaviour and cognitive function provide a scaling of drugs more likely than others to be associated with problems of behavioural toxicity and increased risk of accident.

Table 7.1   Behavioural toxicity (CFFT)
The strength of effect of various antidepressants on CFFT used as a measure of cognitive function

Sertraline 100mg	1.769
Paroxetine 30mg	1.153
Fluoxetine 40mg	0.895
Lofepramine 140mg	0.347
Cericlamine 400mg	0.141
Placebo	0.000
Fluvoxamine 50mg	−0.017
Buproprion 100mg	−0.204
Alcohol 0.75g/kg body weight	−0.333
Milnacipran 100mg	−0.439
Desipramine 50mg	−0.834
Dothiepin 50mg	−1.279
Trazodone 50mg	−1.305
Amitriptyline 25mg	−2.194
Amitriptyline 50mg	−2.644
Mianserin 10mg	−3.205

Table 7.2   Behavioural toxicity (CRT)
The strength of effect (using Cohen's 'd') of various antidepressants on CRT used as a measure of psychomotor speed and performance

Buproprion 100mg	1.143
Desipramine 50mg	1.028
Lofepramine 140mg	0.937
Sertraline 100mg	0.802
Milnacipran 100mg	0.541
Paroxetine 30mg	0.276
Placebo	0.000
Cericlamine 400mg	−0.189
Fluvoxamine 50mg	−0.386
Fluoxetine 40mg	−0.432
Alcohol 0.75g/kg body weight	−0.569
Trazodone 50mg	−1.029
Mianserin 10mg	−1.242
Dothiepin 50mg	−1.601
Amitriptyline 25mg	−2.086

Epidemiological evidence also supports these rankings with road traffic accidents following tricyclic antidepressants (TCA) at a dose equivalent to 125mg amitriptyline per day, being five to six fold greater than patients treated with other antidepressants (Ray et al., 1992). Similarly, patients held responsible by an independent review panel for the cause of their accidents (severe enough to warrant blood transfusions) had a six-fold greater chance of having TCAs and a sixteen-fold greater chance of having benzodiazepines in their blood, than those patients who were assessed as innocent victims of accident (Currie et al., 1995).

Secondly, it is also convenient to measure the behavioural toxicity of drugs using an impairment index (Ii). Here the number of psychometric tests, from a set of studies, demonstrating a significant impairment due to a particular drug dose is expressed as a percentage of the total number of psychometric used in the same series of studies. This measure can be refined using principles of pharmacovigilance (Stather, 1998) to take account of the relative position of a particular drug within a class or within a therapeutic modality. This proportional impairment ratio (PIR) is calculated by dividing the Ii of the named drug by the mean Ii of all the other medications in that group. If the drug is the same as the rest of the class, then the PIR will be 1.00, if better less than 1.00 and if worse greater than 1.00.

Table 7.3 shows the PIR ratings of behavioural toxicity of a variety of psychoactive drugs used in the treatment of social phobia. While there exists evidence (Stein et al., 2004) that these substances have all shown a certain clinical utility in the effective management of the disorder, it is evident from this 'meta-analysis' of controlled studies that some drugs have a higher intrinsic behavioural toxicity than other clinically equivalent compounds.

Table 7.3   Proportional impairment ratios (psychoactive drugs)
Behavioural toxicity of drugs used in the management of social phobia

Drug	No. Studies	No. tests	No. tests impaired	PIR
Fluoxamine	8	168	0	0.00
Buproprion	4	42	0	0.00
Gabapentin	2	164	1	0.03
Fluoxetine	6	90	3	0.15
Clomipramine	2	63	4	0.29
Moclobemide	7	136	10	0.33
Buspirone	11	156	24	0.70
Olanzapine	2	82	16	0.90
Venlafaxine	2	36	8	1.00
Paroxetine	4	26	6	1.10
Atenolol	9	217	53	1.10
Nefazodone	2	62	19	1.40
Sertraline	4	190	64	1.60
Clonazepam	3	76	26	1.60
Alprazolam	24	781	236	2.20

Similarly, Table 7.4 gives the PIRs of a group of hypnotic agents. Again all of these drugs have equipotent clinical activity, but are clearly differentiated in the extent to which psychometric batteries are impaired the morning following nocturnal medication. Of particular interest here is the fact that the presence of behavioural toxicity (impaired morning function) is not simply related to pharmacodynamic variables such as elimination half-life or time of peak blood concentration. Indeed, with hypnotics, as with all other CNS active drugs, the dose administered would seem to be the most important determinant of the presence, extent and severity of behavioural toxicity and, therefore, subsequent accident risk.

In Table 7.5 are presented the PIRs for antihistamines, which illustrates the profound risks of behavioural impairment with sedative first-generation drugs such as promethazine, triprolidine and clemastine.

Safe use of medication in the workplace

There is an increasing concern regarding the effects of medication in the work environment, brought about by an increase in the strictness of health and safety regulations, the popularity of litigation by alleged victims of workplace accidents and an increased understanding of the relationship between CNS active drugs and accident risk. There are also more psychoactive drugs for more widely identified and diagnosed psychological states. If the drug in question has no or very few deleterious effects attendant on its use, this enables safe work and gives the worker the psychological benefit of productive effort and the social support of colleagues and so on, as opposed to being on sick leave and relatively isolated at home.

However, not all modern psychopharmaceuticals are free from adverse effects. The use of these substances is incompatible with safe working practices. It is too simplistic to absent a patient requiring such therapy from the work environment.

The risks which have been demonstrated here to be associated with the use of 'normal'

Table 7.4   Proportional impairment ratios (hypnotic drugs)
Behavioural toxicity of hypnotics

Drug	Dose (min)	Dose (max)	PIR	t/2 hours	t. max hours
Nitrazepam	2.5	10	0.6	25	2.0
Zolpidem	2.5	20	0.9	2	1.8
Temazepam	7.5	60	1.0	10	1.6
Zaleplon	10.0	20	1.0	1	1.0
Zopiclone	2.5	10	1.5	5	1.0
Flunitrazepam	1.0	2	2.6	15	1.2

t.max = time at which peak plasma concentration ocurs
t/2 = mean elimination half-life, i.e. the time at which plasma concentrations reach 50% of their
    maximum level

Table 7.5 Proportional impairment ratios (antihistamines)
Behavioural toxicity of antihistamines

Drug	PIR	χ^2 with 1 d.f.	Impairment
Fexofenadine	0.00	***	↑
Ebastine	0.00	***	↑
Astemizole	0.00	**	↑
Levocabastine	0.00	*	↑
Temelastine	0.00	ns	–
Ketotifen	0.00	ns	–
Terfenadine	0.15	***	↑
Cetirizine	0.18	***	↑
Tazifylline	0.48	ns	–
Cyclizine	0.48	ns	–
Loratadine	0.58	ns	–
Brompheniramine	0.58	ns	–
Azatadine	0.67	ns	–
Mizolastine	0.73	ns	–
Acrivastine	0.83	ns	–
Mequitazine	1.09	ns	–
Chlorpheniramine	1.92	**	↓
Diphenhydramine	2.05	***	↓
Triprolidine	2.21	***	↓
Clemastine	2.21	***	↓
Hydroxyzine	2.25	**	↓
Oxotamide	2.94	ns	–
Promethazine	3.14	***	↓

*   p≤0.05

**   p≤0.01

***   p≤0.001

↑   No impairment with respect to all other AHs

↓   Impairment with respect to all other AHs

–   No difference with respect to other AHs

Adapted from:
Shamsi, Z. & Hindmarch, I. (2000) Sedation and Antihistamines: A Review of Inter-Drug Differences Using Proporational Impairment Ratios. *Human Psychopharmacology: Clinical & Experimental*, **15**, Supp. 1, S3-S30

clinical dose regimens are real enough, and patients using drugs with high behavioural toxicity ratings have been demonstrably over-represented in road, domestic and industrial accidents.

It is accepted that the basis of these measures is derived primarily from laboratory studies of asymptomatic subjects. However, both the limited number of psychopharmacological studies in patients and the more widespread epidemiological surveys of drugs and accidents confirm that a drug's intrinsic potential for increased impairment and raised behavioural toxicity impacts negatively on the safe performance of work-related duties and tasks.

All medicines are prescribed to individual patients and the possible risks of personal injury can only be made in the light of an individual's illness, reaction to medication, psychological and socio-economic status and so on. However, accidents do also happen as the result of someone else's impaired behaviour, and awareness of the impact of medicines on performance in the workplace must be raised as a major health and safety issue. It is possible to minimise the behavioural toxicity associated with some classes of drugs via changing the drug and/or dose treatment regimens. An awareness of the possibilities is to be encouraged.

No attention has been paid here to the pharmacoeconomic considerations of using newer relatively expensive, less behaviourally toxic drugs in contrast to those cheap but behaviourally toxic psychoactive substances first introduced in the 1960s. It is likely, however, that if the legal costs of a serious work-related accident due to a toxic psychoactive drug were to be factored into the equation, the less toxic agents would prove the most economically viable.

There is no suggestion that the use of a behaviourally toxic drug means that an accident will necessarily be caused, but as with intoxication by alcohol, there is more than sufficient cause for concern regarding a patient's relative accident risk in the workplace.

References

Alvarez, F.J. and Carmen del Rio, M. (1994) Drugs and Driving, *The Lancet*, **344**, 282.

Baenninger, A., Costa e Silva, J.A., Hindmarch, I., Moeller, H.J. and Rickels K. (2004) *Good Chemistry: The Life and Legacy of Valium Inventor Leo Sternbach*, McGraw-Hill: New York, pp 168.

Barbone, F., McMahon, A.D., Davey, P.G. et al., (1998) Association of road traffic accidents with benzodiazepine use, *Lancet*, **352**, (9137), 1331–1336.

Barnas, C., Miller, C.H., Sperner, G., Sperner-Unterweger, B. and Beck, E. (1992) The effects of alcohol and benzodiazepines on the severity of ski accidents, *Acta Psychiatrica Scandinavia* **86** (Pt 4), 296–300.

Campbell, A.J., Borrie, M.J. and Spears, G.F. (1989) Risk factors for falls in a community-based prospecive study of people 70 years and older, *J Gerontol A Biol Sci Med*, **44**, (4), 112–117.

Chan, A.W.K. (1984) Effects of combined alcohol and benzodiazepine: a review, *Drug and Alcohol Dependency*, 6, 341–349.

Cherpitel, C.J. (1993) Alcohol and injuries: a review of international emergency room studies, *Addiction*, **88**, 923–937.

Currie, D.J., Hashemi, K., Fothergill, J., Findlay, A., Harris, A. and Hindmarch, I. (1995) The use of antidepressants and benzodiazepines in the perpetrators and victims of accidents, *Occupational Medicine*, **45**, (6), 323–325.

Granek, E., Baker, S.P., Abbey, H. et al. (1987) Medications and diagnoses in relation to falls in a long term care facility, *J Am Geriatr Soc*, **35**, (6), 503–511.

Hemmelgarn, B., Suissa, S., Huang, A. et al. (1997) Benzodiazepine use and the risk of motor vehicle crash in the elderly, *JAMA*, **278**, (1), 27–31.

Hindmarch, I. (1990) Human psychopharmacological differences between benzodiazepines. In: Hindmarch, I., Beaumont, G., Brandon, S. and Leonard, B.E. (eds.) *Benzodiazepines: Current Concepts – Biological, Clinical and Social Perspectives*, pp 73–93, John Wiley & Sons: Chichester.

Hindmarch, I. (1999) Behavioural toxicity of anti-anxiety and antidepressant agents, *Human Psychopharmacology: Clinical & Experimental*, **14**, 137–141.

Honkanen, R., Ertama, L., Linnoila, M. et al. (1980) Role of drugs in traffic accidents, *BMJ*, **281**, 1309–1312.

Kerr, J.S. and Hindmarch, I. (1991) Alcohol, cognitive function and psychomotor performance, *Rev Environ Health*, **9**, (2), 117–122.

Leveille, S.G., Buchner, D.M., Koepsell, T.D. et al. (1994) Psychoactive medications and injurious motor vehicle collisions involving older drivers, *Epidemiology*, **5**, (6), 591–598.

Lord, S.R., Anstey, K.J., Williams, P. and Ward, J.A. (1995) Psychoactive medication use, sensorimotor function and falls in older women, *British Journal of Clinical Pharmacology*, **39**, (3), 227–234.

MacDonald, S., Wells, S. and Lothian S. (1998) Comparison of lifestyle and substance use factors related to accidental injuries at work, home and recreational events, *Accid Ana Prev*, **30**, (1), 21–27.

McLellan, B.A., Vingilis, E., Liban, C.B., Stoduto, G., McMurtry, R.Y. and Nelson, W.R. (1995) Blood alcohol testing of motor vehicle crash admissions at a regional trauma unit, *J Trauma*, **30**, (4), 418–421.

Maxwell, C.J., Neutel, C.I. and Hirdes, J.P. (1997) A prospective study of falls after benzodiazepine use: a comparison between new and repeat use, *Pharmacoepidemiol Drug Saf*, **6**, 27–35.

Mendelson, W.B. (1996) The use of sedative/hypnotic medication and its correlation with falling down in the hospital, *Sleep*, **19**, (9), 698–701.

Mendelson, W. and Rich, C. (1993) Sedatives and suicide: the San Diego study, *Acta Psychiatr Scand*, **88**, (5), 337–341.

Montgomery, S.A., Henry, J.A., McDonald, G., Dinan, T., Lader, M., Hindmarch, I., Clare, A. and Nutt, D. (1994) Selective serotonin reuptake inhibitors: meta-analysis of discontinuation rates, *International Clinical Psychopharmacology*, **9**, 47–53.

Neutel, C.I. (1995) Risk of traffic accident injury after a prescription for a benzodiazepine, *Ann Epidemiol*, **5**, (3), 239–244.

Neutel, I. (1998) Benzodiazepine related traffic accidents in young and elderly drivers, *Human Psychopharmacology; Clinical & Experimental*, **13**, (Supp.2), S115–S123.

Neutel, C. and Patten S. (1997) Risk of suicide attempts after benzodiazepine and/or antidepressant use, *Ann Epidemiol*, **7**, (8), 568–574.

Neutel, C.I., Perry, S. and Maxwell, C. (2002) Medication use and the risk of falls, *Pharmacoepidemiol Drug Saf*, **11**, (2), 97–104.

Oster, G., Huse, D.M., Adams, S.F., Imbimbo, J. and Russell, M.W. (1990) Benzodiazepine tranquillisers and the risk of accidental injury, *Am J Public Health*, **80**, 1467–1470.

Oster, G., Russel, M.W., Huse, D.M., Adams, S.F. and Imbimbo, J. (1987) Accident- and injury-related health-care utilisation among benzodiazepine users and non-users, *J Clin Psychiatry*, **48**, (Suppl 12), 17–21.

Passaro, A., Volpato, S., Romagnoni, F. et al. (2000) Benzodiazepines with different half-life and falling in a hospitalised population: The GIFA study, Gruppo Italiano di Farmacovigilanza nell'Anziano, *J Clin Epidemiol*, **53**, (12), 1222–1229.

Ray, W.A., Griffin, M.R., Schaffner, W. et al. (1987) Psychotropic drug use and the risk of hip fracture, *N Engl J Med*, **316**, (7), 363–369.

Ray, W. A., Thapa, P.B. and Gideon, P. (2000) Benzodiazepines and the risk of falls in nursing home residents, *J Am Geriatr Soc*, **48**, (6), 682–685.

Ray, W. A., Thapa, P.B. and Gideon, P. (2002) Misclassification of current benzodiazepine exposure by use of single baseline measurement and its effects upon studies of injuries, *Pharmacoepidemiol Drug Saf*, **11**, (11), 1–7.

Ray, W.A., Fought, R.L. and Decker, M.D. (1992) Psychoactive drugs and the risks of injurious motor vehicle crashes in elderly drivers, *American Journal of Epidemiology*, **136**, 873–883.

Rurdorfer, M.V., Manji, H.K. and Potter, W.Z. (1994) Comparative tolerability profiles of the newer versus older antidepressants, *Drug Safety*, **10**, 18–46.

Sgadari, A., Lapane, K.L., Mor, V. et al. (2000) Oxidative and non-oxidative benzodiazepines and the risk of femur fracture: the Systematic Assessment of Geriatric Drug Use Via Epidemiology Study Group, *J Clin Psychopharmacol*, **20**, (2), 239–239.

Shamsi, Z. and Hindmarch, I. (2000) Sedation and antihistamines: a review of inter-drug differences using proportional impairment ratios, *Human Psychopharmacology: Clinical & Experimental*, 15 (1) S3–S30.

Skegg, D.C.G., Richards, S.M. and Doll, R. (1979) Minor tranquillisers and road accidents, *BMJ*, 1 (6168), 917–919.

Sobel, K.G. and McCart, G.M. (1983) Drug use and accidental falls in an intermediate care facility, *Drug Intelligence and Clinical Pharmacology*, **17**, 539–542.

Stather, R. (1998) Update on collecting ADRs and new methods of signal generation, *Reactions* **718**: 3–5.

Stein, D.J., Vythilingum, B. and Seedat, S. (2004) Pharmacotherapy of phobias: a review. In: Maj, M. et al., (eds) *Phobias – WPA Series Evidence and Experience in Psychiatry Volume 7*, 117–142, John Wiley & Sons: Chichester.

Tromp, A.M., Pluijm, S.M., Smit, J.H. et al. (2001) Fall-risk screening test: a prospective study on predictors for falls in community dwelling elderly, *J Clin Epidemiol*, **54**, (8), 837–844.

Wang, P.S. Bohn, R.L., Glynn, R.J. et al., (2001) Zolpidem use and hip fractures in older people, *J Am Geriatr Soc*, **49**, (12), 1685–1690.

Establishing a Drug Policy

8 Drug and Alcohol Policies – A Review

David Snashall and Dipti Patel

Background

A recent independent inquiry into workplace drug testing concluded that employers have a legitimate interest in drug and alcohol use amongst their employees in a restricted set of circumstances only.

The suggested circumstances were:

- where employees are engaging in illegal activities in the workplace;
- where employees are actually intoxicated during work hours;
- where drug or alcohol use is having a demonstrable negative impact on employees' performance;
- where the nature of the work is such that any responsible employer would be expected to take reasonable steps to minimise the risk of accident;
- where the nature of the work is such that the public is entitled to expect a higher than average standard of behaviour from employees and/or there is a risk of vulnerability to corruption (for example in the police or prison service).

We might add to these:

- where safety-critical work is inherent to the job (for example the nuclear industry) and/or where statutory regulations apply (for example the railways);
- where professional regulations require a higher than average standard of behaviour (for example the medical profession);
- where employees might be open to blackmail.

There were three other key recommendations of relevance:

- If staff have drug or alcohol problems this is a health and welfare issue as well as a disciplinary matter, and should not be an automatic trigger for dismissal. Wherever possible, employees in safety-critical functions should be redeployed in other roles, and provided with help and support.
- Drug and alcohol policies should not be imposed on employees by managers. Drug testing should only ever be introduced following proper consultation with staff and their representatives, and should be even-handed.

- For the majority of businesses, investment in management training and systems is likely to have more impact on safety, performance and productivity than the introduction of drug testing at work. There is a wealth of evidence that good and open management is the most effective method of improving workplace performance and tacking drug and alcohol problems amongst staff (*Drug Testing in the Workplace – an independent enquiry*. The Joseph Rowntree Foundation, June 2004).

A review of policies (2004)

The above conclusions are unexceptional and likely to be agreed upon by a majority of interested parties. We looked in depth at 15 substance-misuse policies from a wide range of typical industries where the above recommendations might apply. They included policies from:

- pharmaceutical industry
- National Health Service hospital
- rail transport (2)
- retail operations
- university
- broadcasting
- heavy engineering industry
- nuclear industry
- aviation industry
- military
- local authority
- manufacturing industry (2)
- petroleum industry.

Some policies applied internationally.

Some policies were joint alcohol and drug policies incorporating a common approach to both; others tackled the two issues separately with discrete policies. In the safety-critical industries, and particularly where statutory regulations applied, the policies were sometimes expressed as 'standards'.

A common approach was for the policy to have been developed jointly by occupational health, legal and human resources departments. There was not much explicit evidence of employee involvement. In a National Health Service policy, local alcohol and drug advisory service input was sought. Human resources were usually cited as the custodians of the policy, occasionally 'safety, health and environment' or similar. In the case of some multinational enterprises there was a global policy published as an 'umbrella document' that applied differently in each region depending on culture, human rights issues and country-specific legislation. Some of these 'local' policies would be more punitive than supportive in tone depending on who had written them. One policy (heavy engineering) was prefaced by a statement on the subject from the chief executive officer.

Some policies were paper documents, others published on the organisation's intranet or even available in the public domain.

Policy structure

The policies obviously differed in the way they were structured. We have chosen to list 15 generic headings upon which a model drug and alcohol policy could be based.

POLICY AIMS/PURPOSE/OBJECTIVES

These tended to cover four main areas:

- the promotion of good health amongst staff, including the early identification of problems suggestive of drug and alcohol misuse;
- the necessity to deal with staff who are identified as having such problems affecting their work performance, attendance or behaviour at work;
- ensuring safety at work, the quality of the work, services or products, and recognising others may also be affected as co-workers and consumers;
- the good image of the organisation.

APPLICABILITY

This varied according to the industry but a general approach was to include all staff at whatever level. Possible variations were:

- all employees including contractors, non-employees (elected or appointed individuals, students and so on);
- differential applicability (for example safety-critical workers only);
- exemptions (for example during business entertainment or work parties).

SCOPE

This also varied according to the industry. Shift work and travelling were recognised as special cases. Possible variations were:

- timing (for example only effective during normal working hours);
- location (for example regional or national differences);
- work activities (for example remote workers or travellers);
- whether the policy applies to *consumption* on or off premises, or possible *intoxication* or simply *possession*;
- whether alcohol should be on sale within the organisation or whether soft drinks should be subsidised and so on.

RESPONSIBILITIES

The various responsibilities of affected individuals were usually laid out clearly but differed according to the organisation. Management and employees were generally expected to follow the protocols within the policy correctly and the support services such as occupational health departments expected to follow guidelines, especially in relation to rights and confidentiality. The responsibilities of contractors were not always made explicit. Sometimes the essence of the policy was incorporated into the employment contract.

Responsibilities were often outlined for employees, management, contractors, support services, trades union representatives and others.

REGULATIONS AND STANDARDS

Depending on the industry, these were specifically mentioned:

- general (for example Management of Health and Safety at Work Regulations 1999)
- specific (for example The Misuse of Drugs Act 1971 (Modification No. 2) Order 2003, The Misuse of Drugs Regulations 2001, The Transport and Works Act 1992, the Railways (Safety Critical Work) Regulations 1994, The Medicines Act)
- quality assurance (for example BS EN ISO/IEC 17025:2 000 General Requirements for the Competence of Testing and Calibration Laboratories).

DEFINITIONS

Drug misuse

A typical definition was 'the use of illegal drugs controlled under the Misuse of Drugs Act 1971 such as heroin and cocaine, the misuse of legally prescribed drugs (for example tranquillisers or hypnotics) and other substances (for example solvents)'.

Alcohol

Alcohol was generally considered to be a drug but often listed separately in polices because people in general tend to regard it differently from other drugs. In practice, however, the measures needed to deal with alcohol problems in the workplace are similar to those appropriate to other drugs and substances.

Dependency

This was often defined as any drug misuse which interferes with an employee's health, social functioning, performance or behaviour, either physical or psychological.

A positive test result

This was usually related to the accredited laboratory's cut-off level. Throughout the policies there was always a concern to differentiate between consumption of a drug which is illegal – classified under the Misuse of Drugs Act 1971 – and which is legal – alcohol, prescribed drugs, solvents, nitrates and so on. However, any of these drugs, legal or illegal can be consumed in ways which may be regarded as acceptable or unacceptable, and policies need to lay down what is unacceptable in terms of consumption at or around work. Illegality and unacceptability were usually contrasted with concerns about the health and/or performance of the person taking them. One view taken was 'Misuse with dependence is an illness; misuse without dependence is misconduct.'

IDENTIFICATION OF PROBLEMS

There was often a different attitude towards self-declaration which may be seen as a cry for help and an identification by managers or by co-workers coming as a result of performance or behaviour deficits or concerns about an individual's health.

MANAGEMENT PROTOCOLS

The procedures universally differentiated between situations where there is, for example, intoxication at work when the matter is principally a disciplinary issue (at least initially), and where there is declared ill health underlying a performance decrement when the matter is dealt with as a health/welfare problem requiring help and support.

All the policies we surveyed came from large organisations with occupational health departments, who were expected to become the primary case managers in the workplace where the issue was not considered to be one of misconduct. In smaller organisations and in the absence of occupational health or human resource support, case management is more likely to be provided externally by general practitioners or substance-misuse advisory services (and policies less likely to be formulated).

EMPLOYEE RIGHTS

These were expressed as rights to confidentiality in relation to personal or health details and to representation in any disciplinary proceedings. In relation to testing, the avoidance of gender or ethnic bias was sometimes emphasised and the appeals procedure explained.

POTENTIAL ROLE OF AN OCCUPATIONAL HEALTH DEPARTMENT

- Assessment: this might involve the use of validated questionnaires and the occasional need for management of acute intoxication, for example breathalysing for alcohol and urine testing for drugs.
- Monitoring versus treatment: this might involve biological monitoring, for example drug testing, or biological effect monitoring, for example gamma GT estimations to track alcohol intake. These might be done pre-employment or pre-placement in a safety critical post, or might be applied unannounced, randomly, post-incident or 'for cause'.
- On-going monitoring: this would include guidance on dealing with a refusal to cooperate and how to differentiate that from a relapse despite cooperation.
- Counselling: providing in-house or external counselling or employee assistance programmes.
- Prescribed drugs: advice on their use.
- Liason: with GP's or alcohol/drug treatment facilities.
- Alcohol education: training of managers to recognise signs of drug or alcohol misuse and avoidance of collusion when suspicions are vindicated.

ADVICE TO MANAGEMENT

This might cover how to deal with return to work, follow-up after return to work and the imposition of specific restrictions, for example health care workers' access to drugs. Figure 8.1 in the appendix to this chapter shows an example flowchart of the management of a substance abuse issue (supplied by a pharmaceutical company).

OTHER DISCIPLINARY ISSUES

Those covered were:

- violence
- searching employees for drugs
- use of 'sniffer' dogs
- drug dealing or pushing at work
- stealing drugs from the work place (solvents, alcohol, narcotics, and so on)
- pay considerations
- prolonged absence
- warnings and terminations of employment
- spiking
- notification to the Home Office.

RESPONSIBILITIES FOR IMPLEMENTING THE POLICY

This covered the individual(s) or department(s) responsible, the date the policy went active and a review date.

PROMULGATION

These policies were often given to employees on joining (or to visitors when visiting). Some companies gave periodic reminders. Most re-wrote the policies from time to time and directed their employees to the latest version.

SOURCES OF ADVICE

- National
- Local

Comment

These policies represent a typical cross-section of such instruments in use in large British companies in 2004. One company we surveyed found it unnecessary to have an explicit policy except where there was 'client demand'. Another simply used a generic policy available to members of a large trade federation. In the main however, these 15 policies addressed, in a similar way, the general and particular problems relating to substance misuse within their sphere. The need for consultation, although not explicit in most of them, was recognised.

Appendix

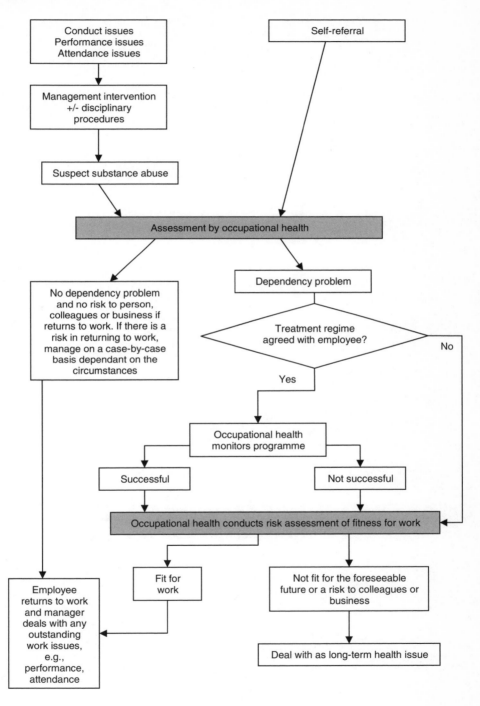

Figure 8.1   Example flowchart of the management of a substance-abuse issue

9 Employers' Liability and Responsibility

Ian Stone

Introduction and overview

TERMINOLOGY

In writing about this subject a number of terms are used to cover the problems and concerns arising from the misuse of alcohol and the use of, with one or two minor exceptions* illegal drugs in the workplace. In this chapter I will refer to all these issues as 'substance abuse'.

A LEGAL AND CULTURAL ISSUE

In this chapter it will be asserted that the question of an employer's liability and responsibility for dealing with substance abuse in the work context is at heart a cultural, as well as a legal, issue. Employers consciously or unconsciously, as demonstrated by their action or lack of action, adopt a stance or an attitude towards drugs and alcohol in the workplace. Whilst the law sets down responsibilities, much of the question of how these responsibilities are discharged rests with the employer. What is an employer's approach to the challenge, inherent in their responsibility and liability, in the work context? This question demands a responsible answer in the United Kingdom where various estimates and surveys demonstrate that a significant proportion of men and women consume alcohol above the weekly-recommended limits, alcohol misuse is costing British business up to £3.3 billion a year and the annual cost of drug abuse is estimated at around £800 million.

Some organisations may already be culturally attuned to an approach that supports an effective stance on dealing with substance abuse: they have recognised that there can be problems and that when these problems arise they need to be handled in a logical, consistent and fair manner. Other organisations will need to face the likelihood that if any policy or policies are to be truly effective then cultural change – 'how we view things around here' – will be necessary. The change may simply be that the employer needs to align the ways in which they handle the challenges of any substance abuse in the work context: the need to bring some consistency and system to what have been one-off, ad hoc responses to individual problems. It is nevertheless essential to emphasise that only when the organisation's attitudes and ways of managing its employees are aligned will any policy be

---

* Khat and ketamine are not controlled drugs, their legal status is the subject of investigation by the Advisory Council on the Misuse of Drugs (see *Drug Misuse in the UK*, an information sheet published by DrugScope, 2004).

effective. For any policy to work and to carry credibility throughout an organisation there must be clear support from the top of that organisation: policies need the endorsement of the managing director, chief executive or their equivalent. This will be a clear signal that this is the approach to be adopted and that in operating the policy, managers will receive backing and encouragement from their seniors. However it happens within an enterprise, there must be obvious and effective support from the top.

THE CURRENT EMPHASIS ON REHABILITATION

Current thinking[1] in dealing with all forms of substance abuse at work puts the emphasis on rehabilitation and action that is aimed at retention rather than bringing the employment relationship to an end. This is based on successful practical experience and is strongly linked to the emergent views and values of the early twenty-first century. ACAS has suggested that any substance misuse should whenever possible be managed as a medical problem, not handled as a disciplinary issue[2]. This approach is supported also by the International Labour Organisation Code of Practice on the management of alcohol-related and drug-related situations in the working context – the code views both aspects of substance abuse as health related and promotes a way of dealing with them that is similar to how other health problems at work might be addressed. The Employment Appeals Tribunal has tended to view alcohol as a health-related issue but the use of drugs as a misconduct issue[3]. If a rehabilitative approach is taken in both areas then this would mean that discipline would be viewed as a last resort to be used only when a more constructive approach had failed to resolve the problem and the requirements of the business and the interest of other employees demanded that the matter be concluded. In the case of employees with alcohol problems then it is quite usual for an employer to make it clear that disciplinary action may have to be taken if the employee does not cooperate with any recovery programme.

The nature of the employer's undertaking will largely determine the balance between a rehabilitative approach and the need to use disciplinary methods. In safety-critical occupations the recourse to a disciplinary procedure from the start, or at an early stage, of problems with some form of substance abuse is more appropriate and more likely. In other industries or occupations the disciplinary procedure could be appropriate where a particular act of drunkenness from an employee who is not 'alcohol dependent' takes place or, arguably much more seriously, where an employee is, say, storing drugs on work premises and is likely to face criminal charges. In this latter case dismissal is likely to be considered. Within an enterprise, that might not as a whole be a safety-critical one, occupations that are 'front of house' may leave less room for a supportive approach unless the employee can be moved to work which removes the danger to the public.

THE CLEAR ROLE OF MANAGERS

It is vital to ensure that any approach which deals with substance abuse at work should make it clear that a manager retains the right to manage. Unless this is clear it will not be possible for management as a whole to discharge its responsibilities in this area. Any policies, no matter how supportive, must continue to make it clear that a manager remains in control. Such policy statements must additionally make it abundantly clear that the manager has an undeniable responsibility for managing the workplace which at all times must also take into account the interests of other employees and the continuing productivity and financial health of the business. It would be all too easy to confuse a rehabilitative approach with laxness or permissiveness and this must be countered at all times. It is also important to point out here that managers may feel confident to identify when one of their staff is affected by alcohol at work – but they are unlikely to possess the skills necessary to identify an employee under the influence of drugs, and they will need help and support with this.

MAINTAINING CONFIDENTIALITY

In dealing with substance abuse at work employers are managing issues that must be progressed in a setting of confidentiality. Information will need to be shared but there must be a clear understanding that it will only be shared with those who have good reason to need to know. This is the only basis on which an employee is likely to cooperate in any meaningful manner and probably the only way to bring any sort of resolution to the situation. The strict maintenance of confidentiality is also vital to ensure that public confidence in the enterprise is not undermined.

FULLY-DECLARED POLICY OR AD HOC APPROACH?

The current situation is that nearly 60 per cent of organisations have some form of policy according to a December 2001 Chartered Institute of Personnel and Development (CIPD) survey[4]. A conclusion that can be drawn from this is that some organisations knowingly prefer not to have a policy or policies, and rely instead on the individual judgement of their managers who will deal with each case as it arises. This can be an attractive reliance on the good sense of those who are used to and comfortable with managing others and this approach may be able to be sustained successfully in the smaller enterprise where staff and managers are known to each other. The downside of ad hoc management is the difficulty of justifying actions, explaining individual approaches and dealing with apparent inconsistencies: especially when challenged by trade unions or in an employment tribunal under employment legislation[5]. All these concerns and more are brought into the open, and management actions and attitudes are challenged, informally and formally, when things do go wrong. The existence of a fair and workable policy may make all the difference.

Why should employers have a policy?

REASONS FOR A POLICY

The primary reason for a policy or policies is to safeguard the well-being of the workforce[6]. This reason is closely followed by the need to:

- ensure the safety of the public;
- safeguard the organisation from unfair claims;
- maintain external image and reputation.

Any policy should therefore include sections that:

- are designed to combat the vulnerability inherent in the position where an employer responds in an ad hoc manner to every situation: they set down a framework of how cases will be handled, whilst allowing managers within that framework some flexibility to take into account the unique nature of each problem;
- clearly set out for employees what their employer expects of them and what would happen if that expectation is not met;
- ensure consistency in the management of any employee and in the management of employees more generally by identifying the stages and sequences involved in handling issues concerning drugs and alcohol at work and who might be involved at each stage. It should also allow stages to be accelerated or expanded to match a specific need and the unique nature of a particular case;
- support the employer in complying with legal, contractual and other requirements, for instance production or service demands: it would be difficult to maintain compliance to the law without the steadying influence of a comprehensive policy;
- are part of a series of policies that set out the employer's stance on a wide range of topics that affect their employees in the work situation: it would be natural to include substance abuse in such a range. It reinforces the message that an employer is responsible for the whole spectrum of their employees' actions and their welfare at work. It is worth noting that for policies to be consistent the employer does need to be sure of their values and of their general approach across all their employment policies;
- assist in arresting the adverse effect of substance abuse on the health of an individual employee. This responsibility has to be balanced with the employer's wider responsibilities;
- make it clear to all their staff that turning a blind eye or covering up undoubtedly difficult situations is no longer acceptable and will not be tolerated by the employer.

ONE POLICY OR TWO?

In those organisations that do have policies on substance abuse, the majority of the employers have produced a combined document covering their overall approach to both alcohol and drugs; the others have issued two quite separate policies. It would seem that the underlying reason for the existence of two distinct policies is that whilst generally, the consumption of alcohol is not illegal, the taking of most drugs certainly is[7]. However, although the legal position is quite different between alcohol and drugs, it is possible in many circumstances for the employer's approach to members of staff who succumb to the undue influence of either to be broadly the same. Of course it has to be borne in mind that the use of Class A, B or C drugs is illegal[8] whilst the use of alcohol is clearly not and this does add an additionally serious tone to situations of drug abuse at work. A circumstance that may lead to differing policy between the two types of abuse may be in safety-critical industries: here employers, mindful of heavy public responsibilities and liabilities, have tended to rehabilitate those with alcohol problems but discipline employees whose problems relate to drug misuse.

LINKS TO OTHER POLICIES

As set out in 'Reasons for a Policy' above, each individual policy would therefore play its part in combating the effects of substance abuse in the work environment. Employees will better understand their employer's stance where they can perceive the same theme and values pervading a range of human resource policies – so that the approaches hang together displaying a similar attitude and telling a consistent story. This would inevitably and helpfully be reinforced by and in return reinforce other employer policies:

- Lateness: problems with alcohol or drugs can be first indicated by a pattern or frequency of late starts and increasingly unbelievable excuses for such lateness.
- Absenteeism: employees with alcohol or drugs problems can have greater levels of absence than other employees.
- Performance: there needs to be a policy covering the effect of the behaviour of the substance abuser on individual or group performance including how to deal with poor performance. An analysis of the reasons might indicate drug or alcohol problems: substance abuse might mean poor judgement, a reduction in the ability to concentrate or difficulties with remembering items.
- Individual responsibilities within work teams which include relationships within such teams and with the organisation more generally: drug and alcohol problems can mean antisocial behaviour or sudden changes in behaviour or mood.
- Adverse effect on other employees: individual members of staff have a responsibility to their fellow workers and substance abuse might mean an increasingly unheeding attitude to other members of staff.
- The effect on the reputation of the organisation: public relations policies should include sections on what is expected of employees and what action would be taken by managers where an employee's behaviour puts this at risk.
- Compliance with legal requirements: in potential or actual breaches of legal requirements it is essential that employees know what is required of them and what might happen if they breach those requirements – the effects of substance abuse can make lack of compliance more likely.

ENCOURAGING EMPLOYEES TO SEEK HELP

A substance-abuse policy should also clearly and firmly encourage employees with problems to seek help. It can frequently be the case that a member of staff with a drug or alcohol problem may not feel confident to approach their manager – so the policy should clearly encourage them to pursue other routes such as occupational health, the human resources department, or to approach another manager whom they trust so that there is every reasonable channel permitted to allow them to declare their concerns and request support. When an employee approaches a manager or another agent of their employer it is essential that this can be done in an atmosphere which maintains proper confidentiality – that is only those who must know will be told, and the employee should know who else will be informed.

DISCIPLINE OR REHABILITATE?

Any policy should set out a clear distinction between a disciplinary approach and a capability or rehabilitative approach and should explain the circumstances in which one or the other would be adopted and the reasons why either approach is being followed. Whilst, as has been said elsewhere in this chapter, employers must choose where to pitch their approaches between a totally disciplinary way of handling the situation and a totally rehabilitative one, there is not total freedom, of course, to make such a choice. The decision will partly be determined by the nature of the enterprise: is it one where the public or others are at immediate risk and drugs and alcohol cannot be tolerated under any circumstances – for instance transport or the operation of heavy machinery? Are there serious criminal charges pending which if proved will result in imprisonment or a heavy fine? The decision will also partly rest on the values and style – 'approach' – 'preferences' – of the organisation. However, personal preferences must sit within what is seen by the employment tribunals and Employment Appeal Tribunal as reasonable employer behaviour. A stance that treated all substance-abuse problems at work as disciplinary cases, leading to warnings and dismissal and ignoring personal distress or mitigating circumstances, is not likely to be defendable in the working climate of the twenty-first century.

GAINING AND MAINTAINING SUPPORT FOR A POLICY

Policies that are determined entirely by the management of an organisation are at risk of constant challenge by individual members of staff, staff organisations or trade unions. A policy that carries the support of the trade unions or staff organisations will mean that there should be fewer challenges to procedure and that there should be consequently an increased ability to concentrate on dealing with the substantive issues, focusing on the employee and their problem. Arriving at an agreed policy may take more time and absorb more management effort, but reaching and maintaining an agreement will greatly reinforce the employer stance on the management of drugs and alcohol at work and do much to gain acceptance and understanding. It is an issue where there is great potential for joint interest, a shared understanding and a common approach.

LEGAL REQUIREMENTS ON EMPLOYEES

A policy can be of great assistance in ensuring that an employee complies with legal requirements as far as substance abuse at work is concerned. Under the Misuse of Drugs Act 1971 an employee can be personally responsible if they are aware that illegal drugs are being used or distributed on the premises at which they work. Any policy therefore needs to set out an employee's obligations and the basis of all such employee duties. In regard to alcohol in the workplace a policy will assist with control and consistency over the legal or other reasons for any restriction applying to alcohol in the work setting. This would cover individual possession and use, whether or not alcohol is permitted on social occasions (for example leaving parties and celebrations), whether or not it is permitted to be consumed in meal breaks and whether there is a required alcohol-free period before the commencement of any period of duty (as in the case of train drivers and airline pilots).

THE REPUTATION OF THE ORGANISATION

The existence of an effective policy on alcohol and drugs will combat risks to the standing or reputation of the organisation, its products or services and its position in the community. Managing the public relations aspects will mean the policy or policies will need to spell out the extent of any rehabilitative approach and the determinants that might lead to disciplinary action. The management of effective public relations might be the overwhelming reason for a board to encourage and support the existence of a policy which will be consistently and fairly applied to the whole organisation.

CORPORATE IDENTITY

The effect of good human resources policies is that they can make a major contribution in pulling an organisation together, strengthening its corporate identity. However, policies will only assist in this way if they represent the considered views of senior management and they have the support of the trade unions or staff associations as well as that of managers throughout the organisation. Staff training and briefings that included meaningful references to the policy, or extracts from it, would further reinforce the consistency of any approach and ensure that all staff were aware of its existence. A substance-abuse policy would be an essential element of such policies, helping to hold the organisation together, and would play its full part in setting employment standards.

POLICIES NEED TO BE TAILOR-MADE

Those charged with the responsibility for drafting a policy often start the task by perusing the policies of other organisations, adapting and editing to form something relevant and useable in their local context. Whilst it is clearly helpful to study policies from other organisations, and it should be noted that the CIPD library holds a considerable collection of substance-abuse policies from a range of employers, any policy does have to be specific to the nature of the organisation and its particular culture. In order to ensure that such a policy is relevant and sharply focused it is advisable, *before referring to other policies*, to determine and set down:

- what the basic message of the policy is to be: what should it say to employees and managers?
- what are to be the essential elements or sections of the policy, the headings of each part?
- what attitude does the organisation wish to adopt on the issue of substance abuse at work?
- what outcome does the organisation want from the policy: what is the purpose of the policy, what is it designed to achieve?

Having clarified the local requirement for a policy in this way it can then be helpful and informative to consult the work of others, produce a draft, consult internally on its contents, agree with management and staff, publish it and ensure it is adhered to.

Employers' responsibilities towards the individual employee

The primary responsibilities that the employer has towards individual members of staff have their origins in an employer's legal duties under the Health and Safety at Work Act. The principal duty under this enabling Act is to ensure the health, safety and welfare of all employees and by implication to protect them from any dangerous acts of other employees. Whilst these responsibilities are concisely encapsulated they are extensive and do reach to many corners of an organisation.

These responsibilities could be summed up as:

- Ensuring a safe system of work. In order to discharge its responsibilities towards the individual employee each organisation will need to ask itself what this means for its own operations in regard to drugs and alcohol at work. Where are the risks to the individual? What safeguards for the individual employee must be present? What are the reporting and alerting protocols for any instance of unsafe working that could put an individual at risk?
- Ensuring that managers and supervisors are competent to apply the organisation's policies on drugs. In order to discharge the employer's responsibility towards the individual worker, knowledge of what is required is not sufficient in itself. Have managers and supervisors received appropriate training and is there advice and expertise available to maintain them at a level of competence? Do managers and supervisors understand and can they enunciate the policy on drugs and alcohol in so far as it affects the individual employee?
- Ensuring consistency in their treatment of an individual employee, and between employees, covered by the policy. Well-written policies will ensure that individual managers interpret and operate them towards their individual members of staff in similar and consistent ways, but there will need to be checks and safeguards. Such monitoring procedures may be with a more senior manager or with the human resources department and should be explicitly built in at various stages of the procedure in each case. The purpose of these is to ensure that responsibilities towards individual employees are discharged fairly and consistently – that the interpretation of the policy and the pace of any procedure is appropriate and reasonable in the circumstances.
- Ensuring that there is clarity in the policy regarding the employer's position, attitude and stance on the issue of drugs and alcohol at work. There is a responsibility to be clear to the individual employee. An overt declaration of intent of which managers and members of staff are fully aware will help to avoid misunderstandings or expectations and approaches which do not stem from the stand on the issue that the employer has taken.
- Providing a policy or policies that are firm but fair and supportive to the individual employee. Not only should the policy stance be clear and well known but there should be also a responsibility to the employee. This responsibility is to be clear about the limits of support and the balance between this and the need to have regard to other employees and the overall interests of the enterprise. The overall interests must include any responsibilities to customers, clients and the wider public.

In addition the employer now has considerable legal responsibilities to the employee under the Human Rights Act 1998. Under this Act an employer will have to consider an employee's rights under Article 8. In summary this sets down an employee's right to a private life which under this Act has to be set against the employer right to protect the reputation of the business. As far as substance-abuse policy is concerned this has implications in such an area as drug testing where an employer would be required to demonstrate that it was relevant to the work context and not just exercising control over a worker's private life.

The employer also has new legal responsibilities in connection with substance-abuse policies towards the employee under the Data Protection Act 1998. Under this legislation an employer must ensure that any testing for alcohol or drugs complies with data protection principles. In particular an employer may only collect or process information about the results of drug testing if the member of staff has given their explicit consent. Exceptions to this protection would include where the employer needs the information to process any legal obligations or in connection with legal proceedings.

The employer has contractual obligations towards the individual employee to provide supportive policies in return for cooperation from that member of staff. Breaches of contract can be matters for the courts and this can therefore take this liability into the legal realm. These contractual obligations would be one basis to any claim the employee might make against the employer. The employer will also have obligations under all formal policies which touch on their approach to the issue of substance abuse and the individual employee.

In recent years when work and the other parts of an employee's life are expected to be kept in balance it can be said that there is a social responsibility placed on every employer not to stand aside from problems of individual employees where those problems have an effect on the way they perform their functions. It is in this area of responsibility where an employee's behaviour is most closely and consistently managed and monitored. The extent of the penetration of this social responsibility into the day-to-day management of staff will be a function of the values and culture of the organisation; but the divide between the world of work and the wider world seems less in recent years than it has been for much of the nineteenth or twentieth centuries. The expectations of employees now challenge the extent and nature of the responsibility of employers.

Employers' responsibilities towards the wider organisation

Under the same legal framework that sets down their responsibilities to individual employees, employers have responsibility for the health, safety and welfare of all their employees. As in so many aspects of dealing with substance abuse at work in any of its forms, the employer must balance their responsibility for individual employees with their responsibilities for the total workforce and the wider interests of the organisation.

In addition to their corporate duties under the Health and Safety at Work Act employers have other legal obligations to the wider organisation under employment law and laws relating to their particular function:

- The Misuse of Drugs Act 1971 makes it an offence to possess, supply, offer to supply or produce controlled drugs without authorisation.
- The Disability Discrimination Act 1995, although it specifically excludes addiction or dependency on drugs or alcohol (as set out in the disability discrimination (Meaning of Disability) Regulations 1996), does include in its provisions any impairments that have resulted from addictions[9].
- The Transport and Works Act 1992 sets down specific requirements for employers in the transport industries and is very specific on railway workers who report for duty whilst under the influence of alcohol or drugs.
- The Data Protection Act 1998 details obligations on every employer towards their employees on the subject of testing for drugs as well as draft guidelines (due for issue in July 2004) which cover the need to justify any adverse impact of testing, minimising the amount of personal information, being able to justify criteria for selection of employees, confining testing to significant occupations, testing impairment rather than substance misuse and ensuring employees are aware that testing is taking place[10].

- The Human Rights Act 1998 now has an impact on testing and screening for alcohol or drugs in the workplace, establishing the worker's rights to privacy to be balanced with the employer's need to prevent any adverse effect on their business or organisation. This has been outlined earlier in this chapter under the employer's responsibilities towards an individual employee.

There is also very specialised legislation which includes obligations towards all employees and the wider organisation. This legislation includes three very significant sets of regulations:

- The Work in Compressed Air Special Regulations 1958
- The Control of Lead at Work Regulations 1980
- The Ionising Radiations Regulations 1985.

Over and above these specific legal requirements there is a general requirement on employers towards their wider organisation and the workforce in ensuring that they apply policies and the law consistently. It is the observance of such responsibilities, or their absence, that contributes to the reputation of organisations as good places to work and as excellent employers.

There is furthermore a responsibility on every employer towards their employees to have clear disciplinary rules, which have been clearly and fully made known to the workforce, so that they know where they stand[11]. Any rules must be sensibly applied, rigid application without due regard to the circumstances could mean that any subsequent dismissal could be seen as unfair. The addition of rules about substance abuse will of course mean a change to the individual contract of employment and can only be introduced with the consent of the employees: at least employees should be consulted and, as has been mentioned earlier in this chapter, a full agreement would be the preferable route. Additions to disciplinary rules are clearly a change to the contract of employment and there should also be an agreement with each member of staff, or a collective agreement. As has also been mentioned earlier in this chapter, employers may take a disciplinary route with an employee who indulges in misconduct or puts others safety at risk while affected by alcohol or drugs.

Summing up

This chapter has attempted to pull together the main features of the liabilities and responsibilities in connection with drug abuse at work that fall on employers. In this chapter it has been suggested that there are three main themes underpinning these issues in the working world of the twenty-first century.

The first theme is that in tackling responsibility and liability in these matters an employer should do all that is reasonable to retain the employee where that member of staff is involved in some form of substance abuse. If it is possible to retain this member of staff whilst working with them to combat their dependency on alcohol or drugs then their employment should be preserved. This theme of course can only be followed where an employee displays some recognition of the inappropriateness of their behaviour and a willingness to be helped.

The second theme in identifying the elements of liability and responsibility is the desirability of bringing staff organisations or trade unions into the production of policy. If a policy on substance abuse is to be of practical use then it must be able to be applied consistently and without confusion or procedural challenge. A workforce needs to know its interests have been fully considered and that any of its members will be fairly and consistently treated: this can be achieved by asking the body or bodies representing the staff to agree and endorse a standardised approach – a policy. Consultation is useful but cannot deliver the support and confidence – or sense of ownership – in a way that an agreed policy can. Furthermore an agreed policy is likely to be a safer and more successful policy as it will be one that encourages observation and compliance.

The third theme in pinning down the essentials of responsibility and liability is that a balance must be maintained between the interests of the employee with the problem, fellow employees and the many interests of the employer. One significant determinant of a balanced position must be the nature of the business of which the problem employee is a part. The question here is whether the interests of each element – employee, the workforce and the employer's concern – have been thoroughly assessed and that this has enabled a fully informed decision to be taken.

In essence it is in the full consideration of these three themes that an employer will be able to be assured that they have met their liabilities and fully discharged their responsibilities in the difficult and challenging area of substance abuse.

References

1.   'Tackling alcohol and drugs in the workplace', City of London Drug Action Team and five other partners, 2001
2.   'Discipline at Work', *ACAS Advisory Handbook*, February 1999
3.   'Alcohol and drug policies', IDS HR Study 771, April 2004, page 10
4.   'Alcohol and drug policies in UK organisations', Chartered Institute of Personnel and Development Survey Report, December 2001
5.   Angus Council v. Edgley (EAT 289/99)
6.   'How to deal with alcohol and drug misuse', Christian Geelmuyden, *People Management*, 25 July 2002
7.   *Drugs and Alcohol Policies*, Tricia Jackson, Chapter 3, published by CIPD, 1999.
8.   'Drug misuse in the UK', information sheets published by DrugScope, 2004
9.   Hutchison 3G UK v. Mason (EAT 0369/03)
10.   'Employment Practices Data Protection Code: Part 4 – Information about workers' health', Information Commissioner's Office (undated)
11.   Claypotts Construction Ltd v. McCallum (EAT 699/81)

CHAPTER

10 *Policy Design and Implementation*

Graham Lucas

The principles of alcohol and drug policies

An organisation's most valuable asset is its workforce. The scope of addictive problems is such that it is not whether an organisation can afford to address the matter; *it cannot afford not to do so*. The motto 'good health is good business' facilitates acceptance of the rationale for vigilance regarding risk factors from alcohol and drugs to which the respective policies are key. The WHO (1980) defined health as 'a state of mental, physical, and social well being'. It dictates how the individual functions in the personal, occupational and community domains, all of which are relevant in considering the significance of problem drinking and the misuse of drugs in a particular organisation.

There are areas of commonality and difference between problem drinking and the misuse of drugs. Therefore, the similarities will be covered collectively, the differences identified and the policies outlined separately, customised according to the nature and structure of the organisation, and the degree to which the operation is safety-critical.

The respective policies should:

- be included in the organisation's overall health and safety policy together with mental and physical components. They should be explained at induction and reiterated in ongoing health education, creating awareness throughout the workforce of the commitment to maintaining a safe and healthy environment;
- ensure that the workforce is fully aware that there is a potentially serious health and safety problem for which each employee is themselves responsible. Likewise, problem drinking and misuse of drugs are regarded as illnesses, and will be handled in exactly the same way as any other clinical condition, be it medical, surgical or psychiatric;
- eliminate or minimise problem drinking or misuse of drugs respectively, and their effects on co-workers, on-site contractors, the local community and the environment. This is achieved by sensitive intervention, reassurance regarding confidentiality, salary, job security and sickness absence, appropriate level of support and treatment, and assisted rehabilitation and return to work.

Both alcohol and drugs cause adverse subjective, behavioural, and health-related effects, including impaired cognitive function, judgement, performance, coordination and gait predisposing to tripping. The effect of drugs is very rapid, as can be that of alcohol, particularly when consumed on an empty stomach. In combination, the effects of each is potentiated. This, and poly-drug misuse is increasingly common and must always be suspected.

The respective policies apply throughout the organisation, not being restricted to safety critical sections only, regardless of the level of seniority. This prevents an 'us and them' attitude, everyone being at risk, and there are no stereotypes (*Tolly's Guide*, Lucas, 2002). Whether problem drinking or drug misuse occurs within the workplace, at home or in the community, adverse occupational effects ensue.

Although drugs are more 'sexy', and attract widespread publicity, they constitute a significantly smaller problem than does alcohol. Unfortunately, public funding is allocated disproportionately in favour of drug services and research.

Despite the Health and Safety Executive's (HSE) *The Problem Drinker at Work* (1991), *Don't Mix It* (1996) and *Drug Misuse at Work* (1998), the majority of organisations, public and private, still have difficulties coping effectively. Policies are mandatory, and the culture of the organisation is focal regarding their effectiveness in practice. The HSE correctly emphasised that the introduction of policies necessitates agreement between management, human resources, the trade unions or workers representatives, with advice from the occupational health physician (OHP). The majority of workers, as with people in general, are in denial of problem drinking or of drug misuse. Emergencies include an ultimatum following domestic rows or violence, occupational or community incidents, accidents, and acute alcohol- or drug-related medical or surgical complications.

From the small- or medium-sized enterprise to the global plc, good management through routine appraisal or other monitoring and feedback is essential. It should be capable of identifying an inexplicable change in personality, behaviour and performance, all of which are crucial parameters in identifying the misuse of drugs and alcohol. Simple observation often suffices for the line manager or co-workers to identify such changes, without any formal clinical input. The question then arises whether the deterioration is due to predictable or unpredictable work-related stress; alternatively, other psychosocial issues, or to some underlying physical or psychiatric morbidity, such as anxiety or depression caused or compounded by problem drinking and drug misuse. Post-traumatic stress and post-traumatic stress disorder can predispose to depression and problem drinking, or the misuse of prescribed medication due to impaired sleep. Hence, the importance of considering mental, physical and environmental health comprehensively; problems in all domains of life may be contributing, and a macro- rather than a micro-approach is essential.

A new drug or alcohol policy cannot be imposed, or modifications made to an existing one, without the closest consultation and agreement between management and the trade unions or workers representatives. However, at recruitment, the respective policies are clarified, and whether they are acceptable rests entirely with the job applicant. This is particularly relevant in the context of any form of biological screening, be it urinalysis for drugs or breathalysation for alcohol. Nevertheless, such objective methods of identification should be recognised as mere components of a comprehensive health and safety programme, the aim of which is to maintain or improve morale, performance and productivity. Also, when required, treatment facilities should be accessed in conjunction with the GP, subject to the employee's formal agreement. Unfortunately such programmes are still seriously under-resourced within the NHS, as are those for any other form of minor psychiatric morbidity. However, excellent results are often achieved by community drugs and alcohol teams together with other organisations such as Narcotics Anonymous, Alcohol Anonymous and the British Doctors' and Dentists' Group.

The employee's motivation to engage in an addiction treatment programme is often easier when the referral is initiated from the workplace, in keeping with the alcohol or drug policy. The common response when the employee is referred by the GP to a treatment facility is often 'Yes doctor, I know I need help but I can't take time off – what would they say at work? I'd lose my job.' Hence the importance of the policy addressing and clarifying these specific issues.

The effect of mind-altering substances on a worker must be avoided, particularly in those physically or mentally safety-critical jobs. The City banker or stockbroker on cocaine who makes faulty decisions at the computer screen is financially hazardous for the organisation, himself and his clients; the crane operator or cruise boat captain with a similar habit is physically dangerous. The misuse of drugs or problem drinking may precede recruitment, and may have been acquired at school, college or at a previous workplace.

The legal aspects are dealt with elsewhere. Suffice to say that its implications dictate the importance of drugs and alcohol policies to clarify the position of the organisation, co-workers, and the afflicted employee who risks a criminal charge. The employer is contravening the law and the Health and Safety at Work Act (1974) by colluding. The co-worker who well-meaningly but misguidedly covers up is actually more treacherous than a 'whistleblower'. Should an accident occur, injured co-workers or contractors are more likely to sue the employer than the culprit.

To reiterate the general principles of both policies are the same, each being customised according to the size of the organisation, the nature of its operation and the degree to which it is safety-critical.

Definitions

Here, as in the literature generally, the terms 'drugs' and 'substances' are used interchangeably. The definition of illegal drugs excludes alcohol.

Drug misuse is defined as intentional or unintentional use of illegal drugs or prescribed medication outside the recommended dosage.

Dependence on alcohol and drugs can be physical, psychological or both. Availability of a continuing supply is crucial. If not, withdrawal becomes physical; or more commonly, psychologically intolerable, being time-consuming at work, exemplified by nicotine and caffeine although not considered here.

Problem drinking is said to occur when alcohol consumption, irrespective of the amount, adversely affects personal, occupational or community life, mental and/or physical health, and requires some form of treatment.

Contributory factors include work-related and domestic stress, interpersonal tension, bullying, unsocial hours, shiftwork, monotony, lack of supervision or a traumatic incident, particularly if constituting a near-death experience, causing residual post-traumatic stress or post-traumatic stress disorder. There are specific jobs where the culture is perceived as requiring drinking, as in business entertaining, or when there is lack of supervision, financial resources are available, and there are opportunities to drink 'respectably' in working hours. (Sceptics state this describes the culture of the House of Commons!) However, throughout industry there has been a gradual reduction of drinking expectations, particularly in the City and other entrepreneurial occupations. Nevertheless, binge drinking after work is on the increase.

Alcohol policy

In the employment context, 'problem drinking' is a more appropriate and functional definition than 'addiction', 'abuse' or of any ICD-10 (International Classification of Diseases) or DSM IV (Diagnostic and Statistical Manual of Mental Disorders) categories. In 1981 the HSE referred to it 'adversely affecting the standard of *his* work, and requiring help'. Currently, such use of 'his' is not only politically but also factually incorrect, as it increasingly refers to 'her'.

Alcohol compromises safety, working relationships, morale and productivity. Therefore, its use before or at work is totally unacceptable in the majority of jobs, particularly in transportation, construction, health care and the emergency services to mention a few. Even agricultural workers and gardeners enjoying a glass of beer with their lunchtime sandwiches after sweating in high summer could pose a risk.

The TUC and CBI have long been unanimous in advocating that every organisation, whatever its size, should have its own alcohol policy. The HSE's 1981 initiative was formally endorsed by the Secretaries of State for Employment, Health and Social Services. The importance of local needs and the culture of individual organisations were recognised in formulating the policy. The idea originated in 1977 when the National Council on Alcoholism identified the need for such guidance.

However, firms were slow to develop policies (Lucas, BMJ, 1987). Moreover, only 15 per cent of the Scottish organisations surveyed had a copy of *The Problem Drinker at Work* (1991). The Post Office later produced a very useful training video 'Someone like you' outlining the identification process and describing correct, and incorrect handling of the problem drinker in the workplace.

The majority of those so affected are at work. Hence the current concern regarding the ever-increasing prevalence of binge drinking, made more alarming by recent changes in UK licensing laws, the impact on shift work being particularly relevant.

It must be emphasised, however, that most people drink sensibly, consuming alcohol in moderation, recognising the risk of escalation to problem drinking, health education creating awareness and hopefully prevention. Quoted workplace costs of problem drinking vary, but they exceed those due to industrial strife.

WHY HAVE A POLICY?

As little as two to three units of alcohol can impair functional effectiveness and exacerbate anxiety and depression, and poor timekeeping with sickness absence ensuing. Later, it can cause impaired memory and premature intellectual deterioration, compounded by head injuries from falls, all unacceptable occupationally. The employee who previously gained respect for being 'capable of holding their drink', is actually to be pitied as it signifies a tolerance to the hazardous effects of very high blood alcohol levels.

Social anxiety is extremely common and strategies are required to cope with the constant temptation to drink for its anxiolytic effect. Therefore, basic alcohol counselling and relapse-prevention programmes include assertive skills, and stress, anxiety and anger management.

Alcohol is not illegal unless it results in drink-driving above the permitted level, or hazardous work-related, domestic or community incidents. An airline pilot is automatically reported to the Civil Aviation Authority (CAA), as is a doctor to the General Medical Council (GMC), and an officer in the armed services is disciplined following a drink-driving charge.

Joint Aviation Regulations and CAA regulations (JAR-FCL3, 2000) are appropriately stringent regarding alcohol consumption by pilots prior to flying, 'eight hours from bottle to throttle' being the minimum requirement. Restriction to some four units is also recommended during the preceding 24 hours prior to take-off. This is essential because even with normal hepatic and renal function, alcohol excretion is only 15 mg per cent per hour. Likewise, one unit of alcohol increases blood alcohol concentration by 15 mg per cent. Therefore, for drivers, machine operators, scaffolders and others in safety-critical jobs, a pint of beer or half bottle of wine at lunchtime is hazardous as some alcohol remains in the bloodstream for the ensuing three hours, that is until the end of the working day. Late-night drinking presents the risk of starting work with a hazardous blood alcohol level. A significantly higher rate of accidents occur in the morning and at the beginning of night shifts compared with other times.

A director of education was drinking a bottle of vodka a day, but despite having a first in mathematics, he was incapable of manipulating the simplest of figures and his short-term memory had deteriorated significantly, covered up by prudent delegation and evasion. Only his wife's threat to contact the CEO led him to consult his occupational health physician.

The armed services culture has changed significantly: alcohol was previously expected as part of mess life and lunchtime drinking was the norm – all now unacceptable.

In 1994, 90 per cent of UK organisations reported that alcohol consumption constituted a problem, albeit to a relatively minor degree: 17 per cent described a major problem resulting in impaired work performance, productivity, poor timekeeping, significant sickness absence (3–5 per cent alcohol related), risk to safety, adverse effect on working relationships and morale, unacceptable behaviour and disciplinary problems.

The purpose of an alcohol policy is to clarify employers' and employees' respective obligations in terms of the Health and Safety at Work Act, and to make management and HR departments aware of the adverse effects of alcohol.

IMPLEMENTING THE ALCOHOL POLICY

The following stages are recommended:

1   Ascertain the scope of a suspected alcohol problem.
2   Appropriate consultees should be involved, directly:
    a) the occupational health physician (OHP) at initial referral to the occupatioal health department (OHD), and confidentially with treatment providers;
    b) following treatment and prior to re-entry to assess the likelihood of satisfactory ongoing performance. (Understandably, employers may introduce the question of the chances of relapse in the 'foreseeable future'. In alcohol-related illness, no absolute guarantee can be given, just as is the case with coronary heart disease following bypass surgery.)
3   In smaller organisations, the owner or manager has greater personal knowledge of their workforce and is themself more capable of identifying significant change in behaviour, performance, timekeeping and sickness absence of each employee. This is probably the commonest scenario, and a simple policy clarifies respective roles in the identification, intervention, help, treatment and rehabilitation processes. Also, it helps a GP providing

occupational health sessions in a purely clinical context without 'on the shop floor' knowledge of the culture or personalities.

4   Union or employee representatives are key if there is a wish to challenge applicability of the policy.

5   Clarify the quantity and timing to which alcohol consumption is to be limited. Safety-critical jobs preclude the use of any alcohol, contravention being a legal matter.

6   Formulate the optimum method of identifying an employee's alcohol problem, intervene sensitively, and offer effective and immediate help appropriate to the severity of the condition. If indicated, specialist treatment facilities should then be accessed urgently in conjunction with the GP, subject to the employee's formal agreement. Normally, these are the NHS and the community alcohol and drug team. Unless such effective facilities are available, identification and sensitive intervention will achieve nothing. However, NHS resources are grossly inadequate, in this area and private treatment is prohibitively expensive unless the organisation provides or the employee themselves has private medical insurance.

7   Communicate the alcohol policy within the organisation.

8   Continue workforce health education on the effects of alcohol with emphasis on the respective responsibilities of the organisation and of the individual employee for themself, and co-workers.

9   Ensure that management have received essential training in implementing and monitoring the policy.

10   Document financial and safety aspects.

11   Clarify that treatment is also beneficial for the family, the organisation as regards productivity, safety and well-being of co-workers, contractors, the local community and the national economy.

12   Do not collude, 'turn a blind eye' or transfer the employee to a less safety-critical location; it is counterproductive. Because of whistleblowers, general recognition of the legal position and the introduction of alcohol policies such a well-meaning but hazardous response is now less frequent. Denial of problem drinking, and secret drinking at work and home is common. As every GP, OHP and general physician knows, it is extremely uncommon for a patient or employee to state, 'I've got a serious alcohol or drug problem' or 'I'm severely depressed and anxious...' Therefore, managerial and co-worker awareness is essential in identification and intervention.

13   Consider dismissal as a possible expedient in the short term, but not in keeping with caring and basic corporate social responsibility. Also, it is costly in terms of labour turnover, recruitment, induction and training costs. Inevitably, more severe health problems will develop, personal and occupational life disintegrates, and the individual's problem drinking is transferred to another organisation, common in the licensed trade, or to the community if unemployed.

14   Awareness of management's sensitivity facilitates self-identification and a request for help, ahead of obligatory managerial 'for cause' intervention. Nevertheless, however well-formulated the policy and supportive the employer, the employee must themself be motivated. The decision regarding treatment is the individual's as with any clinical intervention. Well-meaning persuasion by employer, health care professionals or loving partner can be counterproductive.

15   Alcohol Concern, the Medical Council on Alcoholism and other organisations are

available to advise on the formulation and customising of policies in addition to the HSE.

16   Routine job appraisals to discuss impaired performance, poor timekeeping and unexplained sickness absences, provide the opportunity for medical referral and treatment.

17   A dangerous incident or accident necessitates immediate 'for cause' intervention.

18   A formally identified senior manager should be the reference point to action help or treatment, and to coordinate within the organisation and externally before and during sickness absence, and to facilitate subsequent re-entry.

19   Sickness absence, salary, job security and pension rights should be confirmed provided the recommended treatment programme is accepted.

Refusal of the offer of initial assessment help, or the discontinuing of a treatment programme already in progress is not itself a disciplinary matter. However, subsequent behaviour problems or impaired performance can then be subject to disciplinary action. However, each case must be evaluated individually. Moreover, this scenario can be referred to as 'constructive coercion' (Taylor and McCann, 1995).

20   If relapse follows recommended treatment, this should again be handled sensitively and a further programme be offered.

21   If treatment is unsuccessful, assuming that there are no outstanding disciplinary problems, conditions of service sometimes allow of consideration of ill-health retirement.

22   Clinical confidentiality is mandatory. However, re-entry can be facilitated by line manager and co-workers being aware of the condition, given the rehabilitee's formal agreement.

23   The organisation should regularly review the operation of the policy.

SCREENING

Breathalysation has to be considered in all safety-critical industries to reduce risk. It can be:

- at selection;
- routinely or randomly, throughout or for part of the workforce only;
- for cause, that is following a hazardous incident, accident, evidence of drinking in contravention of company regulations or arriving under the influence of alcohol;
- during rehabilitation following return to work after an addiction treatment programme. This is reassuring for managers who, however supportive, are understandably apprehensive: it is in the employee's best interests to avoid disputed accusations.

However, screening remains extremely sensitive and it is obligatory to have the formal agreement of management, HR, trade unions or workers' representatives. It reduces risk to co-workers, contractors and others involved in the organisation, and to the local community.

Used appropriately, breathalysation can be a valuable preventive measure, but it is only a component of a comprehensive clinical assessment. However sophisticated ancillary medical investigations become, there is no substitute for history-taking, preferably with the spouse, partner or relevant key carer to provide an objective account, subject to the employee's agreement. Also clinical examination should include both mental and physical aspects. Therefore, it is essential for the occupational health physician to have adequate facilities to carry out such an assessment.

Implications of introducing alcohol screening

Formal agreement to such a process must be included in all new employment contracts. However, those already employed are not legally required to agree to such changes in terms and conditions of service. If imposed, the individual may resign and the organisation could then face a subsequent claim for constructive dismissal. In addition to the contractual agreement, formal consent should precede each breathalysation, as is the case in drug testing. Medical confidentiality is mandatory; managers merely need to be informed whether the employee is fit or unfit for work. Even when 'for cause' breathalysation is positive, the possibility of an underlying medical condition, including head injury, must always be considered.

PREVENTING ESCALATION

Alcohol policies can prevent the escalation of problem drinking by:

- alerting the workforce to the risks at induction, and through ongoing routine health education;
- identifying early risk signs in self and others;
- encouraging to request help, be it counselling, utilisation of an employee assistance programme, to their general practitioner, community mental health alcohol and drugs team, or to a formal addiction treatment programme.

Unless effective help is quickly achieved, the employee becomes disillusioned and the policy loses credibility. Also, the condition could deteriorate, and an accident occur with unfortunate consequences for the employee and others. Moreover, the organisation could be seen to be culpable.

Health education on alcohol and problem drinking should encompass all the above. In addition it should cover the following:

- advice on the adverse effects on health, behaviour and performance at induction and ongoing;
- recognition that to present an inappropriately restrictive, rigid attitude is counterproductive;
- safe limits are up to 21 units per week for men, and up to 14 units per week for women. However, consumption of the weekly quota in one day, within a few hours, is extremely dangerous (Cantopher, 1996);
- drinking alone should be discouraged, particularly if feeling stressed, anxious or depressed;
- drinking slowly with food is preferable;
- drinking water is recommended to counteract the dehydrating diuretic effect of alcohol which predisposes to a hangover. This can be aggravated by coffee due to the diuretic effect of caffeine, particularly relevant in work-related flying;
- each individual's tolerance varies, and there is a range of common causes which can predispose to increased susceptibility to alcohol. These include tiredness, post-viral debility, low-grade fever, the coincidental taking of an antibiotic, or of over-the-counter minor analgesics for headache or musculo-skeletal pain;
- however sophisticated a residential addiction treatment programme, the prognosis for

maintenance of indefinite abstinence is significantly better when the rehabilitee engages effectively with Alcoholics Anonymous;

- involvement of the partner or the key caring person is invaluable from the initial workplace assessment to monitored re-entry, subject to the employee's agreement;
- the organisation Al-Anon can be very supportive in coping with a spouse's or partner's devious behaviour.

Health education can also facilitate self-identification of problem drinking:
- The definition of problem drinking is helpful.
- The **CAGE** test. This is a mnemonic for four pertinent questions. Have you ever:
  - been **c**oncerned about your alcohol consumption?
  - felt **a**ngry when criticised for drinking?
  - felt **g**uilty about your drinking?
  - required an **e**ye-opener in the morning?
- Another useful mnemonic for self-identification of vulnerability in general is **HALT**: Do you feel:
  - **h**ungry
  - **a**ngry but covering tension, irritability, resentment
  - **l**onely
  - **t**ired?

SUMMARY OF IMPLEMENTATION OF AN ALCOHOL POLICY

The OHP, in conjunction with other key personnel, is properly involved in drafting and routine revision of the policy, which varies according to size and structure of the organisation and nature of the operation. However, awareness of its content and implications throughout the workforce is essential and is facilitated routinely by ongoing health education.

Drug misuse policy

The Health and Safety Executive classes any use of illegal drugs as 'misuse'. In the workplace, the crucial issue is whether illegal drugs have been taken rather than whether the drug is 'used' or 'abused' (Beswick, 2002). Drug misuse is illegal in the workplace as it is in the community, notwithstanding recent changes relating to cannabis.

The ever-cheaper Class A drugs including heroin and cocaine are increasingly causing drug-related deaths. Even highly intelligent people are under the misconception that cocaine is safe, binges occurring in conjunction with alcohol. However, this combination is cardiotoxic, and deaths from heart attacks and strokes are reported in relatively young employees who binge following a hard week's work (Schifano et al, 2003). The problem can be brought to work, or originate in the occupational setting. In a recent survey (Smith A et al, 2004), one in four workers under 30 admitted to misusing drugs in the previous year. At acute and chronic levels, drugs impair cognition, perception and motor skills. If human error has caused an accident or injury, drug misuse may have contributed. The gap between the prevalence of drug misuse in the employed and in the unemployed respectively is narrowing.

The 1996 National Drugs Campaign Survey (Taskey et al, 1999) reports around 16 per cent of respondents had used 'any drug' in the preceding three months, 12 per cent had used 'any drug' in the preceding month. Cannabis was the most widely used; 16 per cent of those between 16 and 24 had used it during the preceding month.

An effective workplace drug policy must describe the range of effects of Class A, B and C drugs including: alteration of thought processes, perception and feelings; impairment of judgement, concentration and level of consciousness; and sudden unprovoked mood changes, irritability, verbal and physical aggression. Also, certain drugs including cocaine, amphetamine, cannabis and MDMA (ecstasy) and LSD can cause a psychosis. That is a severe mental illness, and the possibility of such an illness being drug induced should always be considered. Such features are occupationally hazardous, particularly so in transportation, construction, emergency services and health care. However, to identify specific occupational groups is unrealistic as virtually all have a safety component, although not 'safety critical' in the accepted sense: gardeners using cannabis could injure themselves or let a bonfire get out of control.

Again, following identification, sensitive intervention is crucial, for example 'Your performance is not up to its usual standard, nor is timekeeping and there has been inexplicable sickness absence – could it be that you are not feeling well and not sleeping well?...' However, intervention is simplified if it is on a 'for cause' basis following an accident or incident, such as unacceptable behaviour or risk taking.

Each hospital trust has an occupational health department, some providing a service to local industries in formulating a drug policy.

However, it is illogical to formulate and publicise a policy without having the ability to respond appropriately either with in-house or outsourced facilities, whether identified objectively or following a personal request. To date, relatively few organisations have an occupational health department, or an occupational health physician or nurse, even on a sessional basis. Instead, GPs with an interest in occupational health run sessions. The workplace is a component of any community and provides the ideal setting for any such positive public health measure, as has been achieved with smoking.

Without such facilities, only lip service can be paid to what should be effective crisis intervention and essential confidence is lost, the policy being perceived by the workforce as a useless paper exercise. Scepticism ensues, and a valuable opportunity is irrevocably lost. Reassurance regarding the spontaneous accessing of help can be facilitated by confirming normal rights to sickness absence, confidentiality, pay and job security, as with any other illness. This is on the understanding that the employee cooperates with the recommended treatment and rehabilitation. Obviously, if this is refused and behaviour and performance continue to be unsatisfactory, the matter then becomes an administrative or disciplinary issue.

The armed services properly hold comprehensive personal records; mental and physical health being routinely assessed in the 'Pulheems' categorisation, and work performance is reported on regularly (Mackay and Lucas, 1986). Also, there is considerable knowledge about the partner and family. In civilian life, this is sometimes obtained in large corporate organisations. However, statistically these constitute a minuscule proportion of the country's workforce. Health-related data regarding the majority of employees is much less well documented, and labour turnover is frequently rapid as is the case with casual employment.

The drug misuser, co-workers and others can be harmed mentally and physically, and the environment and community adversely affected. Drug-seeking behaviour can become all-embracing, including impaired performance and harm extending beyond the workplace itself.

The components of a drugs-misuse policy include:

- Aims – to clarify why it exists: for health and safety, and to confirm its application throughout the workforce regardless of seniority;
- Responsibility – all managers and supervisors are involved; however, it is preferable to have an identified senior manager with overall responsibility, as with an alcohol policy;
- Definitions of drug and substance misuse;
- Rules regarding drug-induced unacceptable behaviour.

The advantages of an effective drug policy include:

- early identification and effective intervention;
- reduction of sickness absence or 'presentism', the misuser continuing at work but not functioning effectively due to drug seeking, or behaving irresponsibly or dangerously;
- improved performance, productivity and morale is achieved by an effective response to a request for help;
- reduction of accidents or untoward incidents;
- improvement of general health of the workforce;
- an awareness that help is available. Therefore a spontaneous request signifies an employee's confidence and trust in management, and in the organisation as a whole being caring. This is highly relevant in demonstrating a duty of care and mandatory corporate social responsibility.

Adopting a drug policy is basically good working practice providing that it is presented with an alcohol policy within the overall context of health and safety. If these two policies are seen to be separate, they defeat their own object by stigmatisation. Whether there is or is not an alcohol or drug problem, legal aspects and positive health care and safety strategies are clarified.

The misuse of drugs can be identified in an individual by:

- inconsistencies in behaviour or concentration, inexplicable poor timekeeping or frequent sickness absences;
- change in personality;
- unusual variation in energy and work performance, or of a section's productivity. Regular routine job appraisals facilitate discussion of such changes;
- inappropriate or dangerous incidents or accidents affecting the misuser and co-workers.

IMPLEMENTING THE DRUG POLICY

- Awareness is best achieved through education about the nature of acute and chronic effects of drugs on mental and physical health, and behaviour.
- A clear definition of what constitutes drug misuse is required.
- Aims – why is it necessary? To confirm:
  - its application irrespective of seniority, or nature of work;

- throughout the organisation, irrespective of the degree to which the specific work of an individual section is safety critical.
- With whom does responsibility ultimately lie for its operation? It is essential to have a senior member of staff to support the vulnerable employee and the line-manager effectively. This ensures a smooth process from the ideal situation of self-identification, or following obligatory intervention, to in-house or outsourced treatment, assuming such is available. Unfortunately as with problem drinking, essential NHS programmes are seriously under-resourced.
- Rules – the organisation's expectations of its employees to undertake the total exclusion of drugs must be clearly stated.
- Entitlement to sickness absence, for treatment and rehabilitation as with any other illness. This should include documented assurance that a relapse will be covered.

DRUG TESTING

Some organisations take a rigid approach: and a positive drug test can result in immediate dismissal. This is counterproductive both the for organisation and the subsequent recruitment of that individual by other organisations because of loss of skills, cost of labour turnover and for drug-related community crime. It could end in a fatality, resulting in predictable and justifiable criticism and even litigation. Analogies include a hotel sacking a chef with a salmonella infection, or a construction company sacking an epileptic without any continuity of help in obtaining mandatory treatment. Drug testing is claimed to be precise and evidential. However, it is only qualitative, not quantitative. A reliable result cannot be achieved without the most thorough 'gold-standard' programme including supervised specimen collection, transportation, storage and toxicology, with 100 per cent security and confidentiality throughout. Any drugs policy which includes testing has to be customised according to that organisation's specific requirements.

The Faculty of Occupational Medicine's *Guidelines on Testing for Drugs of Abuse in the Workplace* (1994) recommended 'that occupational health staff have a duty to help ensure that any testing programme is undertaken appropriately within an ethical framework and in a manner which recognises the individual's human right'. The latter applies even if the testing is being conducted as a disciplinary rather than as a medical or health screening matter.

Although the decision whether to test remains an administrative one, the occupational health care physician can contribute to drug testing in a variety of ways:

- They should brief management on factors predisposing to drug misuse and the effects on mental state including behavioural and cognitive aspects. Assuming that testing proceeds, then methodological and technological advice ensures the scientific validity of the process.
- Those testing positively should be offered psychiatric and physical assessments to identify possible underlying causes, and an appropriate intervention programme should then be put in place in conjunction with the GP, subject to the employee's formal agreement and in accordance with the company policy.
- Any drug testing programme is subject to medical review, itself a component of a

comprehensive occupational health programme. It is the statutory duty of occupational health staff, whether in-house or out-sourced, to advise management on the technical and procedural aspects of the testing process.

The potential enormity of the consequences of a positive result must be considered, including criminal proceedings, domestic disruption – even the question of child custody – and the risk of dismissal, potentially affecting re-employment. Hence integrity of toxicological procedures, chain of custody, transportation of specimens, quality assurance and confidentiality must be beyond reproach. Any opinion may be legally challenged in court. Therefore the occupational health physician's role is key. Thus the 'quick test' must be regarded with suspicion, whether or not seen as expedient by management. As with any scientific procedure every effort must be demonstrated to exclude false positive results – only a gold standard is acceptable.

Planning a drug-testing programme

The OHP advises on medical aspects and the employer is responsible for outcome and rehabilitation facilities.

Prior to implementation, senior management should endorse a policy statement on workplace testing for drug misuse including:

- objectives
- procedures
- confidentiality confirmation
- support for self-referral
- availability of treatment and rehabilitation facilities
- disciplinary aspects
- groups to be targeted:
  - whole or part of workforce, routinely or randomly
- health education effects on performance and health
- timing of testing:
  - pre-employment – to be clarified in advance to applicants who then have a choice whether to proceed or not
  - at promotion or internal transfer – to be forewarned
  - for cause or post-accident – indications to be defined specifically, and responsibility clarified for notifying employees of the reason for testing and which manager is responsible for requesting the test. 'Post-incident' reasons must be defined in advance
  - periodic – can be useful, but the element of uncertainty is lost
  - unannounced – this would stand up to strict statistical criteria. Therefore the basis for individual or group selection to be agreed to exclude bias
  - during rehabilitation and subsequently – with employee's agreement, management and testing agency jointly monitor
  - clinical indications – result remains within normal medical confidentiality.

A steering committee decides:

- which tests are undertaken – drugs tested for to be agreed in advance. Geographical community culture may dictate drugs tested for; local knowledge and liaison with laboratories is helpful

- target groups – to be agreed in advance
- testing schedules – to be decided ahead of implementation, applicable to routine and unannounced testing
- staff training to be comprehensive for management, HR, OHD and the workforce in general.

Conclusion

Conscientious employees may resort to the misuse of drugs or to alcohol in an effort to cope with intolerable stress, albeit inappropriately and dangerously so.

Considering the serious physical complications of problem drinking and the misuse of drugs, it would be cost effective to improve NHS facilities for acute detoxification and essential ongoing rehabilitation for both. This would prevent inevitable deterioration with ensuing personal, family, occupational and economic loss.

The current pattern of binge drinking and drug availability – particularly crack cocaine – necessitate occupational vigilance. Hopefully achievable through respective policies being understood, and seen to be beneficial throughout the workforce.

References

1.   World Health Organization. Health aspects of well-being in working places; report on a WHO working group. Prague, 18–20 September 1979. *Euroreports & Studies 31*, 1980. Copenhagen: WHO
2.   Occupational Mental Health: Lucas EG, In *Tolley's Guide to Managing Employee Health*, edited by Leslie Hawkins. London: Tolley, 2002
3.   *The Problem Drinker at Work*, Health and Safety Executive. London: HMSO, 1991
4.   *Drug Misuse at Work: a guide for employers*, Health and Safety Executive. Sudbury: Health and Safety Executive, 1998
5.   *Don't Mix It!: a guide for employers on alcohol at work*, Health and Safety Executive. Sudbury: Health and Safety Executive, 1996
6.   Health and Safety at Work Act 1974. Elizabeth II 1974. Chapter 37. London: HMSO, 1974
7.   *Alcohol in Industry*, Lucas EG. BMJ 1987 Feb 21; 294(6570):460–1
8.   Joint Aviation Authorities/Joint Aviation Requirements. JAR-FCL3 Flight Crew Licensing (Medical). Printed and Distributed by Global Engineering 1 Dec 2000
9.   *Problem Drinking at Work: notes for the occupational physician*, Taylor, DJW, McCann, M. 2nd Edition (1995) London: Medical Council on Alcoholism
10.   *Dying for Drink. A no-nonsense guide for heavy drinkers* Tim Cantopher. The Book Guild Ltd, 1996
11.   Review of the literature on illegal drugs in the workplace, Beswick, Johanna et al. (*Health and Safety Laboratory series report* WPS/01/02) Sheffield: Health and Safety Laboratory (an agency of the Health and Safety Executive) 2002
12.   Review of Deaths related to taking ecstasy, England and Wales, 1997–2000, Schifano, F, Oyefeso A, Webb L, Pollard M, Corkery J, Ghodse AH. BMJ 2003 Jan 11: 326(7370):80–1
13.   The scale and impact of illegal drug use by workers, Andy Smith, Emma Wadsworth, Susanna Moss, Sharon Simpson. (*HSE Research Report 193*. Prepared by Cardiff University for the Health and Safety Executive 2004) Sudbury: Health and Safety Executive, 2004
14.   *Drug Use in England – Results of the 1996 National Drugs Campaign Survey*, Taskey T, Raw M, McNeill A, O'Muircheartaigh C, Bowden C & Houston J. London: Health Education Authority, 1999
15.   Occupational Mental Health: Mackay CJ, Lucas EG. In *The Psychosomatic Approach: contemporary practice of whole-person care* edited by Margaret J. Christie and Peter G. Mellett. Chichester: Wiley, 1986

16. *Guidelines on Testing for Drugs of Abuse in the Workplace.* London: Faculty of Occupational Medicine of the Royal College of Physicians, 1994

PART III

Tools for Managing the Problem

11 *Addressing Psychosocial Problems at Work – SOLVE*

David Gold and Joannah Caborn

The International Labor Office, the secretariat of the United Nations specialized agency responsible for safety and health at work, addresses the problems of drugs and alcohol at work through a holistic comprehensive educational program known as Addressing Psychosocial Problems at Work or otherwise by its short title SOLVE.

Stress, tobacco, alcohol and drugs, HIV/AIDS and violence (both physical and psychological), all lead to health-related problems for the worker and lower productivity for the enterprise or organization. Taken together they represent a major cause of accidents, fatal injuries, disease and absenteeism at work in both industrialized and developing countries. These problems may emerge due to the interaction between home and work, they may start at work and be carried home (or into the community) or vice versa. SOLVE focuses on prevention.

The combined effects of these psychosocial factors have considerable negative ramifications for workers, employers, the worker's family and society. For the worker, these problems can result in isolation, stigmatization, injury, illness and even death. For the organization or enterprise, these factors can result in increased absenteeism and accidents, reduced productivity, increased recruitment, training and insurance costs and decreased profits, and therefore a lack of competitiveness. The family invariably suffers the full brunt of the loss of income, reduced welfare, missed opportunities for children, psychological trauma, lack of self-respect and injuries, to the extent that the family may break up altogether. For society, the impact may be seen in terms of increased social costs, decreased consumer spending, increased crime and adverse economic development.

Background

The scope of psychosocial problems in the world is considerable. If one looks at Europe for example, according to the European Union's 2000 survey of working conditions over one-quarter of European workers suffer from stress, which is one of the primary causes for use of sick leave. Just under 25 per cent of all workers in Europe suffer from overall fatigue. And almost 1 out of every 20 workers experiences physical violence from members of the public. These three psychosocial issues in Europe alone account for over one million lost work days.

The World Health Organization published a study in 2002 which identified the top ten health risks in the world. The number of such factors is countless and the report does not attempt to be comprehensive but concentrates on a selection of real risks to health – often the actual causes of major diseases for which the means to reduce them are known – and produces some startling findings about their true impact. The ten leading risk factors globally in order of importance are: underweight; unsafe sex; high blood pressure; tobacco consumption; alcohol consumption; unsafe water, sanitation and hygiene; iron deficiency; indoor smoke from solid fuels; high cholesterol; and obesity. Together, these account for more than one-third of all deaths worldwide (WHO World Health Report 2002). SOLVE addresses seven out of ten of these top health risks. For example, unsafe sex is a leading cause of transmission of HIV/AIDS; high blood pressure is one of the results of high stress levels; tobacco and alcohol abuse are addressed directly; and iron deficiency, high cholesterol and obesity will be addressed with the new SOLVE modules on sedentary lifestyles and dietary problems.

The ILO divides occupational fatalities into five main categories: circulatory problems, respiratory diseases, cancer, contagious diseases, and accidents and violence. Psychosocial problems can be contributing factors to any of these causes of death. Increasingly the psychosocial problem in question may in fact emanate from the workplace itself. The combination of poor health and safety conditions and a poor psychosocial working environment can literally be fatal. Therefore the successful implementation of the SOLVE methodology will help to mitigate these fatalities at work.

This data on occupational fatalities also indicated that these problems, although in different proportions, are present in all regions of the world. Therefore SOLVE continues to contribute to preventing workplace primary health problems worldwide.

Psychosocial problems are interrelated

Not only do the five psychosocial focal points of SOLVE address some of the most important global health issues, but research also indicates that these five issues are interrelated. This means for example that problem drinkers are more likely to use tobacco and drugs than those persons who do not drink heavily.

Multiple risk factors are not equal in all occupational categories. Those who come into frequent contact with the public are at higher risk of violence than those who don't. In one study, one-third of nurses claimed to be victims of violence at work. In addition to the risk of violence, stress levels for nurses are also high because of constant rotation of shifts and lack of adequate numbers of personnel to handle the workload.

In another study of almost 1000 police personnel, about 800 had at least one unhealthy lifestyle behavior. Sixty-one percent of them said they would seek advice from their workplace for stress problems. Fewer said they would seek advice from their workplace about their alcohol or tobacco use. This study was done two years after the organization introduced a comprehensive drug and alcohol policy, hired drug and alcohol counselors and required all personnel to take a six-month course on drug and alcohol use.

The ecological model

The model in Figure 11.1 proposes that psychosocial issues are determined by many

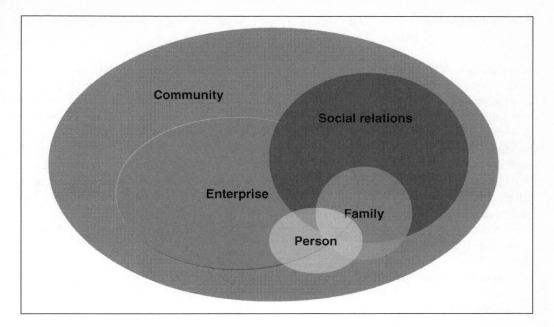

Figure 11.1   The ecological model

different overlapping factors. The model suggests that behavior has both situational and psychological influences. The psychological factors are those within the person's own realm of thought and emotion. Individuals bring their personal influences, as such as our attitudes, beliefs and opinions, to the different circles of their lives: families, social circle of friends, workplaces and the wider community. Each of these environments has its own impact on an individual's life. For example, if someone in the family is dying from HIV/AIDS one's ability to concentrate, one's mood and one's attendance at work may very well be affected. For prevention programs to be successful in changing behaviors and attitudes they need to be comprehensive, that is, they must address beliefs, attitudes, behaviors, and environmental factors in multiple realms.

The impact of psychosocial problems

EFFECT OF PSYCHOSOCIAL PROBLEMS ON THE WORKER

When there are high levels of psychosocial problems at work, the following represent some of the effects that can be present for the individual worker:

- Accidents may be more likely to occur because the worker is working with diminished awareness and a high potential for distraction.
- Family or social problems may occur such as marital discord, child behavior issues or conflicts with and pulling away from friends.
- Impact on behaviour at work, including perhaps increased absences.
- Stigmatization and discrimination may be directed at those individuals perceived as being different or having a potentially debilitating condition such as AIDS.

- General physical and mental health may deteriorate, leading to pain, suffering and, in extreme cases, death.

The Health Belief Model in Figure 11.2 was developed in the 1950s as social psychologists in the United States Public Health Service tried to explain the lack of public participation in health screening and prevention programs. It is a psychological model suggesting that individuals' attitudes and beliefs determine health behaviors and therefore can be used to predict participation in health programs. It supposes that an event acts as a trigger to a series of decisions about how to respond to a potential health problem. By graphically representing it as a decision tree, we make the potential consequences of a negative decision apparent, which we suggest could include increases in psychosocial problems. If the person withdraws from the decision tree the model becomes a vicious cycle, and we see the potential for negative synergistic effects of multiple psychosocial problems. The elements of the model, based on their description in the US National Cancer Institute's publication 'Theory at a Glance', are as follows:

- **Perceived susceptibility**. One's subjective perception of the risk of contracting a health condition: 'I won't get cancer from smoking, because I only smoke ten cigarettes a day,' or 'I know that most lung cancer sufferers are smokers, so I want to stop smoking because I don't want to get cancer.'
- **Perceived severity**. Feelings concerning the seriousness of contracting an illness or of leaving it untreated (including evaluations of both medical and clinical consequences and possible social consequences): 'Even if I do get cancer, many types are treatable

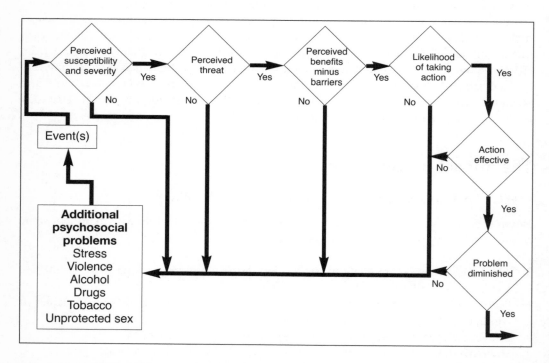

Figure 11.2   The health belief model (modified)

today, so it won't have a big impact on me,' or 'Some cancers are untreatable, and the treatment is often drastic and painful, so I don't want to put myself through that.'

- **Perceived threat**. The decision point based on the combination of the perceived susceptibility and perceived severity of a health condition: 'There is therefore no threat to my health or my wellbeing from smoking ten cigarettes a day,' or 'The threat to myself from smoking is therefore big enough for me to want to do something about it.'
- **Perceived benefits**. The believed effectiveness of strategies designed to reduce the threat of illness: 'I could save a lot of money and have more time with my family.'
- **Perceived barriers**. The potential negative consequences that may result from taking particular health actions, including physical, psychological, and financial demands: 'Would my coworkers tease me if they found out I was in trying to quit?', or 'Craving a cigarette and not having one is going to ruin my day.'
- **Likelihood of taking action**. The composite of the perceived benefits and barriers together with the person's impression of their self-efficacy: 'Will I be able to cope with the teasing and the craving?'

If there is not a perceived threat, action will not be taken. Or if there is a perceived threat, but the perceived barriers are larger than the perceived benefits, nothing will be done about it. Positive action to eliminate the unhealthy behavior will be taken only when the perceived threat is high and the perceived benefits outweigh the barriers.

EFFECT OF PSYCHOSOCIAL PROBLEMS ON THE ENTERPRISE

When there are high levels of psychosocial problems for individuals at work, some of the effects for the enterprise or organization as shown in Figure 11.3 could include:

- **Increased absenteeism**. If psychosocial problems are highly prevalent in the workforce, more workers may be absent more often This is one of the most immediate costs to employers.
- **Turnover**. Worker turnover will mean loss of skills and knowledge for the enterprise or organization. A high turnover rate is a sign to workers and employers that the institution is not well, and seeing their coworkers leave will decrease the sense of wellbeing and morale at work. The resulting need for increased recruitment and training represents a significant cost for the enterprise.
- **Indirect costs**. The enterprise also faces rising costs related to insurance premiums, the retirement fund, safety and health training and other provisions, medical assistance and counseling.
- **Diminished capacity**. Resulting from issues such as high turnover and declining morale the enterprise will suffer declining profits and organizations will be less able to provide high quality services.

Should a wave of increased health problems impact on the wider community, the number of available and appropriately skilled workers can decrease, leaving the enterprise or organization with less resources locally and with no option but to broaden the scope of their employee search to neighboring communities, which also comes with increased costs.

A study was carried out by the University of Michigan quantifying the costs of health risk factors. The Health Management Resource Center used the data from nine separate

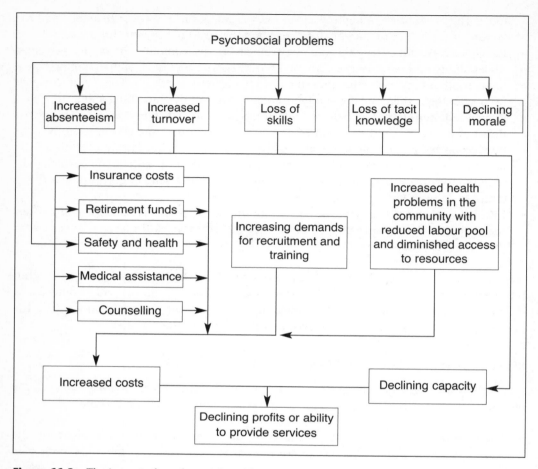

Figure 11.3   The impact of psychosocial problems on enterprises

studies of US corporations and combined the results in a meta analysis to form a database covering two million workers. A clear relationship was demonstrated among health risk factors and health risk costs. It was found that eliminating one health risk factor for one worker translated into a savings of $150. However, increasing one health risk factor for one employee resulted in a costing of $350, more than twice the amount. The study concluded that programs designed to keep healthy people healthy, in addition to reducing the health risks of those with multiple health risks, will probably provide the greatest return to the employers.

The ILO's response

SOLVE is an interactive educational program which was developed by Dr David Gold, Mr Behrouz Shahandeh and Mr Vittorio Di Martino of the International Labour Office. The first training program was run in March 2001 at the International Training Center of the ILO in Turin, Italy. The purpose of SOLVE is to deal with and eventually prevent psychosocial problems in the workplace.

SOLVE assists workplaces to develop and integrate policies concerning psychosocial issues into their already existing policy framework. SOLVE also gives enterprises the materials and ideas needed to plan strategies for mitigating the existing problems and for preventing new ones from emerging. SOLVE's association with the ILO assures a tripartite approach to these issues, requiring active participation from and cooperation between workers, employers and governments.

THE FOCUS OF SOLVE

SOLVE focuses on five primary psychosocial issues: stress, alcohol and drugs, violence, both emotional and physical, HIV/AIDS and the use of tobacco. Research has shown that these issues do not exist in isolation from each other. All of them are inter-related to the others. For example, if a work environment has high levels of stress, the stress can lead to greater levels of violence as a pressure-release valve and potential use or increased use of alcohol and drugs as a way to escape from the harsh reality of the stressful workplace. In addition to the existing five psychosocial issues which SOLVE addresses, the program will soon include five additional psychosocial issues: sleep deprivation, gambling, sedentary lifestyle, addiction to new technologies and dietary issues.

The SOLVE programme provides a powerful tool for combating many of the psychosocial issues that one can encounter at work in an integrated way, ensuring that addressing one problem is not being undermined by interference from another issue.

THE GOAL OF SOLVE

Based on the above scientific knowledge the following goal for the SOLVE program has been established: to integrate the psychosocial issues of stress, tobacco, alcohol and drugs, HIV/AIDS and violence as well as other psychosocial problems, into a comprehensive organizational policy and development of action based on the policy.

Building a holistic policy

The SOLVE program builds an analogy to this policy development using a forest and trees. Trees in a forest become stronger when they grow as a group, rooted firmly in the earth by interlocking their roots and branches. These trees are able to withstand high winds and protect each other from pounding rains and damaging hail storms. As a forest, they have more impact on their environment than a single tree would and as leaves and branches fall and decompose, the soil becomes richer. In the same way, the SOLVE strategy is to develop inter-related policy statements for all psychosocial issues as a whole, because the issues correlate with each other. Like the forest, a comprehensive and holistic psychosocial policy has more impact and is more effective in diminishing the problems than would separate policies for each issue. The policies are rooted firmly in and based on commonly held values such as non-discrimination, empowerment, worker involvement, personal growth and prevention. Treatment always needs to remain an option for those persons for whom prevention fails.

SOLVE needs to be dynamic as change is everpresent. In order to respond to change, processes need to be managed in predictable cyclical phases. Managing change will often start with a new idea, thought or concept, such as the information introduced in a SOLVE training course. On the basis of the information, a strategy is developed to implement the new ideas. Once a plan or policy is in place, responsible individuals and teams carry out the action steps towards achieving the desired results as outlined in the strategic goals and objectives. To assess whether the desired results were achieved, evaluations are performed and the original concepts and strategies can be reviewed and improved according to the new situation, commencing the cycle again. In healthy organizations, this process is open, inclusive and continual.

The SOLVE cycle as shown in Figure 11.4 begins with the introduction of the SOLVE Policy-Level Course in an enterprise or organization. The result is the broadening of the enterprise policy to include psychosocial issues in an integrated way. The organization can then tailor its particular efforts to the specificities of the psychosocial problems it is facing. Using the SOLVE MicroSOLVE modules on stress, tobacco, alcohol and drugs, HIV/AIDS and violence, awareness is raised and tools are provided to alleviate the problem in the workplace and to make the policy work. Continual evaluation of the psychosocial environment at work and responding to the issues found with new policies and actions continues the transformation of the workplace into a more productive and satisfying workplace where everyone benefits.

THE SOLVE EDUCATIONAL PROCESS

The SOLVE methodology moves from concept to policy to action. There are four SOLVE courses which drive the change process:

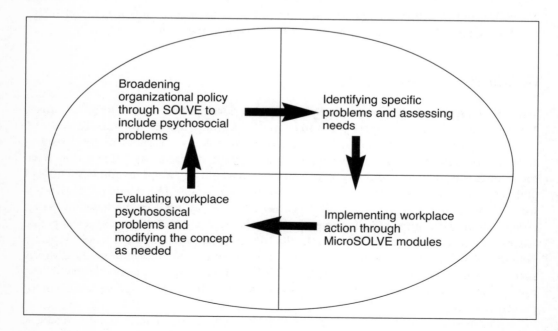

Figure 11.4   The SOLVE cycle

- **SOLVE for Managing Directors** is aimed at top executives. Often the first contact with an enterprise or organization is with the directors or senior officials. Their commitment to action on psychosocial problems is key for achieving successful change in the workplace. SOLVE offers a two-hour presentation and discussion session to explain why it is in the company's and the workers' interest to reduce psychosocial problems at work and what SOLVE can do to contribute to that aim. This course uses an interactive approach incorporating case-study analysis and group discussion.
- **The 32-hour or four-day SOLVE Policy-Level Course** is the flagship of the SOLVE program. It helps enterprises include psychosocial issues in an integrated way into their existing policies. This course is highly interactive, using case study analysis, simulation exercises and policy development activities to reach its objectives. It may be conducted over four days or over a longer period of time, dividing the course into smaller units. It is designed to work best in groups of 16 participants. Ideally the group should consist of four workers' representatives, three government officials and eight employers or their representatives. During the course, six simulation exercises are linked together by a story line that starts on the first day of the workshop and ends on the last day. The story is an ongoing scenario with problems that require participative high-level management decisions for resolution. The simulation exercise is designed so that each participant in the course is actively involved in a role-playing capacity. The last element of the course is dedicated to action planning. At the end of the course participants are required to develop an action plan that will indicate how the SOLVE concepts will be applied in their respective organization or enterprise within the three months after the course is completed.
- **SOLVE for Workers** is a one-hour orientation course for workers, workers' representatives and supervisors. It is designed to demonstrate how multiple psychosocial factors can impact the worker at work, during leisure activities and at home. It also provides an opportunity for the participants to become familiar with the comprehensive corporate policy. SOLVE for workers uses exercises, group discussion and individual action planning to achieve its objective.
- **MicroSOLVEs** are subject-specific courses relating to one of the five psychosocial problems covered in SOLVE. They are the action-oriented follow-up to the policy-level SOLVE activities and are designed for workers and supervisors in enterprises that have already completed the Policy-Level Course and have developed a comprehensive policy that addresses psychosocial issues. MicroSOLVE elements come in sets of three for each topic: module one addresses recognition of the problem, module two addresses action and module three prevention. Each module is about 90 minutes long.

THE EVALUATION OF SOLVE

SOLVE, being an instrument for cyclical change, has its own built-in evaluation process. This process serves to demonstrate what impact SOLVE is having and how to adapt the program to better fit the changing conditions in workplaces and the changing faces of psychosocial issues that emerge in workplaces. SOLVE has four evaluation mechanisms. The first one is an 85-item questionnaire which confidentially gathers information about participants' attitudes, knowledge, perceptions and beliefs regarding the five psychosocial problems addressed. This is administered before the SOLVE Policy-Level Course over the internet (or on paper for those without access to the internet). The results of this questionnaire are received and archived by a university in France. In three to five years, each person will be asked to answer the same questions once more as a means of measuring improvement in their psychosocial health. The second evaluation mechanism is a 12-question multiple-choice pretest and posttest to measure the effectiveness of SOLVE training in improving the technical knowledge base of participants. The third evaluation is a six-item qualitative narrative written by participants after the course ends, giving them a chance to say what they liked and didn't like about the course and how it could be improved. The fourth mechanism measures the impact which each individual has on their workplace three months after the course is over. The participants report about the action which they carried out and the impact it had on their workplace. There is a fifth mechanism being developed that will study the impact SOLVE has on absenteeism, turnover and productivity in enterprises which have run SOLVE programs.

WHERE IS SOLVE TODAY?

Educational courses

Over 600 persons have successfully completed the SOLVE Policy-Level Course. They have been held in Belgium, Cameroon, Canada, France, India, Italy, Malaysia, Namibia, the Philippines, Senegal, South Africa, Sri Lanka, Swaziland, the United States and Zambia. Participants have included government officials, university professors, employers and workers, officials from six United Nations agencies and the Athens Olympic Committee. Early 2004 saw the rollout of SOLVE throughout Canada by means of the Joint International Association of Machinists and Aerospace Workers / Air Canada, Employee Assistance Program.

There have been Course Director's Courses in a number of places, including Turin and Rome (Italy), Cape Town (South Africa), Montreal (Canada), Bangkok (Thailand), Manila (Philippines), Brussels (Belgium), Douala (Cameroon) and Penang (Malaysia). Some of these courses have included participants from other countries, thus creating capacity to implement SOLVE both nationally and regionally. There are now over 180 SOLVE Course Directors in 37 different countries.

SOLVE for Workers and MicroSOLVE modules are being implemented in numerous enterprises.

Universities

A number of universities in Asia, Europe and Africa are actively building means to incorporate SOLVE into curricula in schools of public health, occupational health, occupational psychology and industrial relations.

Translations

English, French and Thai versions of the SOLVE manual have been printed and are available for use. The SOLVE manual has been translated in draft into Bulgarian, Spanish, Portuguese, Russian and Italian. Translations into Chinese and German versions are foreseen.

Sector adaptations

In concert with the WHO, SOLVE for the Health Sector has been drafted and was tested in 2004, and for Public Administration have also been successfully tested. SOLVE for the Maritime Sector is currently being developed in the Philippines and SOLVE for Firefighters is being drafted in Geneva. SOLVE for the Air Transport Sector is under discussion.

Internet

The SOLVE homepage is located at www.ilo.org/safework/solve. There is a public section offering information about SOLVE, frequently asked questions and a listing of courses. Promotional material can be read online or downloaded for use. There is also a private section (password protected) that serves as a repository for instructors of the latest materials as well as material under development.

Manual

A new edition of the SOLVE manual will be authored in 2005. The new manual will be in a book format including five additional psychosocial issues: sleep deprivation, inadequate nutrition, lack of regular exercise, gambling and addiction to new technologies. The materials for SOLVE course participants will be published separately.

SOLVE continues to grow and positively influence workplaces in many countries. It has the capacity to improve working conditions, productivity and workers' health in agencies, institutions and organizations throughout the world.

12 *Specialist Care*

Alexander Baldacchino

Introduction

There is a growing public and political awareness of the extent of drug and alcohol use.[1] It is recognised that a substantial or significant number of people at work will be experiencing drug- and/or alcohol-related problems.[2] Problems with alcohol and drugs are suffered by people in varying degrees, ranging from occasional excess consumption to an addiction or dependence, which may affect the person and their whole lifestyle. Patients often progress from mild misuse of alcohol and other drugs to more extreme stages so it is important to try to address any problem at an early stage, seeking medical assistance where necessary. There are different reasons why individuals seek help. It could be as a result of a perceived change in one's own personal circumstances and/or due to influence by family or a significant other.

At a personal level alcohol and drug misuse has many effects including:

- health problems caused by the alcohol and drug consumption itself including liver and brain damage and other serious conditions such as epilepsy and heart disease;
- consequential health problems caused by the effects of alcohol such as malnutrition, injuries and gaps in memory and high risk behaviour, for example needle stick injuries and deep vein thrombosis due to intravenous use of illicit drugs like heroin and cocaine;
- difficulties in sustaining employment, meaningful relationships, ability to pursue educational interests and other activities that enhance the individual's quality of life status.

Having a family member with an alcohol and/or drug problem can seriously affect the family, where family members and friends can become anxious, depressed or alienated. Financial problems caused by the purchase of alcohol and drugs, coupled with reduced earnings potential, also impact on the family.

The increasing frequency of drug testing in the workplace will result in an increasing number of individuals identified as having substance-abuse related problems. The focus of this chapter is to explain the context, processes and philosophies of care that are universally provided to individuals once it has been recognised that they have substance-related problems and are referred for specialist treatment.

It is not a unique experience for people responsible to refer an individual for treatment that they find the whole experience of 'treatment' as mind boggling and incomprehensible. This chapter also attempts to highlight the pharmacological and psychological components of this treatment package that have been evidenced to help motivated individuals resolve their substance-abuse related problem.

A tiered approach to drug and alcohol services

Requests for help with substance-misuse problems are usually initially received by the general practitioners and primary care teams who can provide a range of responses. These include:

- initial discussion and support;
- advice regarding non-hazardous drinking levels and ways to reduce drinking;
- counselling and therapy for the individual;
- counselling and therapy for the family;
- treatment options including medication to relieve the physical effects of stopping drinking and taking drugs, and to help to reduce the incidence of drinking and taking drugs in the longer term;
- referral to a specialist nurse, often within the practice, for individual help;
- referral to another agency for clinical care with information about treatment options available;
- referral to a voluntary agency for lay counselling;
- linking with a mutual help association such as Alcoholics Anonymous;
- longer term support and monitoring.

There are other agencies that are also working in the community together with the primary care teams in order to respond to referrals due to drug- and alcohol-related problems. These include:

- Community pharmacists:
  - providing services related to needle exchange
  - dispensing, and in some cases supervising consumption, of methadone
  - dispensing other medicines used in the treatment of drug misuse, for example lofexidine, naltrexone
  - advice and health education, including advice on secure handling and storage of medicines
  - promotion of healthy lifestyles
  - referral to appropriate agencies
  - advising on safe sex and supplying condoms.
- Social work community care teams:
  - overall management and care of people with drug problems
  - assessment
  - care planning
  - social skills training
  - counselling (non-specific)
  - advice and information
  - education
  - monitoring and evaluation of planned care
  - links to community services.
- Non-statutory agencies with a specific remit for the care and treatment of drug and alcohol problems:
  - advice and information

- education
- counselling
- social skills training
- support
- advocacy.
- Generic statutory services:
  - housing and employment services
  - education and children's services
  - neighbourhood resources and community education.
- Wider community services:
  - police and judiciary system who are increasingly involved in harm-reduction initiatives (needle and syringe exchange schemes) and treatment (arrest referral schemes, enhanced probation, drug treatment and testing orders).
- Organisations providing useful information:
  - NHS 24, Alcohol Focus Scotland, UK Alcohol Concern and Drugscope amongst many others.

The aim of the above mentioned services is to either provide local approaches to alcohol and/or drug problems with the promotion of positive health through community plans and information, or provide non-specialist counselling and support and initiate appropriate referral to specialist services in addiction if appropriate. Using a public health model these services are described as being within a Tier 1 service. They meet the support and treatment needs of the majority of people with alcohol and drug problems.

A Tier 2 service provides specialist support to people with drug and/or alcohol problems that is provided by trained staff or volunteers who give advice, training and support to those providing local services. They also provide a link to specialist substance-misuse/addiction services. They usually offer low-threshold, open-access services and their core competence is in structured counselling techniques, which is different from advice and information giving. Examples of Tier 2 services are needle exchange schemes working under the remit of harm reduction teams, alcohol advisory services, advocacy groups, homelessness and addiction services. Other agencies listed above also provide Tier 2 services, for example non-statutory addiction services.

The Tier 3 and 4 agencies provide local or regional specialist drug- and alcohol-problem services. Such services usually operate from within the Primary Care Division of the National Health Service responsible for the particular geographical region. These agencies usually work in conjunction with the local general mental health services, general hospital including accident and emergency departments, the prison services, maternity services and addiction teams within social services dealing with particular issues such as child protection, criminal justice and housing. Tier 1, 2 and 3 services should be available in all parts of the United Kingdom.

Tier 4 services are less common. These services are usually based in a research or academic unit to provide particular expertise to complex cases that need an in-patient residential treatment approach and form part of a managed care network structure.

Tier 3 and 4 services provide a specialist assessment process and define treatment plans and priorities. They usually instigate and/or advise prescribing substitutes such as methadone. They provide the specialist support and leadership to shared-care treatment pathways and community and/or home detoxification programmes. They provide a specialist psychiatric, medical and psychosocial opinion of individual cases that will identify specific and complex treatment needs. Examples are: an individual with severe enduring mental illness such as schizophrenia and concomitant opioid dependence; severe benzodiazepine dependence with a history of epilepsy and depression; alcohol-related brain damage with associated memory problems and chaotic intravenous cocaine use.

Philosophy and aims of a care for a substance user

Treatment of substance misusers incorporates many approaches which sometimes may seem to be in conflict, ranging from 'harm reduction' approaches aiming to reduce the biological, psychological and social 'harm' a substance misuser is causing to themselves and their community, through to total abstinence. Also people presenting to drug and alcohol treatment services include those presenting with a broad range of problems with a clear recognition that not all people require (or may not want) a prescription to overcome their drug or alcohol problem. Any philosophy of care must recognise:

• Any service can offer a comprehensive range of interventions.
• Any service can offer the opportunity for the individual to work through their problems in a framework where harm reduction and/or abstinence are seen as part of the same spectrum and not opposing constructs.
• A service can offer a person-centred, needs-led service and will respond appropriately to requirements following a full and comprehensive assessment.
• The service delivers evidence-based practice within nationally agreed quality standards.
• The service works in partnership with other agencies in the community to provide a full range of high quality interventions.
• The service respects confidentiality unless there is concern that the individual's behaviour is a risk to themselves or others.

Assessment and treatment of substance users

ASSESSMENT

Due to the dynamic nature of substance-use problems, assessment for this group of patients is an ongoing process and continues throughout the period of engagement with the service. When first presenting or re-presenting at the treatment services, an initial assessment is necessary to identify the appropriate therapeutic and treatment responses. Such assessment may be brief or in depth according to the type of service and/or patient's needs.

Major areas examined in the assessment are: historical and current drug and/or alcohol use; past and present state of physical and mental health; and the family and social situation. Most information is acquired from interviews with the patient and family. Mental state and physical examination, certain medical investigations and toxicological analysis of urine or saliva are routinely undertaken in order to provide objective evidence of recent drug use.[3]

The assessment process is a multidisciplinary procedure and is considered as the start of a long and hopefully beneficial therapeutic process.

It is therefore not a static and meaningless reportage of facts. It tries to prioritise needs of the client being assessed by:

- being alert to patients' anxieties about engagement into treatment and provide explanation of options, processes and procedures;
- helping in implementing a treatment plan;
- helping to initiate a range of therapeutic interventions;
- helping to liaise with a variety of agencies and professionals;
- helping to identify the extent and the nature of social deficits, psychological problems and other human needs of the individual;
- helping to identify areas where social work intervention may be required including housing issues;
- helping to identify the needs of any children for whom the patient has responsibility and possibly liaise with Child Protection Services;
- helping to advise on therapeutic options that require Community Care Assessment;
- helping to establish the presence or absence of a dependence syndrome.

The dependence syndrome

The dependence syndrome[4] is a collection of presentations that describe in the previous 12 months:

- if the individual had a strong desire or sense of compulsion to take the substance they have been using (including alcohol);
- if the individual had difficulty in controlling substance-taking behaviour (in terms of its onset, termination or level of use);
- if the individual exhibited withdrawal symptoms (depending on the substance in question). Do they take the substance to relieve or prevent withdrawal symptoms?
- if the individual increased the dose of the substance in order to achieve effects originally produced by lower doses (tolerance);
- if the individual progressively neglected alternative pleasures or interests because of the substance used;
- if the individual continued to use the substance despite clear evidence of overtly harmful effects (for example liver problem, depressed mood states or social issues).

The individual is considered to be dependent on the substance if they can relate to three or more of the above statements during the previous year. Most individuals presenting to Tier 3 or 4 specialist services are usually severely dependent before they access such services.

TREATMENT OF OPIOID DEPENDENCE

Opiates act on central opioid receptors of which there are believed to be five types: μ (mu), κ (kappa) σ (sigma), δ (delta) and ε (epsilon). However, the euphoria and physical dependence is considered to be mediated through μ receptors outside the central nervous system. Opioid receptors mediate the release of endorphins, which exert presynaptic inhibition on the synapse in the locus coerulus, thus regulating the release of noradrenalin in normal amounts. In opiate dependence, there is continuous stimulation by the exogenous opioids, resulting in a reduction in endorphin activity and at the same time, a relative inhibition of central neuronal activity.

Methadone is a synthetic (opioid) agonist with a half-life of one to two days. It has good oral bioavailability and reaches peak blood concentration at four hours after oral administration. It is useful in maintenance prescribing because 'once daily' dosing is possible. Buprenorphine is a partial μ opioid agonist; that is, it has both agonist and antagonist properties. In patients on high doses of opiates, it can have antagonist properties and thus precipitate withdrawal. It passes through the oral mucosa and it is generally administered sublingually. LAAM is a potent, long-acting opioid with duration of action of 72 hours. It was licensed for use in the UK, but was later withdrawn because of serious side effects. Hydromorphone is only available in the US.

Replacement prescribing, as part of a treatment programme, will only include the use of medications licensed for that purpose:[5]

- standard treatment is provided with methadone mixture (1mg/1ml)
- methadone oral concentrate (10mg/1ml) used very rarely in a specialist setting
- buprenorphine hydrochloride (Subutex®) 0.4mg, 2mg and 8mg sublingual tablets.

Methadone tablets and injectable Dihydrocodeine (DF118) and all other opiate-based analgesics are not licensed for the treatment of opioid dependence.

Prescribing is only considered once a person has been adequately and comprehensively assessed and the individual is experiencing signs and symptoms of the opioid dependence syndrome. Prescribed treatment is usually only considered once a person is fully engaged with the general practitioner or specialist services and has agreed on a treatment plan with their key worker following discussion covering all of their options. A written agreement is also signed by the staff and service users in order to clearly set out the expectations users may have of the service and the service has of those in treatment. The doses used will reflect the person's regular use of opiates, usually heroin. There are different ways of determining an appropriate dose of methadone without giving too little for the individual to go back to illicit heroin to stop from withdrawing or too much that carries the risk of overdose and potentially death. One technique is methadone tolerance testing where the dose is gradually increased after several days of measuring subjectively and objectively signs and symptoms of opioid withdrawal.

COMMUNITY MAINTENANCE

One way of helping drug misusers to reduce illegal heroin use and the crime, morbidity and mortality associated with drug dependence is community maintenance treatment, that is by stabilising clients on a substitute drug for as long as it is necessary to help them avoid returning to previous patterns of drug use. Secondary aims are to reduce injecting behaviour and crime associated with requiring money to buy illicit drugs. Community maintenance treatment generally consists of drug administration, and the provision of psychosocial treatment and motivational interventions.

The main findings of literature available is that:[6]

- community maintenance is effective across a wide range of age and ethnic groups, and among clients with a long history of opiate misuse;

- higher doses of methadone and buprenorphine are associated with better outcomes;
- higher doses of methadone (> 50–65mg per day) appear to be slightly more effective than buprenorphine (2–8mg per day);
- those maintenance programmes that provide more and better psychosocial services have a higher effectiveness;
- contingent reinforcement is an effective method to reduce drug use and promote client use of other services;
- treating opiate dependence with methadone or buprenorphine in a primary care setting is feasible and effective.

COMMUNITY DETOXIFICATION

Detoxification programmes and withdrawal programmes are used interchangeably. The term 'detoxification' is sometimes used to describe a programme in which the client is opiate-free within days or weeks. However, withdrawal programmes in which opiates are the basis of treatment are often also described as detoxification. The important factor is that clients are opiate-free at the endpoint of the programme.

The main findings of the literature state:[6]

- A wide range of different models of community detoxification is present. It is not really important how long the opioid detoxification programme takes but what is important is that there is a bio-psychosocial approach with adequate and well-prepared follow-up support and specialist advice organised prior to the actual pharmacological detoxification. Relapse rates range from 19 per cent to 83 per cent after an opioid detoxification is complete.
- Lofexidine appears to be slightly more effective at reducing withdrawal symptoms and, importantly, has considerably less adverse effects on blood pressure than clonidine. Lofexidine and clonidine are described as alpha adrenergic agonists and relieve the physiological symptoms of opioid withdrawal such as a sweating and other 'flight or fight' responses that our body tries to compensate for when threatened and/or frightened and feeling anxious.
- Buprenorphine taken as sublingual tablets could have an important role in detoxification but further UK-based studies are required in order to determine if it is more efficacious than methadone-based detoxification.
- The role of using methadone alone appears to be limited in a successful detoxification as it was associated with particularly high dropout rates. This is usually because methadone itself creates a prolonged withdrawal phase after completed detoxification and this created an ideal situation for individuals to go back to using heroin and/or other opioids unless there is a strong supportive therapeutic infrastructure with possibly symptomatic prescribing of lofexidine.
- Counselling and/or behavioural psychological treatment is associated with improved outcomes.
- Prescribing maintenance naltrexone following detoxification can be effective at maintaining abstinence from opiates, reducing illicit opiate use and retaining people in treatment. Naltrexone is an opioid antagonist that blocks opiate receptors thus minimising the effect of any other opioids if naltrexone is taken regularly. Identifying and involving a significant other during detoxification and subsequent prescribing of

naltrexone is seen as good practice in order to guarantee regular naltrexone intake by the patient and also to provide an informal and personal supportive network that is already in place

RESIDENTIAL REHABILITATION

Residential rehabilitation refers to all programmes that include detoxification, maintenance and, finally, abstinence within a residential setting. Residential rehabilitation involves communal living with other drug misusers in recovery, group and individual relapse-prevention counselling, individual key working and improving skills for daily living.

The literature on residential rehabilitation deals with treatment within a therapeutic community and the provision of counselling, psychosocial services and social activities within a residential setting. A therapeutic community can be described as a drug-free environment in which people with addictive problems live together in an organised and structured way to promote change towards a drug-free life in the outside society.

The main findings of the literature available indicate that:[6]

- residential rehabilitation is effective in terms of reduction in illicit opiate use, improved employment status, reduction in high risk behaviours and reduction in crime rates;
- retention in and completion of treatment are more important than length of treatment in influencing outcomes;
- residential rehabilitation programmes that provide more health and treatment services and encourage client participation are more effective.

TREATMENT OF SEDATIVE-HYPNOTIC DEPENDENCE

Benzodiazepine dependence has been well described.[7] There are two distinct clinical populations in which dependence is manifest. The therapeutic dependent individual is often in receipt of long-term prescriptions from a single prescriber and is not otherwise involved in the inappropriate use of other drugs or dependent on drugs of other classes. The prescribed dose is usually within the normal therapeutic range.

Meantime the non-therapeutic dependent individuals are usually polydrug users. The usual patterns of illicit benzodiazepine use are with opiates (including prescribed methadone), psychostimulants and alcohol. There are also some individuals who take illicit benzodiazepines as their 'drug of choice' without other drugs. These individuals often target several medical practitioners, frequently take high doses and are part of the addiction subculture.

The size of the problem is difficult to determine. However, in the non-therapeutic group perhaps 28 per cent of current benzodiazepine users will satisfy dependence criteria though not all of these will necessarily require pharmacological support to withdraw.[8]

There are good reasons to advise patients to withdraw and to avoid any long-term prescribing. These include doubts over long-term efficacy, risks of adverse effects and evidence of neuropsychological impairment. There are also concerns about a paradoxical effect with release of aggressive behaviour.[9] Long-term prescribing is also associated with problematic monitoring in that urine tests routinely available are qualitative only and do not distinguish between different benzodiazepines. Oral Fluid Testing (OFT) can at least indicate very recent benzodiazepine use but is expensive and not yet widely available.

Finally the risk of diversion into the illicit market is clearly a significant one. A specialist assessment will identify any underlying pathology (organic or psychological) that makes the individual take benzodiazepines for example to relieve anxiety to help them sleep. As a result the following is advisable:

- The treatment of anxiety is primarily psychological.
- The treatment for misuse of benzodiazepines is primarily counselling.
- Relaxation and sleep hygiene programmes should be sought.
- If prescribing is deemed necessary it will involve only diazepam, and will be low dose, should involve rapid reduction (30mg to 0mg over 12 weeks) and should not be repeated.

TREATMENT OF DEPENDENCE ON STIMULANTS, CANNABIS, HALLUCINOGENS AND VOLATILE SUBSTANCES

Abrupt discontinuation of use of these substances does not produce severe physical withdrawals. However, there might be profound pscyhological dependence and occasionally mental health-related problems. There is no specific pharmacological intervention unless the person is presenting with abnormal beliefs, hallucinations and mood disorder when it is not advisable to prescribe antipsychotics until the individual has been guaranteed drug free for more than 72 hours.

TREATMENT OF ALCOHOL DEPENDENCE

Individuals drinking in excess of 21 units (males) or 14 units (females) per week should have a more detailed drinker history taken.[11]

Medication may not be necessary if:

- the patient reports consumption is less than 15 units/day in males and 10 units/day in females and reports neither recent withdrawal symptoms nor recent drinking to prevent withdrawal symptoms;
- the patient has no alcohol on breath test, and no withdrawal signs or symptoms.

A body of evidence, based on randomised controlled trials (RCTs), has shown that benzodiazepines are currently the best drug group for alcohol dependence detoxification.[12] Although the evidence is mostly derived from inpatient studies, the conclusions are generalisable to primary care.

Acamprosate is believed to act by modulating disturbance in the gamma-aminobutyric acid/glutamate system associated with alcohol dependence, reducing the risk of relapse during the postwithdrawal period. It is a safe drug with few unwanted side effects, and is not liable to misuse. Its value is in the first months after detoxification. Acamprosate is not effective in all patients so its efficacy should be assessed at regular appointments, and the drug withdrawn if there has not been a major reduction in drinking. Where it appears to be effective, good practice suggests prescribing for 6–12 months. It is an assumption that, as long as there is a system of monitoring compliance and efficacy, this information is also applicable to primary care.[13]

Acamprosate will usually be initiated by a specialist service within a few days of successful detoxification. If a specialist service is not available, the GP can offer acamprosate, monitor its efficacy and provide links to local support organisations.

Disulfiram's function is to deter the patient from resuming drinking. If taken regularly there is an unpleasant reaction when alcohol is consumed. It has unwanted effects in some patients, and carries special warnings. There is evidence for the use of supervised disulfiram and none for its non-supervised use. It is offered for six months in the first instance, with regular review. Supervision is agreed by the patient to increase the likelihood that the medication is taken even at times of ambivalence.[13]

Units of alcohol

One unit of alcohol	8g pure alcohol
	¹/₂ pint ordinary strength beer
	1 small glass (125ml) table wine (10–12%)
	1 pub measure (25ml) spirits
One can (500ml) of strong lager/cider	4 units
One bottle (70cl) of:	
Table wine	8 units
Sherry	15 units
Spirits	30 units

Psychological interventions for individuals with substance misuse problems

Psychological interventions for relapse prevention are based around 'talking therapies' which can involve one-to-one, couple, family or group approaches and encourage self-help as part of the treatment and support options. These interventions can be broadly grouped into four main categories:

- Building motivation based on motivational enhancement therapy which focuses on eliciting the individual's intrinsic motivation for change[13] and contains certain therapeutic strategies. These include expressing empathy, avoiding argument, detecting and 'rolling with' resistance, highlighting discrepancies in the history and drawing out the individual's own discomfort about the behaviour.
- Cognitive restructuring including cognitive behavioural therapy, relapse prevention therapy and coping skills training. In relapse prevention therapy individuals unlearn the patterns of drug-taking behaviour, implement substitute behaviours and rehearse healthier approaches to dealing with situations that previously triggered thoughts of drinking.[14]

- Behavioural and coping skills training including social skills training, stress management, community reinforcement approach and family therapy. These often focus on general skills (such as communication and assertion skills) rather than on specific skills for avoiding substance use. Emphasis is placed on changing the individual's social environment by developing and rewarding stable employment, healthy leisure activities and relationships that do not involve substances.[15]
- Implementing the 12-step model based on the Alcoholics Anonymous approach which refers to the stages of growth through which the individual must progress in order to achieve and maintain sobriety. The individual is expected to acknowledge the need for help and aim for complete abstinence.

Conclusion

All the above approaches have shown positive outcomes when used as adjuncts to pharmacological procedures. The psychological interventions do not have a standardised single agreed protocol for the delivery of these treatments and the setting, duration and personal qualities of the therapist may all play a part in determining their effectiveness. The result of a recent meta analysis suggest that a combination of coping skill training and motivational enhancement therapy provide a good foundation for treatment effectiveness.[12]

For the pharmacological and psychological interventions described above it should be noted that in most specialist services these are not carried out in isolation but as part of an ongoing relationship with individuals in contact with the service. As highlighted earlier the use of non-statutory services and other agencies, categorised in different tier structures in the interventions provided by the specialist service, are vital in order to help move the individual to a situation where they are able to be aware of their capabilities without the need of intoxicants to help cope with everyday situations. This is what is known in specialist terminology as 'the care pathway'. The component of an effective integrated care pathway are:

- **Accessibility**. A specialist service is able to identify clear referral criteria and entry points in order that the most appropriate support can be offered at the right time to the right person in the right place;
- **Assessment**. This has already been highlighted in this chapter. Effective assessment is an ongoing process and should feature throughout the pathway.
- **Planning and delivery**. It is important that the keyworker or care coordinator ensures that the biological (medication), psychological (therapies) and social (housing, education) support required are delivered at the appropriate points of the care pathway.
- **Information sharing**. The purpose of sharing personal information on individuals between partner agencies is to ensure access to the appropriate treatment, care and support services to those individuals. Meanwhile confidentiality is still respected and qualified consent from the individual concerned is still an important component.
- **Monitoring and evaluation**. This is continuous and regular collections of key information in order to determine if something is going to plan and whether any change in activity is necessary. It is through evaluation that one is able to determine if the pathway and its components are effective, efficient and acceptable.

Treatment works[16] and as an employer one needs to appreciate that dependence is a chronic relapsing condition. The evidence suggest that if an individual is well assessed and needs prioritised with the active participation of the patient, one is creating the right environment for a successful treatment programme.[17] This success is guaranteed if adequate psychosocial therapeutic interventions[18] are in place together with, when needed, good use of the limited pharmacological agents licensed to prescribe in these conditions.

References

1. Condon J and Smith N (2003) *Prevalence of Drug Use: Key Findings from the 2002/2003 British Crime Survey*, London: Home Office (Findings 229)
2. Independent Inquiry into Drug Testing at Work (2004) *Drug Testing in the Workplace*, York: Joseph Rowntree Foundation
3. Ghodse AH (2002) *Drugs and Addictive Behaviour: A Guide to Treatment* (3rd edn), Cambridge: Cambridge University Press.
4. World Health Organisation (1992) *ICD-10 Classification of Mental and Behavioural Disorders*, Geneva: WHO.
5. Department of Health (1999) *Guidelines on Clinical Management. Drug Misuse and Dependence*, Norwich: The Stationery Office
6. Simeons S, Matheson C, Inkster K, Ludbrook A, Bond C (2002) *The Effectiveness of Treatment for Opiate Dependent Drug Users: An International Systematic Review of the Evidence*. Scottish Executive Drug Misuse Research Programme, Effective Interventions Unit (EIU), Edinburgh: The Stationery Office
7. Ashton CH (1989) The Treatment of Benzodiazepine Dependence. *Addiction* 1535–1541
8. Woody GE, O'Brien CP, Greenstein R (1975) Misuse and abuse of diazepam: An increasingly common medical problem. *International Journal of the Addictions*, **10**: 843–848.
9. Bond A (1993) *The Risks of taking Benzodiazepines in Benzodiazepine Dependence* (Hallstrom Ed.), Oxford, Oxford Medical Publications
10. Scottish Intercollegiate Guidelines Network (SIGN) No 74 (2003) *The Management of Harmful Drinking and Alcohol Dependence in Primary Care, A National Clinical Guideline.*
11. Edwards G, Marshall E and Cook CCH (2003) *The Treatment of Drinking Problems: A Guide for the Helping Professions* (4th edn). Cambridge: Cambridge University Press.
12. Slattery J, Chick J, Cochrane M, Craig J, Godfrey C, MacPherson K, Parrot S (2002) *Prevention of Relapse in Alcohol Dependence*, Health Technology Board for Scotland (HTBS)
13. Rollnick S and Miller WR (1995) What is motivational interviewing? *Behavioural and Cognitive Psychotherapy* **23**, 314–315
14. Marlett G and Gordon J (1985) *Relapse Prevention and Maintenance Strategies in the Treatment of Addictive Behaviours*, New York: Guilford
15. Azrin NH (1976) Improvements in the community reinforcement approach to alcoholism. *Behaviour Research and Therapy* **14** (5), 339–348
16. Gossop M, Marsden J, Stewart D and Rolfe A (2000) Patterns of improvement after methadone treatment: One year follow-up results from the National Treatment Outcome Research Study (NTORS). *Drug and Alcohol Dependence*, **37**: 15–21
17. Saxon AJ, Wells EA, Fleming C, Jackson R, Calsyn DA (1996) Pre-treatment characteristics, program philosophy and levels of ancillary services as predictors of methadone maintenance treatment outcome, *Addiction*, **91**: 1197–1209
18. McLellan AT, Arndt I, Metzger D, Woody G, O'Brien C (1993) The effects of psychosocial services in substance abuse treatment, *Journal of the American Medical Association*, **269**: 1953–1959

NB: References 3, 5, 6, 10 and 11 are considered by the author as suggested reading and/or textbook reference material.

13 *Drug Screening and Detection*

John Christofides and Martyn Egerton

Introduction and background to workplace drug testing

Drugs and alcohol cause impairment of performance due to effects on concentration, attention and motivation; but also, perhaps more importantly, due to changes in reaction times and ability to make rational judgements. The overall effect is to reduce the employee's efficiency and productivity, and consequently to adversely increase personal or company liability. The aim of workplace drug testing or any employment drug-testing programme is to ensure the health and safety of employees at work and the public at large.

Testing procedures may be required for the investigation of industrial incidents or injury to a third party, for example following a public transport accident. Occasionally testing will form part of an investigation when unidentified substances are found in the workplace. Drug analysis will also form part of the management of those undergoing treatment for drug addiction. In short, drug testing is carried out for clinical management, clinical toxicology, forensic toxicology and medico-legal reasons and it is the last category that is of relevance to workplace testing. The following subdivisions may be considered cause for workplace testing:

- Pre-employment testing where a negative result might be a condition of employment.
- Random testing during employment where an employee consents to being tested without prior notice.
- Regular testing during employment where an employee consents to being tested at predictable intervals.
- Cause for testing arising from a high index of suspicion flagged when an employee is tested following an accident at work or has clinically verified behavioural problems.
- Cause for testing arising from a low to medium index of clinical suspicion of drug use where an employee's absenteeism or lateness for work has been flagged.

Drug analysis can be performed on a number of body fluids and tissues. The analytical techniques employed range from simple screening procedures suitable for use in the workplace to those requiring extensive laboratory facilities.

To date most drug analyses have been based around laboratory testing of urine samples with an increasing shift to preliminary screening in the workplace and use of saliva (also called oral fluid) and hair. It is less common to test for drugs of abuse in blood samples.

Drug tests are categorised as either screening or confirmatory procedures. Screening tests are quick, sensitive methods used mainly to exclude the presence of a drug. Confirmatory tests use a different technique and chemical principle from the screening test and can identify and accurately measure the concentration of a specific drug or drug metabolite. Thus, positive findings of a screening test should always be verified by a confirmatory test.

Drug availability does vary on a geographical and social basis and employers may wish to consult with local laboratory and addiction agencies before deciding which drugs to test for prior to commissioning drug analysis.

The principle classes of drugs tested in Europe are opiates, cocaine, amphetamines (including ecstasy), barbiturates, benzodiazepines and cannabinoids. A variety of other drugs may require testing including methadone, phencyclidine (PCP), buprenorphine, dipipanone, β-blocking drugs, antihistamines, decongestants, laxatives and diuretics. In any drug-testing setting it is important to define which drugs are acceptable and which are not. Agencies involved in testing must therefore establish policies that clearly define these differences and procedures that can confidently differentiate between the two.

Workplace drug testing is very similar to that used in a clinical setting for managing drug addicts. In practice the main differences are around the legal defensibility of the sample handling process and in the cut-off concentrations used to define a positive result.

The US transport industry was the first body of civilians subjected to workplace testing during the early 1980s. A brief historical review[1] is a salutary reminder that well-intentioned actions can founder without the underlying prerequisites of informed consent to drug test and the laboratories to provide accurate methods of analysis.

There were objections to workplace testing from trade unions and suggestions of deteriorating worker/management relations. However, these objections gradually subsided during the evolution of workplace testing and there is currently widespread if reluctant acceptance of the benefits. This was partly alleviated by the introduction of legally drawn company policies that were transparent and that also informed employees on all aspects of testing.

The consequences of a positive test following a job application are far-reaching as is testing positive whilst in employment. In the former an applicant may not be employed, but the established employee will have to be referred to the company occupational health team, investigated, counselled for possible treatment options and ultimately may be dismissed. The repercussions for the employer in terms of a wrongful dismissal can be extensive.

Following the transport industry, the US oil and nuclear industries became involved in drug-testing programmes, but again, insufficient consideration was initially given to standardising company policies and procedures for the collection of urine samples. The situation was also complicated by the variability in the performance of the testing laboratories. There was much costly litigation during the early years of workplace testing particularly involving so-called accredited laboratories that had given out wrong results.

Some of these early blunders were avoidable in hindsight despite valuable lessons learned from the testing of US forces returning from Vietnam. One apocryphal story has it that the chaplain of a ship's company tested positive for opiates for which no explanation could be found. It was later discovered that the chaplain had a particular fondness for poppy seed bread and the morphine contained in the seeds was enough to give a positive screening test. This simply highlights the need to confirm initial screening tests with an independent confirmatory test.

The US government finally intervened in workplace drug testing and in 1986 the Reagan administration directed the heads of all Federal agencies to formulate policy statements together with guidelines as to how to implement employee-testing programmes for Federal employees. It was expected that State and local governments and heads of private sector companies would follow suit. The legal implications ran deep into the economy even suggesting that contracts should not be awarded to companies that failed to implement a suitable employee-testing programme. That same year, 1986, was when the National Institute on Drug Abuse (NIDA) convened discussions between top employers and trade unions and they formulated the following principles:

- Random testing within a mutually acceptable workplace testing programme was legally defensible.
- Individuals must give informed consent.
- All positive results from screening must be confirmed by an alternative analytical method.
- The results must remain confidential.

NIDA, later known as SAMHSA (Substance Abuse and Mental Health Services Administration), also worked on laboratory accreditation and made joint recommendations to the US Department of Health and Human Services (DHHS) in 1987, which issued guidelines for the entire process of urine testing covering procedures for:

- collecting urine
- the testing process
- interpreting and evaluating the results
- implementing quality control
- document control.

The result was to ensure test accuracy, confidentiality and privacy of the employee so that the process was legally defensible. The DHHS Mandatory Guidelines[2] evolved into an Act of Congress in 1994 and was finally incorporated into the US Department of Transport rules published in 1994 covering urban road transport, railways and aviation. In 1995 the law covered companies comprising more than 50 employees but by 1996 this was altered to cover smaller companies as well.

Workplace drug testing has been sporadically introduced into the UK during the 1990s partly to supply a demand for testing US employees working in the UK. Further introduction into the UK workplace was mainly led by the transport and nuclear industries. The US NIDA urine testing guidelines provided the basis for workplace testing in the UK but these have been superseded by the United Kingdom Laboratory Guidelines for Legally Defensible Workplace Drug Testing[3]. These guidelines were prepared by a steering committee representing UK analytical laboratories and other interested parties including the Forensic Science Service, the Laboratory of the Government Chemist (LGC), the London Toxicology Group (LTG) and Cardiff BioAnalytical Services[4] (which runs a national external quality assessment for urine drug testing schemes throughout the UK and Europe).

The UK Guidelines give an overview of the best practice for laboratories providing a workplace testing service for drugs in urine and should be followed wherever workplace testing is undertaken. Their objective is to provide a set of criteria for service providers to ensure that the procedures are capable of legal scrutiny, to protect the rights of the specimen donor and to define quality criteria that are transparent and recognisable by the layperson.

The scope of the document considers the various stages of the workplace testing process and are built on the older NIDA guidelines. They also cover those instances where part of the process may take place within the customer's organisation (known as 'point-of-care' testing or 'near-patient' testing), in which case the laboratory provider has a duty of care to ensure that the customer understands the full implications of the testing process.

The general principles within the guidelines can be used for specimen types other than urine.

Drug metabolism

A level of understanding of drug pharmacology is required to avoid misinterpretation of analytical results.

Drugs enter the body through the mouth, by smoking, nasal inhalation or injection (see Figure 13.1). They then enter the blood circulation by absorption from the digestive tract, from the mouth or mucous membranes of the nose, or are absorbed through the lungs.

After entering the circulation, drugs are distributed throughout the body. The extent of distribution and ultimate biological effect varies with the extent of binding to blood proteins. A general rule of thumb is that the more the drug is bound, the less the biological effect of the drug, for example 95 per cent of nicotine is unbound and free to exert its effect whilst only 4 per cent of diazepam is free in the blood. Protein binding particularly

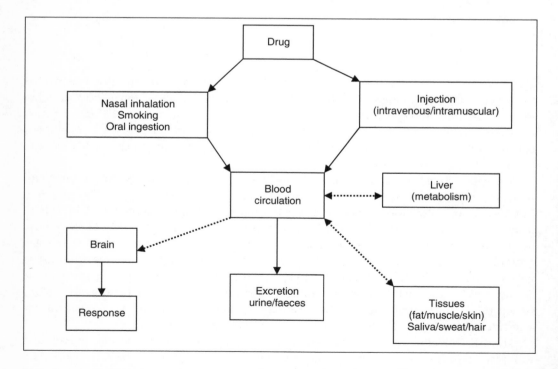

Figure 13.1   The various routes of drug introduction into blood and subsequent distribution

influences the transfer of drug across various membranes in the body, hence underlining the fact that different forms of a particular drug may be found in urine compared to saliva.

Elimination from the body is mostly through the urine and faeces and traces are detectable in sweat. A proportion of the drug will be excreted unchanged (known as the parent drug) while the rest will be chemically transformed by the body, usually in the liver, then excreted as metabolites. Metabolites are biologically deactivated forms of the parent drug that have been chemically transformed so as to render them more water soluble to enable easy excretion.

The presence of drugs within the circulating blood allows them to be incorporated into other tissues, for example fat, and also to pass into the sweat, saliva and hair follicles. The proportion of drug that passes into different tissues will vary greatly and much care is required in comparing drug results from say a urine sample with those from a saliva or sweat sample, even from the same subject.

The detection of a drug in a urine sample must be interpreted with caution. It will not necessarily give the information being sought by the front-line caring professional nor answer such questions as:

- Does the presence of a drug account for the subject's impairment?
- How long ago did the subject take the drug?
- Is the subject physically or psychologically dependent on the drug found?

The dose of drug taken, the route of elimination and the method of detection will all determine how long that it remains detectable in a sample after ingestion. There is significant variation in the rate of elimination of drugs between individual subjects. The duration of detection for some drugs is given in Table 13.1 In this context, the half-life is the time required for the concentration of a drug to fall by 50 per cent. This information together with knowledge of the sensitivity of the testing procedure will provide an approximate time window when a drug will be detected following its entry into the body. The larger the dose of drug taken the longer the drug will be detectable.

The principal factors influencing the drug concentration in blood and consequently in urine can be summarised as:

- Apparent availability of drug dose
  - purity of the drug (for example ecstasy can vary from 0 to 80 per cent)
  - chemical alteration of a particular drug (for example cocaine and crack cocaine)
  - route of administration
  - the time elapsed between taking the drug and collecting the sample
  - co-administration of other drugs (including alcohol) that influence metabolism.
- How the body distributes, metabolises and excretes a drug:
  - protein binding
  - volume of distribution of the drug in the body (an important theoretical function which relates the dose given and the blood concentration) and may change for example in pregnancy
  - urine concentration
  - liver and kidney function.

Following drug intake, the concentration of a drug in the blood will rise initially as it enters

Table 13.1   Recommended maximum cut-off concentrations (ng/ml or µg/l) from the UK
Laboratory Guidelines

Drug/class	Screening test	Average duration of detection
Opiates (total)	300	2 to 3 days
Cocaine metabolites	300	2 to 4 days
Amphetamine group	300	2 to 3 days
Benzodiazepines group	200	2 to 7 days
Cannabis metabolites	50	3 to 10 days
	Confirmatory test	
Morphine (total)	300	
Cocaine metabolite (benzoylecgonine)	150	
Amphetamine	200	
Benzodiazepines – individual drugs	100	
Cannabinoids as THC	15	

the circulation. The peak level may be reached in a few minutes or a few hours depending on the route of administration and the nature of the drug. The concentration will then fall as the drug is distributed throughout the body and as it passes out of the circulation into the tissues. This concentration will then continue to fall as the drug is broken down (metabolised) and then excreted. Thus the concentration of drug found in saliva, oral fluid or urine would rise then gradually fall as the blood concentration falls. If the half-life of a drug is 24 hours then it will take 8 days for the drug concentration to fall to 1 per cent of the original level.

For many drugs the parent substance may be eliminated quite rapidly from the blood, however, the metabolites may remain for a much longer time. It is preferable to measure the drug's metabolite in urine rather than the parent drug. Table 13.2 lists some principal metabolites. It is however important to know which entity is being measured in the analytical process, something that is not always made clear by testing laboratories or suppliers of testing devices. For example, some kits claim to measure morphine when they are more accurately measuring a mixture of opiates including morphine, a metabolite of heroin.

The rate of transfer of drugs to the sample (urine, saliva or sweat) will reflect the blood concentration and hence the dose taken. Transfer of drugs from blood to saliva may depend upon the rate of saliva production, while the concentration of a drug in the urine will depend upon the dilution of the urine, which is principally influenced by the amount of fluid consumed. The dilution of urine can vary several fold in the course of a 24-hour period and it is for this reason that the concentration of a drug in urine must be interpreted with extreme caution when correlating impairment.

Table 13.2   Principal metabolites of drugs found in urine

Drug	Metabolites measured
Heroin	Morphine
	6-monoactetylmorphine
Morphine	Morphine-3-glucuronide
Cocaine	Benzoylecgonine
	Methylecgonine
Cannabis	δ9-tetrahydrocannibinol carboxylic acid
Benzodiazepines	Often detected as oxazepam

Methodology

UNDERSTANDING THE CHARACTERISTICS OF METHOD PERFORMANCE

The performance of an analytical method can be defined using the following terms: sensitivity, specificity, accuracy, precision and recovery. These parameters are fundamental in defining the quality of results obtained from a method but will not necessarily be familiar to the lay reader. Nevertheless, it is important to gain at least a passing knowledge of their meaning and application in order to make informed comparisons between different commercial tests for point-of-care testing devices.

The analytical *cut-off* is a fundamental performance characteristic of any drug-measuring device. First, however, we define the *maximum sensitivity* or *detection limit*. This is defined as the lowest concentration at which a drug or drug metabolite may be analytically detected, that is the concentration at which the presence of a drug can reliably be distinguished from no drug present at all. This is an important concept that then leads to the definition of cut-off. In essence, the cut-off concentration for an individual drug device defines when the drug is *present* (positive) or *not present* (negative).

By definition, the cut-off concentration is higher than the maximum sensitivity and may be pitched at different concentrations above the maximum sensitivity depending on the manufacturer's intended *response range*. The response range of the testing device is that range within which the device can be assumed to give a reliable positive signal. In summary, the order that links these various concentrations is: the response range concentration is higher than the cut-off transitional concentration, which is higher than the detection limit. The cut-offs are published in the UK Guidelines[3] and have largely been adopted by device manufacturers and laboratory service providers alike. The actual cut-off concentrations are discussed later in this section with particular reference to workplace testing

Drug-testing devices have therefore been designed by the manufacturers to give a signal at a certain concentration that is consistent with the reliable presence of a drug. The positive response from a drug-testing device, however, gives no indication of how big the drug dose was, nor how long ago the drug was taken. Given the wide variation in urine concentrations between subjects on similar drug doses, deciding on a consensus cut-off concentration has been fraught and recently revised upwards for opiates in the US to take into account the 'poppy seed defence' discussed later. Users of drug-testing devices should therefore appreciate that any time window of detection quoted by a drug device manufacturer or a service provider is merely a rough guide to how long drugs stay positive and cannot possibly accurately predict how long a drug remains detectable. Users should also be aware of the variations in commercial devices so that they can confidently apply devices of different sensitivity and cut-off to different situations. The choice of cut-off concentration will vary according to the setting. A low cut-off concentration may be appropriate for use in a workplace setting where high sensitivity testing is required but may be inappropriate in a drug treatment clinic where subjects use large doses of drugs more frequently. Metabolites of cannabis and some benzodiazepines may persist for several weeks during a period of abstinence following prolonged use; the choice of a suitable cut-off concentration may need to be appropriate for each individual situation. Some examples of the recommended cut-off values are quoted in Table 13.1. It is important to specify which cut-off concentration has been used when performing a test for a drug.

The concept of *specificity* is also important and defines the accuracy of a test result. One can simply define this as the degree of trueness of the result or conversely the extent of interference with the method. Devices from different manufacturers will measure the precise nature of the substance present with varying degrees of trueness or accuracy. However, a more precise definition would be that the specificity of a method is the degree of certainty that the drug found by a testing procedure is actually the named drug present. It applies to both laboratory-based and point-of-care tests. This is because some particular screening tests have to be grouped together as they detect classes of drugs collectively. Thus the collective term 'opiates' includes morphine, codeine, dihydrocodeine and pholcodine, while 'amphetamines' includes amphetamine, methyl-amphetamine, ecstasy (MDMA), ephedrine and pseudoephedrine (last two are both decongestants). The variations in sensitivity and specificity seen in commercially available point-of care drug-testing kits does give cause for concern and is discussed further in the next section.

Specificity also gives an indication of how strongly a test device responds or cross reacts to a particular drug or drug metabolite. Variation in the 'strength of response' or cross reactivity within classes of drugs can be misleading if not fully understood. For example a benzodiazepine screening device may respond strongly to temazepam but much more weakly to lorazepam. The finding of a negative benzodiazepine result may be interpreted as the subject not having taken a drug. This may not be strictly true and may simply reflect the device's poor response to that particular drug. Users of drug devices should always familiarise themselves with the manufacturer's performance information not least of which is the drug cross reactivity list.

LABORATORY-BASED PROCEDURES

Drug detection assays are usually based upon initial immunoassay screening and gas-chromatography mass-spectrometry confirmation of positive results.

Immunoassay procedures use antibodies, raised in animals, to bind the drug. Just as the human immune system recognises infection from a bacterium and produces antibodies to bind and neutralise the intruder (antigen), so the laboratory employs this antigen-antibody phenomenon to recognise a particular drug and signal its presence. Immunoassay drug testing devices contain antibodies mixed with a signalling mechanism. This complex consists of the drug of interest chemically attached usually to an enzyme, but fluorescent compounds and radioisotopes can also be used. When no exogenous drug is present in the urine sample, the antibody binds the complex, it remains inactive and there is no signal. When urine containing a drug is added, the antibody recognises it, the complex is activated and generates a signal in direct response to the presence of the drug. The amount of drug present in the sample is in direct proportion to the extent of activation of the signalling mechanism. The signal is then measured by monitoring subtle chemical changes brought about by the released complex and these may be coloured or fluorescent. This particular methodology called enzyme multiplied immunoassay technique (EMIT™) was developed by Syva in the 1970s and later acquired by Dade-Behring. The principle has been applied to both laboratory-based and point-of-care drug testing.

There are many creative variations of this principle enabling it to be used in both large automated analysers and in simple point-of-care devices. The laboratory-based analysers such as the Olympus and Hitachi use EMIT™ technology with a throughput of approximately 800 tests per hour[5]. Other laboratory-based commercial immunoassay technologies include: Microgenics™ CEDIA (cloned enzyme donor immunoassay), Abbot Diagnostics™ FPIA (fluorescence polarization immunoassay), Cozart'™ ELISA (enzyme linked immunosorbent assay) and Randox Evidence™. Although still based on immunoassay, the Evidence'™ utilises an innovative 'biochip array technology' using highly specific antibodies and claims 3600 tests/hour.

Essentially the same immunoassay technology was adapted and used in the commercial manufacture of point-of-care testing devices and this is dealt with in the next section. Immunoassays do provide a rapid screening tool for drug screening especially on a 'rule out' basis. The urine sample can be analysed directly without purification and results are available in a few minutes. The tests can be made very sensitive enabling low concentrations of drugs to be detected and therefore they currently provide the mainstay of frontline screening.

A general limitation of immunoassay procedures is their susceptibility to interference and lack of specificity. Firstly, this may be the result of an exogenous chemical such as bleach or glutaraldehyde deliberately added to the urine sample in order to disrupt the reaction mechanism. Secondly and perhaps more important is the particular problem of substances that have similar molecular structures and will bind to the antibody giving a positive result. Two notable examples are interference with the opiates and amphetamines assays as dealt with in the previous section. This may be particularly relevant when selecting a near-patient device for measuring opiates. One must be aware that manufacturers may claim to offer morphine-specific tests when in fact the device also suffers interference from over-the-counter preparations containing codeine, dihydrocodeine or pholcodine.

In contrast, many other drugs-of-abuse immunoassays (cannabinoids, cocaine, methadone, barbiturates and buprenorphine) are more specific for the named drug and relevant metabolites. However, sample adulteration by dilution and chemical disruption will always pose a problem irrespective of specificity. All manufacturers and laboratories that practice GLP (good laboratory practice) will advise that any positive immunoassay result should always be confirmed by a separate test, usually a chromatographic one.

Chromatographic procedures rely on the physicochemical properties of a drug (for example polarity or water solubility) to separate individual drugs from the sample matrix (that is the carrier medium such as urine or saliva). Typically, the sample must first be purified by partitioning (transferring) the drugs from their original matrix (urine or blood) into an organic solvent such as chloroform. After concentrating the purified extract, it can then be further separated and measured by a chromatographic procedure. The extract of the sample is passed along a flat surface or through a column containing a silica-based matrix. Individual components within the purified sample separate out due to molecular interactions with the matrix.

Chromatographic procedures are generally much slower than immunoassay but have the potential to estimate several drugs within a sample and can be tuned to look for one drug, a range of drugs or unexpected compounds. The three principal chromatographic techniques are thin-layer chromatography (TLC), high-performance liquid chromatography (HPLC) and gas-liquid chromatography (GLC).

In TLC, a purified extract of urine is applied onto a thin layer of silica on glass and the drugs separated with organic solvent. Individual drugs are qualitatively detected by visualising with a dye as a series of spots on the plate, which can be identified by their characteristic migration distance. In HPLC and GLC, again, a purified extract of urine is applied to a column of silica maintained in a closely controlled temperature environment. The component drugs are separated either by a flowing solvent (HPLC) or inert gas (GLC) and identified by the time taken to pass through the column, the retention time. The individual drug amounts are detected and measured by their response to a UV detector (HPLC) or to an ionising flame (GLC).

ToxiLab™ is a commercially available TLC based system. The kit includes all the required reagents, standards and a library of photographs showing various drug metabolite patterns. The library allows the operator to identify many different drugs in urine by visually matching patterns of coloured spots.

The REMEDi™ Drug Profiling System from Bio-Rad is a commercially available automated HPLC system that identifies individual basic drugs and metabolites from their UV spectra. The manufacturer claims reliable results within 20 minutes. As a laboratory-based system, the capital outlay for REMEDi™ is much higher than ToxiLab™ or an in-house TLC method.

Mass spectrometry is a process of detection achieved by fragmentation of drug molecules under controlled conditions. It may be considered the gold standard of drug-testing procedures not only in toxicology but also in forensic analyses and testing in sports. Mass spectrometry comprises a specific and sensitive detector and is usually linked first to a chromatographic separation procedure (GC or HPLC). After initial purification and separation the component drugs are bombarded with electrons into smaller fragments. Each fragmentation pattern forms a virtually unique characteristic 'fingerprint' for the drug or drug metabolite. The technique has the highest potential for trueness of a result, that is the highest specificity (compared to the low specificity of opiate and amphetamine immunoassays).

Sample throughput ranges from one to twenty samples per hour with several drugs being measured on each sample. Chromatographic and mass spectrometry procedures are currently only available as laboratory-based techniques, requiring a high level of staff expertise for reliable use. The capital outlay for GCMS or HPLCMS is typically £100–150k. In contrast the capital outlay for GC or HPLC equipment without an MS detector is £15–30k, which although cheaper, lacks the ultimate specificity and sensitivity available with an MS detector. In short, capital outlay is low for TLC, is medium/high for HPLC and GLC but high for GCMS or HPLCMS. However, all chromatographic techniques require a high degree of expert operation and interpretation.

POINT-OF-CARE DEVICES

A development of the laboratory-based immunoassay technique has allowed the antibodies and other reagents to be immobilised onto devices that can be used in the clinic near the subject. The sample is applied either by dipping the device into the urine sample or by applying a few drops of urine to a slide using a pipette. The sample diffuses through a wicking support and interacts with antibodies to develop the presence of a line for a negative result. This logic of the positive/negative signal is confusingly reversed so that most devices, with a few exceptions, indicate the presence of a drug by the absence of a line and the presence of a line indicating the absence of a drug. These devices cannot be adjusted in any way and have a fixed cut-off point. They are designed by the manufacturer to show the presence of a drug above a fixed concentration.

The devices are generally easy to use after basic training and provide a result to the clinician within a few minutes of the sample being applied. Inclusion of several antibodies into zones within the device enables multiple drugs to be detected within a single testing unit. More elaborate devices are available that incorporate the testing unit into a urine sample cup. Not only does the cup act as a convenient urine collection container, but also by separating the integrated reagents from the sample, the remaining urine can be used for further chromatographic confirmation.

A recent MHRA Evaluation Report[6] examined 16 point-of-care (POC) devices available in the UK for the detection of drugs of abuse in urine. The devices tested included both single and multiple test devices. The single and multiple test devices included: Acon™, DrugSCREEN™, InstaCheck™, SureScreen™, SureStep™ and Triage™[8].

The report highlighted the same specificity issues that are inherent with all antibody-based procedures as well as issues particularly associated with POC devices:

- Interference particularly of note were the over-the-counter preparations: Boots poppy seed bar, codeine linctus and pholcodine interfering with the opiates and morphine devices, Nytol with some methadone devices and occasionally Ranitidine and Ibuprofen with other devices.
- Problems of misinterpretation occurred due to the inherent use of reverse logic in most devices.
- Manufacturers' batch-to-batch variation combined with variation in the subjective interpretation of the presence or absence of a line led to variability in the reporting of results particularly when the concentration of a drug was close to its cut-off.
- Manufacturers' product variability led to a relatively high device failure rate.

The use of such devices within a clinic also poses challenges to accurate record keeping and quality assurance, which are much more closely controlled in a laboratory environment.

Recent advances in technology have enabled the same principles to be applied to saliva swabs. The lower concentrations found and the subjectivity of interpretation have been overcome by the use of a hand-held reader to interpret the test result. Further development in this area should improve the quality of POC results and record keeping through electronic prompting for information and recording[7].

What to test: suitable samples

URINE AND BLOOD

Historically, mass testing was first carried out using urine on US personnel returning from the Vietnam conflict. Much is now known about urine testing and the interpretation of test results in relation to recent drug use:

- There is a greater concentration of drug available for testing in urine compared to blood allowing the use of cheaper and simpler laboratory methods.
- The test is less invasive than venipuncture required for blood collection.
- The urine drug detection window is most commonly 1–3 days but may be extended to weeks in the case of chronic abuse of cannabis and the benzodiazepines.
- The window of detection for blood drugs is much shorter than urine; for example heroin metabolites and cocaine are detectable for only minutes to hours compared to between one to two days in urine.
- More than adequate volumes of urine can be collected allowing for further testing.
- Urine collection may be considered humiliating by some employees, hence the balance required to maintain privacy during the collection process against the necessity to ensure that a particular urine sample was produced normally by a particular employee and not exchanged or adulterated surreptitiously.
- Although it might be easier to validate the source of a blood sample and also virtually to abolish adulteration, there are health and safety and possibly religious issues to consider with blood samples.
- Perhaps the overriding issue lies in the lower concentration of drug metabolites found in blood compared to urine that will therefore require more sophisticated laboratory-based instrumentation and hence increase overall costs.

ORAL FLUIDS

Oral fluids consist of saliva, secreted by the salivary glands, other mucosal secretions and transudates drawn into the mouth across concentration gradients, for example by the presence of high salt concentrations. The concentration of drugs within these fluids will vary according to the type of fluid. Passage of drugs into saliva is often dependant upon the degree of acidity of the saliva, which in turn depends on the rate of saliva production. Other mucosal secretions and transudates resemble more closely the concentrations found in blood. There are significant advantages and disadvantages to using oral fluids:

- Drug concentrations are usually lower than in urine providing a greater challenge to analytical procedures.
- In addition to the above, drug metabolites appearing in saliva and urine may be different, therefore requiring different method specificities.
- Oral fluid is subject to contamination from residual food, medicines and confectionery.
- Supervised collection is straightforward and much less invasive than for urine or blood.
- The detection window for drugs will be different from urine and generally shorter.
- The volume of saliva produced may be diminished in the presence of some drugs known to cause 'dry mouth syndrome'.

HAIR

Drugs are deposited in hair through the growing follicle. Hair on the crown of the head has an approximate growth rate of one centimetre per month. Analysis of hair sections therefore provides an opportunity to examine drug history over a much greater time window. Hair analysis is demanding, as it must be first extracted from the hair by a digestive process before sensitive analysis by GCMS or HPLCMS to detect the low concentrations that may be expected:

- Testing is technically demanding, relatively expensive and indicates a drug detection window of weeks to months.
- Sample tampering is less common.
- Drug concentrations are influenced by washing, dying and colouring processes.
- Fashions for short hair may negate the use of this testing medium.
- Occasional drug use may not be detected as concentration of the drug will be below the detection limit of the assay.

SAMPLE ADULTERATION

Various attempts are made to tamper with samples for drug testing in order to conceal drug use and occasionally to give false positive results. Concealing drug use may be achieved to a greater or lesser extent by:

- substitution
- dilution, either by adding water to the sample or drinking water before the test
- adding substances to degrade the drug or the testing reagents (such as bleach, glutaraldehyde, ammonia, hydrogen peroxide and detergents).

Substitution with drug-free urine may be made by concealing containers and less commonly by self-catheterisation. The laboratory will test for sample dilution and common adulterating agents as well as sample temperature, which should fall within the range of 32–38°C within four minutes of providing a workplace urine sample.

Creating false positives is rarer in workplace testing and more often found in clinical testing. This typically happens with methadone when a patient wishes to appear positive for a drug in order to divert the drug to the street. The chain of custody procedure for urine collection will virtually eliminate specimen tampering. However, no collection protocol can totally eliminate those most determined to beat the tests.

COLLECTION OF SAMPLES

The reasons for requesting an employee to submit to a drug test must be clearly documented in the company policy and have been dealt with in the introduction. In situations where there is a challenge to the results of a positive test result, there are UK guidelines[3], which should be followed:

- For urine samples, it is preferable to divide the sample into two portions (A and B). Sample A is used in the initial analysis while sample B is deep frozen in a secure environment. With the donor's consent, the B sample (see also Appendix) can be released to a recognised accredited drug-testing laboratory working within the UK guidelines.

- The release must be supported by a chain of custody together with the original quantitative results obtained on the A sample.
- The second laboratory must only test for named drugs identified to it. It must respond within 10 working days saying either that there was no drug found or that the named drug was found at a level that is consistent or inconsistent with what was found in the A sample.

CONSENT

An employee must be fully informed of the reasons for and the procedures to be employed during drug testing as laid down in a written and available company policy. Once released by the accredited testing laboratory, the results should only be received by a medical physician (MRO, Medical Review Officer) who has knowledge of substance abuse and has appropriate training or experience to interpret and evaluate an individual's positive test result in the light of declared information. Where the subject is a minor, local legislation on competency for consent must be followed.

ENSURING SAMPLE INTEGRITY

The nature of drug use requires that comprehensive measures be in place to ensure the integrity of each sample. This is both to avoid cheating on the part of the subject and also to protect the testing employer and agency against accusations of unfairness. The UK Workplace Drug Testing Guidelines give extensive advice on the procedures required and should be consulted for particular details whilst the general headings are given below:

- The subject (the Donor) providing the sample is the correct individual undergoing the test.
- The sample collection procedure should protect the dignity and human rights of the subject.
- Sample collection should be conducted by suitably trained personnel (the Collection Officer). The security of the premises designated for the procedure must be adequate and only named personnel granted access.
- The Collection Officer must adopt procedures to minimise the risk of adulteration of the sample either by the subject, the person supervising the collection or a third party.
- To deter tampering of the sample, the Collection Officer will ask the Donor to remove any unnecessary outer garments that might conceal false samples, water containers and so on. All taps in the WC must be sealed or closed off and the toilet water coloured with a bright blue vegetable dye.
- After washing hands, the Donor remains in the presence of the Collection Officer and must not be allowed access to any chemicals (soap, bleach and so on) which may adulterate the sample.
- The sample containers should be clearly identified with a unique identifier from the time of collection through to the time of disposal following any period of post-analytical storage.
- Suitable records must accompany the entire process recording each stage from sample

collection, transportation, analysis, storage and disposal to issuing of results and this is known as the 'chain of custody'. All links in the chain must be documented and be able to be reconstructed in court if necessary.

An example of a typical protocol issued to the donor is given in the Appendix to this chapter.

If the organisation requesting the drug-testing service (the Customer) takes responsibility for the collection then the analytical service provider (the Laboratory) has a duty of care to ensure that the relevant parts of the UK Guidelines are implemented by the Customer.

High standards of quality are required throughout the drug-testing process, from the time the test is initiated and the decision to perform a test through to the action taken as a result of the test.

The following steps, set out as part of a quality management process, are crucial to ensuring that a test is relevant, just, fair and true:

- A clear line of responsibility should be in place covering each stage of the process with those responsible having recognised and recorded training.
- Documentation of each stage, as the subject is called, the sample collected, analysed and the result reported will ensure transparency and fairness on both sides.
- Laboratories offering drug testing should be accredited under a nationally recognised quality management scheme. This will vary from country to country.
- Each laboratory should participate in a national external quality assurance programme[4] for workplace testing for drugs of abuse. Such programmes distribute samples of unknown drug composition for testing on a regular basis. The results for each laboratory will be compared against the consensus of results and against any information available about sample composition. Details of laboratory performance within that programme should be open to inspection.
- Where analysis is performed in the workplace, steps are taken to ensure quality is maintained. This can include use of an accredited supplier of testing devices and sample collection equipment that confirm to current directives for *in vitro* diagnostics. The organisation should participate in local or national external quality assurance schemes. There must be close monitoring of staff training in using devices according to manufacturer's instructions and comprehensive record keeping.
- Following a drug test the sample should be stored for a length of time such that any questions relating to the testing of the sample are resolved. Where an initial test is performed in the workplace the sample should be stored in a manner likely to minimise sample degradation. This usually involves freezing at $-20°C$.
- Close control of factors likely to affect health and safety should be included within any testing procedure. This becomes particularly relevant when testing is performed in the workplace and should aim to prevent infection, cross contamination and safe disposal of materials.
- Facilities need not be elaborate but need to include a work area that is easily decontaminated and so should be free of soft furnishing with separate sinks for decontamination and hand washing.
- Disposal of biological materials must be in accordance with local environmental and infection control standards and should include measures to prevent any breach of confidentiality through labelled sample pots, tubes or testing devices.

As in all other areas of drug testing, close cooperation with local laboratory-based testing services can be valuable for advice on local regulations and guidance on best practice.

Auditing of procedures and results is a valuable tool in verifying a testing procedure. This can cover:

- sample collection procedure to confirm that each step of the protocol is followed;
- sample analysis by retesting of a random number of samples;
- sending samples to another laboratory or testing centre for comparison;
- confirming that documentation has been properly completed for each testing procedure;
- finally a comparison can be made with other testing services to compare positive rates for drugs in similar populations.

A successful workplace drug-testing policy is one where each individual's role is clearly defined and identified. There must be full informed consent obtained from the employee and it is the job of the company's MRO to ensure that the procedure is conducted in a dignified, courteous and confidential manner.

Appendix – Chain of custody drug testing

Example of information for the donor on urine collection procedure

1   The collection of urine for drug testing will be carried out according to a legally binding procedure known as the *'chain of custody'*.

2   This is an internationally recognised process that tracks the handling and storage from point of urine collection to final disposal of the specimen. It ensures that the entire drug-testing process is conducted in such a way as to give accurate and reliable information.

3   Laboratories that undertake workplace or school drug testing must adopt these legally defensible procedures in order to satisfy the courts should there be a legal challenge to the laboratory results. It is of benefit to all parties concerned that samples are collected and tested according to statutory procedures.

4   The collection site is at XX. You will be given a mutually convenient appointment to attend following arrangements made between your employer's MO/GP, school's MO/GP or a solicitor (if applicable) and the laboratory.

5   *Please bring photographic identification containing your signature with you* (for example passport or new style driving licence) for presentation to the collection officer. Without this, the collection cannot proceed.

6   You will be asked to check that your name and address is correct on the consent form and then date and sign that you consent to the sample collection.

7   After signing, the collection officer will ask you questions relating to any drugs and medicines consumed during the last 14 days including over-the-counter preparations. The collection officer will also initiate the laboratory's chain of custody documentation.

8   *The procedures for collecting urine will allow you complete individual privacy during urination*. The laboratory will always provide a collection officer of same sex as the donor.

9   Before the start, the collection officer will ask you to remove any unnecessary outer garments (overcoat, jacket, hat and so on) and hand these over together with bag or briefcase for safekeeping during the collection procedure. You may place valuables in a safe deposit box and keep the key with you during urine collection.

10   You will then be asked to **wash and dry your hands** with inspection of your hands by the collection officer.

11   After washing and drying your hands you will be asked to choose **one** large seal-wrapped urine collection beaker (100ml) and **two** smaller seal-wrapped tamper-evident containers (25ml) which will comprise the A and B test samples. You should check the integrity of the wrapping in each case. You will then be asked to pass a urine sample into the **single large beaker** in private behind a closed toilet door with the collection officer waiting outside the door.

12   Please fill the collection beaker between half and three quarters full with urine. After providing the required volume you may pass excess urine directly into the WC but **do not flush it or wash your hands until instructed to do so**. Failing these requirements you will have to wait and repeat the entire process after drinking some water.

13   Replace the lid of the collection beaker and give it to the collection officer who will then inspect your hands.

14   Finally, you will be asked to wash and dry your hands after completion of the above process.

15   Upon receiving the specimen, the collection officer will invite you to observe whilst he/she notes the urine volume and measures the urine temperature. ***During this procedure you will both maintain sight of the collection beaker and the two tamper-evident A and B containers***. The collection officer will transfer the urine in equal volumes from the beaker to the two containers, screw on the lids and snap them shut activating the tamper-evident mechanism.

16   You will be asked to sign your name on two sticky-paper labels. These will be countersigned by the collection officer together with the date and time and placed on the two containers. The collection officer finally confirms that the sample is acceptable by completing the final section of the consent form.

17   The process will have to be repeated if more than four minutes elapse between passing the sample and handing it over to the collection officer or if the volume is less than 50ml or if the collection officer has reasonable suspicion of sample tampering.

18   You will be asked to read and sign a statement on the chain of custody form certifying that the specimens identified on the form are in fact the specimens you consented to and actually provided.

19   The screened results are normally available within 24 hours if all results are negative. Confirmatory testing may take between five and ten extra working days. Printed results are sent back to your company MO or GP as required. Results may also be faxed to an agreed secure number.

20   The laboratory may accept requests for drug testing directly from private individuals. The current cost is £XX inclusive of confirmation but exclusive of alcohol testing which is an additional £XX. Payment should be made by cheque before testing starts (payable to XX).

21   If you have any questions please contact XX via the general laboratory number given above.

References

1. S.B. Karch, *Drug Abuse Handbook*, CRC Press LLC, 1998
2. Department of Health and Human Services, Mandatory guidelines for Federal Workplace drug testing programs, *Federal Register*; 1994;**59**:29903–29931
3. *United Kingdom Laboratory Guidelines for Legally Defensible Workplace Drug Testing* Version 1, March 2001, www.wdtforum.org.uk
4. *UKNEQAS for Drugs of Abuse in Urine*, Cardiff Bioanalytical Services Ltd, Cardiff CF10 5DP
5. S. George, Laboratory Screening for Drugs of Abuse, Rila Publications Ltd, *CPD Bulletin Clinical Biochemistry*, 1999;**3**: 85–90
6. *Sixteen Devices for the Detection of Drugs of Abuse in Urine*, Medicines and Healthcare Products Regulatory Agency, MHRA 03078, 2003
7. NACB, *Laboratory Guidelines for Evidence-based Practice for POCT Drugs of Abuse Testing – Draft Guidelines*, http://www.nacb.org/lmpg/poct_lmpg.draft.stm. Accessed February 2005.

14 *Screening New Employees*

John Harrison

History of screening

Occupational health is concerned with the promotion and maintenance of health at work. Historically, its focus has been occupational hazards and their association with the occurrence of occupational diseases. Assessment of fitness for work was concerned with the identification of pre-existing medical conditions that would render workers incapable of performing their duties or that would make them at increased risk of a further deterioration in their health. The risk assessment demanded a comprehensive understanding of the work environment: the activities of the job, the way in which the activities were carried out and the measures in place to protect workers from the hazards. Whilst this approach is still the cornerstone of practice, the remit of occupational health has extended to include wider issues related to employability and performance at work. In 1995, the World Health Organisation revised its definition of occupational health so as to focus on three objectives:

- the maintenance and promotion of workers' health and working capacity
- the improvement of work environment and work to become conducive to safety and health; and
- the development of work organisation and working cultures in a direction, which supports health and safety at work, and in doing so also promotes a positive social climate and smooth operation and may enhance productivity of the undertaking. The concept of the working culture is intended, in this context, to mean a reflection of the essential value systems adopted by the undertaking concerned. Such a culture is reflected in practice in the managerial systems, personnel policies, principles for participation, training policies and quality management of the undertaking[1].

This was followed by the formulation of a new concept of good practice in occupational health. In 1999, the London Ministerial Declaration* launched 'good practice in health, environment and safety management in enterprises' (HESME), which recognises that the responsibility for health at work is not solely that of the occupational health professional, but also that of employers and employees. HESME underscores the importance of work activity, work organisation and the work culture in influencing health and well-being of workers and their families. It also encourages a convergence of traditional occupational health and public health, indicating that the health of workers cannot be considered in a societal vacuum.

---

* The third ministerial conference on environment and health held in June 1999 in London

This shift in emphasis of the approach of occupational health is relevant to the consideration of the issues surrounding the screening of workers for drug misuse. At the beginning of the twenty-first century, there are concerns about the emergence of a 'big brother' intrusion into the privacy of individual lives and about the increased involvement of the State in individual lifestyle choices. On the other hand the relentless progression of the global economy and the associated need to be competitive means that companies and governments must explore ways to boost productivity and reduce labour costs. Intuitively, it does not make good business sense to permit employees to be at work under the influence of drugs, because of the health and safety implications as well as the detrimental effect that this will have on work performance. In addition, attention is being paid to factors that affect the long-term employability of workers because of social insurance costs and the impact of ageing populations on the solvency of pension funds[2]. But where should the balance lie? In the western world privacy acts and human rights legislation mean that employers must act with a sense of proportion and be able to justify their occupational health policies. The concept of partnership is an important one and policies for screening employees for drug misuse should include discussions with all the stakeholders before they are implemented.

Alcohol is the main drug of misuse affecting fitness to work. Concerns about alcohol at work are not new. There is evidence of discussion about alcohol in the workplace at the end of the nineteenth century[3] as well as political and legislative remedies. Throughout the twentieth century the US appears to have led the way in the introduction of alcohol at work policies, until the last two decades when drug and alcohol policies became issues in Europe and Australasia.

A historical review of the cultural influences in the US identified five different eras that affected approaches to workplace drugs and alcohol dating from a pre-revolution era, characterised by imported attitudes and beliefs from England, through the temperance era, a progressive era, a post-World War II era and culminating in the present 'war on drugs' era[4]. The complex issues surrounding the introduction of drug testing in the workplace have been summarised to include public opinion, employer self-interest, collective bargaining agreements, the precedent and influence of employee assistance programmes and developments in legislation affecting the workplace[5].

Testing for alcohol and drugs seems to have originated in the US Department of Defence in the 1960s as a response to drug usage in the military during the Vietnam War[6]. It is suggested that drug testing in the core institutions in America would not have been politically possible without including a clear link to drug treatment. In Europe, the link between testing and provision of treatment is less well established[7]. Workplace drug testing is becoming more prevalent in the UK and Scandinavia, but it is suggested that quality control of the drug testing processes is very variable. A European Workplace Drug Testing Society has been established with the aim of improving the quality of testing. In Ireland, pre-employment testing for drugs of abuse is on the increase[8] but in Italy conflicts between an individual's right to privacy and an organisation's right to safeguard its interests have had to be overcome[9].

Testing for drugs and alcohol in the workplace can take place in three situations: pre-employment screening, for cause testing (for example following an accident) and unannounced testing[10]. Pre-employment screening for drugs and alcohol is the least contentious aspect of a comprehensive testing programme because it occurs before a contract of employment is finalised. However, even this form of screening is not without its sensitivities. In the US it is suggested that courts often consider that the individual right to privacy is subordinate to the public's right to safety and, in addition, employers have more freedom to test job applicants than when testing employees already working for a company[11]. In the UK case law has determined that employers may set their own conditions of employment in relation to health and safety. Testing for drugs and alcohol is permissible, as long as informed consent is obtained and the testing is carried out appropriately. Kloss states that 'there are no legal objections to the practice at the pre-employment stage as long as it is realised that applicants are free to refuse the test if they wish'[12]. There are no legal requirements for systematic testing, although the Transport and Works Act 1992 has proved to be a stimulus for the introduction of testing. This requires an employer to exercise 'due diligence' to prevent an offence being committed by the employee during the transportation of goods and people. An offence will be committed if the employee is found to be unfit to carry out such work through drink or drugs and if the level of alcohol in the breath, blood or urine exceeds the prescribed limit.

Trade unions have raised some objections to testing programmes:

- Testing should be about competency to perform a specific job.
- The concept of a 'voluntary' submission to a test may be more apparent than real.
- Testing can be viewed as an invasion of privacy: blood tests are intrusive, and direct observation of urination is degrading and a violation of personal rights.[6]

Recently, a Trades Union Congress (TUC) report *Testing Times*▲ was critical of employer enthusiasm for drug and alcohol testing at work. An initial survey for the on-going Independent Inquiry into Drug Testing has found that 80 per cent of employers would be prepared to drug test employees if they thought that productivity was at stake. The Rail, Maritime and Transport Union (RMT), which represents workers on UK railways, has accepted with regret the need for testing that is required by legislation[6]. The TUC argue that, whilst there may be a case for testing in safety-critical jobs, workplace testing is a costly waste of time and a gross infringement of an individual's privacy, testing should never be random and that every workplace should have a policy on drugs and alcohol use drawn up by managers in consultation with union representatives.

Pre-employment testing

RATIONALE

The introduction of drug and alcohol testing into the pre-employment health assessment must be done only after careful consideration of a number of questions. Why is it being done? Who will do it, how and where? What will happen when the results are received? The cost of testing is also a consideration. It is generally assumed that such pre-employment testing will improve health and safety at work, work attendance, work performance and productivity.

Little attention is paid to the treatment aspects of drug and alcohol abuse when considering pre-employment testing in isolation. Indeed, the relationship between a company's occupational health service and job applicants is a strange one in that, until a

---

▲ In Hazards Magazine http://www.hazards.org/testingtimes/drugtesting.htm (accessed 26/1/04)

job offer is confirmed, it is questionable as to whether a caring relationship exists. It appears that there is no legal duty to inform the applicants of the results of testing[6] although one would expect there to be a professional or moral duty to do so. The applicant who tested positive would be unlikely to be offered the job and this would end the relationship with the occupational health service. However, good practice would require at least the provision of some health education and advice about how to modify behaviour or how to access help. A formal referral to another agency could only take place with the expressed permission of the individual.

The finding of a positive result may lead to coercion of someone to accept treatment at an earlier stage than might otherwise have happened. Is this beneficial with respect to treatment outcomes? It has been suggested that confrontation from treatment professionals is correlated with a poor outcome, although the results are contingent on a range of factors, such as the treatment setting, the treatment philosophy, client characteristics, the client's view of the relationship with the confronter, whether the confrontation is viewed as legitimate, the client's perception of the confronter's motivation and the level of emotional intensity involved during the confrontation[13]. It is possible that being denied a job because of the finding of a positive screening test result might provide the impetus to seek treatment, with a view to obtaining employment in the future. There is evidence that employees who have tested positive to drugs during on-site testing are more likely to remain in treatment than self-referral patients, who tend to have problems that are more chronic and more severe[14].

An earlier workplace study also found that self-referred workers had poorer treatment outcomes than workers who were identified via the company's alcohol policy[15]. The weight of evidence seems to suggest that patients mandated into treatment, either by the courts or the workplace, do at least as well as 'voluntary' patients, based on US studies[16]. However, these studies included doctors who tended to do well as a result of early intervention[17, 18]. On the other hand, it has been argued that dismissal of a job applicant following a positive drug test at pre-employment assessment, whilst legal on the basis of the risks attendant on employing a drug addict, might encourage prospective employees to conceal information about drug or alcohol problems and might dissuade them from consulting their own physicians, in case the information reached their employers[12]. Ultimately, there is a lack of research data on the effect of pre-employment screening for drugs and alcohol and treatment outcomes.

RELATIONSHIP BETWEEN INCIDENTS AND SUBSTANCE AND ALCOHOL USE

With respect to health and safety at work, the link between the occurrence of fatal accidents and drug usage seems strong. In a study of 459 deaths occurring at work in Alberta, Canada, 40 workers tested positive for alcohol, 28 for prescription drugs and 22 for non-prescription drugs. The only illicit drug found was cannabis, which was found in 10 workers[19]. Fatalities due to motor vehicle accidents, falls and being caught in or under equipment were associated with alcohol usage.

In an Australian study of all work-related fatalities occurring between 1982 and 1984 16 per cent of fatalities had a non-zero blood alcohol concentration, based on all fatalities for whom a blood alcohol measurement was documented (59 per cent of all work-related fatalities). The median blood alcohol concentration was 104 mg per cent. Once again, fatal vehicle accidents occurred significantly more frequently when the blood alcohol concentration was greater or equal to 50 mg per cent[20].

The situation is less clear cut for non-fatal accidents at work. A relationship between problem drinking (measured using Mortimer-Filkins test scores), self-reported alcohol intake and work injuries was explored in a sample of 833 employees[21]. Significant relationships between problem drinking and work injuries and injury-related absences were found, but not between high alcohol intake and injuries.

Problem drinkers were 2.7 times more likely to have injury-related absences than non-problem drinkers. Another study in the US has found that various measures of drug use are not associated with work injuries, but are linked to being sacked or resigning from a job[22]. The possibility that it is problem behaviour that explains a link between problem substance use and work injury has been explored using cases of injury occurring in a cohort of 26 413 workers[23]. However, problem substance use was assessed indirectly using employee assistance programme data, disciplinary records and evidence of dishonesty. The relationship between problem substance use and injury was weak, whereas the relationship between problem behaviour and injury was strong.

A different approach has been taken in a study of 832 workers, selected at random, looking at drinking patterns and the occurrence of hangovers and their experience of work problems[24]. Workplace drinking and coming to work with a hangover predicted work-related problems after controlling for usual drinking pattern, heavy drinking, significant job characteristics and background variables. Overall drinking and heavy drinking outside the workplace did not predict workplace problems. It appears, therefore, that problem drinking or problem substance use may not necessarily cause problems at work, although the evidence is conflicting.

Studies looking at non-fatal accidents may be flawed by the under-reporting of accidents, particularly if there is a possibility of alcohol being the cause and there is a likelihood of sanctions being taken against workers. On balance it seems that alcohol consumption and misuse is likely to be related to accidents, both at work and outside the workplace. However, the precise relationship is not well understood[6].

OCCUPATIONAL SUPPORT

Screening new employees is likely to be undertaken by company occupational health departments, if there is one. Most occupational health services are to be found in large organisations, such as the National Health Service or Transport for London or multinational companies, such as oil companies. Small- to medium-sized enterprises (SMEs) do not have good access to occupational health services[25]. (Small enterprises are defined as having 50 or less employees; medium enterprises have 50–250 employees and large enterprises have greater than 250 employees.) SMEs account for 99 per cent of the private sector business and 56.8 per cent of total employment; 21 per cent of businesses employ fewer than five employees, with clear implications for screening. In such circumstances the responsibility is likely to be outsourced and issues such as confidentiality of testing may be difficult to address satisfactorily.

A study of UK companies revealed that 16 per cent of companies employing 101–200 people had a drugs and alcohol policy, compared to 70 per cent of companies employing more than 10 000 people. A similar finding has been reported in the US[6]. A reason given for this discrepancy is that small companies often do not perceive that they have a problem with drugs and alcohol. A recent survey of provision of occupational support in 4950 companies in the UK estimated that 3–15 per cent of companies provided such support, mainly hazard identification and risk management. Concern for the well-being of employees was the commonest reason given for providing occupational health support, although this often took second place to health and safety. Issues relating to drugs and alcohol were not raised in relation to employee well-being. The only reference to drugs and alcohol in the report was in relation to the introduction of drug and alcohol testing by a train operator.

Guidelines for testing

In the UK, the Faculty of Occupational Medicine of the Royal College of Physicians published guidelines on testing for drugs of abuse in the workplace[26]. The guidelines explicitly focus on drugs, rather than alcohol, although some of the guidelines are relevant to screening for alcohol. The guidelines comment that the concept of testing for drugs of abuse appeals to many in management and society in general because it is seen as both evidential and decisive. The reality however is that unless testing is very carefully undertaken it will be neither.

An important ethical consideration for occupational health professionals is how involved they should be in what is essentially a policing activity? Occupational health is perceived by some workers as a tool of management and unthinking endorsement of a poorly constructed testing policy will reinforce this. A policy must recognise individual human rights and the clinical and scientific processes that must be followed to ensure that correct decisions are taken with regard to challenging employees with positive results and about future employment and/or treatment. Occupational health practitioners, as clinicians, have a duty of care to job applicants, even though the applicants have not yet joined the company. It is essential that individuals understand fully the testing process and what will happen to the results. An All Party Parliamentary Drug Misuse Group has reported on drug testing[27]. A number of criteria must be satisfied to ensure that the Data Protection Act 1998 is not contravened:

- Has the sample/data been obtained fairly and lawfully?
- Was it excessive for its purpose?
- Is the data accurate and up to date?
- Is it stored securely?

CONSENT

The need for explicit consent for testing is also stressed by both the Faculty of Occupational Medicine and the All Party Parliamentary Group. The need for consent is required 'unless the processing is necessary for exercising or performing employment rights or obligations'[27]. This means that employees will not lose their jobs if they do not comply. However, it is unclear as to how this affects job applicants, who are not yet employees. The likelihood is that refusal will terminate the recruitment process.

PURPOSE

It is important that the purpose of any drug testing programme is identified and defined at the outset. There are numerous reasons for implementing a programme the choice of which will affect the implementation. The Faculty of Occupational Medicine recommends setting up a steering committee involving key personnel. The company occupational physician will take responsibility for the medical aspects of the programme. There are a number of considerations including informed consent, confidentiality, referral for testing, clinical assessment, obtaining specimens, chain of custody when transporting specimens to the laboratory, accreditation of the laboratory and the role of the Medical Review Officer.

The training of staff involved in the testing programme is an essential element. Clinical facilities must include a suitably prepared toilet for the collection of urine samples. There is no doubt that stringent testing procedures imply that the worker may try to cheat the testing process and clinicians may feel uncomfortable with this, as may the workers themselves.

STANDARDS

In addition to the standards for the collection of specimens, adherence to strict standards for the labelling, packaging and transportation is necessary to ensure that there is no possibility that any positive results of tests have come from the wrong person. Such results may have a major effect on employability and, as such, must be defensible. A chain of custody involves correct identification of the donor; informed consent; declaration of the use of other medication or foodstuffs, such as eating poppy seeds; tamper-proof production of urine samples; correct transfer of urine to container, which is labelled and sealed in a tamper-proof package; dispatch to the approved laboratory; correct acceptance of the specimen and analysis; correct identification and notification of the report and delivery of the report. Any break in the chain renders the test invalid.

MEDICAL REVIEW OFFICER

An important role in the drug testing process is that of the Medical Review Officer (MRO). This role is fulfilled by a physician who has had special training in the drug testing procedures and who is responsible for the interpretation of the test results. If the tests indicate that illicit drugs have been taken, there is a responsibility to inform the Chief Medical Officer at the Home Office of the UK Government. The MRO does not have to be an occupational physician, but in the case of workplace testing the relationship between the occupational physician and the employees means that it can be advantageous for the occupational physician to take this role. However, it must be clearly understood that one of the jobs of the MRO is to inform the employer of a verified positive result. In the case of a pre-employment drug test this may mean a withdrawal of the job offer. This is a departure from the normal practice of occupational physicians who would normally advise about fitness for work or about adjustments to working arrangements. They also look at the relationship between the work environment and health, which may be particularly relevant when exploring causes of substance misuse. Since the advent of the Disability Discrimination Act 1995 unqualified decisions of being unfit for a job are no longer acceptable without exploring reasonable adjustments. However, drug and alcohol addiction or dependency is not considered to be a disability under the Act.

The MRO is responsible for approving the validity of the entire testing process. Positive results must be verified by reviewing the chain of custody process and the MRO must interview the applicant to inform them of their legal rights and to double check the history for other possible explanations for the positive result[28]. It is also necessary to ensure that the laboratory processes are satisfactory, which means that the MRO must have appropriate laboratory scientific training, as well as knowledge of substance-abuse disorders. The American College of Occupational and Environmental Medicine has concluded that suitably trained MROs would have the following:

- knowledge and clinical training in substance-abuse disorders, including detailed knowledge of alternative medical explanations for laboratory-confirmed drug test results;
- knowledge of issues relating to adulterated and substituted specimens and possible medical causes of an invalid result;
- knowledge of the 'procedures for transportation drug and alcohol testing programmes', the DOT• 'MRO guidelines' and DOT agency rules applicable for any employer for which the MRO provides services.[29]

It is also suggested that knowledge of the pharmacology of drugs of abuse, pharmacological treatments for standard medical conditions, issues relating to the prescription of controlled drugs and laboratory testing methodology and drug rehabilitation will be advantageous. This must be maintained by a minimum of 12 hours of continuous professional development in topics relevant to the work of MROs, over a three-year period.

Results of screening

How should a positive screening test, obtained at the pre-employment stage, be interpreted and what action should be taken? In most cases, a positive result will lead to rejection of the applicant. This is on the basis that applicants knew in advance of taking the test that this would be the outcome and that, in such circumstances, a positive result is indicative of a substance misuse problem. However, caution is necessary to ensure that false positives do not lead to incorrect employment decisions. The MRO has a key role to obtain a full drug history, to exclude the use of some over-the-counter preparations and some foodstuffs, such as poppy seeds[27]. The analysis of heroin metabolites can help to distinguish between results due to heroin or morphine abuse and eating poppy seeds. Heroin is metabolised to 6-monoacetylmorphine (6-MAM) and this metabolite may be detected up to 24 hours after intake[30]. The presence of only morphine-3-glucuronide may be due to heroin usage, but it may be due to prescribed medications or poppy seeds. Thus, when measuring for the presence of opiates it is necessary to obtain a variety of information including urinalysis for prescribed drugs and metabolites. False negative results may occur if the urine concentration is very dilute. This is important when considering the possibility that job applicants may try to cheat the testing process. Additional testing of dilute urine specimens is possible, using gas chromatography – mass spectrometry, and this has been shown to be able to identify drugs in the urine, that would have otherwise been missed[31].

In the case of alcohol, the detection of urine or blood ethanol in the absence of other markers of alcohol misuse is more problematic. The use of alcohol is socially acceptable and it is not illegal. Driving a motor vehicle on a public road in the UK with a blood alcohol

---

• Department of Transport

concentration greater than 80mg/100ml is an offence; the level is lower in some other countries. The finding of a blood alcohol concentration, or equivalent, at this level would be a cause for concern in the context of a pre-employment clinical assessment. However, the detection of a low concentration of alcohol could be construed to be acceptable. Other markers of alcohol misuse are necessary to form a picture of inappropriate drinking behaviour that would justify rejection of the job application. Screening tools, such as the alcohol use disorders identification test (AUDIT), might be considered, but this relies on the honesty and self-assessment of the applicant. Objective screening tests include the measurement of gamma glutamyltransferase (GGT) and carbohydrate-deficient transferring (CDT). CDT is more specific than GGT and it may be better at detecting moderate alcohol consumption and recent alcohol consumption. A workplace study of the use of these tools found that 22 per cent of a transportation workforce were positive for alcohol misuse on at least one of the tools[32]. However, excluding the AUDIT questionnaire reduced the numbers testing positive by approximately one third. Tests, such as GGT and CDT, will detect recent alcohol misuse, whereas the AUDIT questionnaire is concerned with drinking behaviour over a longer period of time. It seems likely that reliance on testing for alcohol will detect only those job applicants with severe addictions. Extending testing to include CDT will increase the likelihood of detecting large alcohol intakes within about two weeks of testing and measurement of GGT will detect large alcohol intakes within the previous six weeks.

It can be argued that, if the aim of pre-employment testing is to protect the public and other employees at work from the effects of alcohol misuse, a longer-term view of drinking behaviour is desirable. Social factors in the workplace, such as perceived drinking by friends and co-workers, have been found to be strong predictors of work-related drinking[33] and so individuals with a history of drinking in excess of recommended norms might be at an increased risk of alcohol misuse if the work culture encourages this.

One would not expect to find many positive test results following pre-employment testing. Applicants know in advance that they will be tested and people with addictions are unlikely to present themselves for testing. The situation may be different when considering testing at the workplace. Experiences from Ireland reveal that ethanol and cannabis are the most frequently detected substances[8] but opiates and amphetamines have been detected. A recent pilot drug testing programme in the UK mining industry has detected two heavy cannabis users as a result of pre-employment testing[34]. Anecdotal reports from other UK industries is consistent with these findings.

Two studies from the US have indicated that employees who tested positive for illicit drugs have worse employment outcomes than those who do not[35]. Both involved the postal service, although they were conducted independently. These organisations did not reject new employees on the basis of the drug testing. In the US Postal Services blind longitudinal study quoted by Logan, 4396 applicants were hired irrespective of their drug test result. Follow up over an average of 1.3 years of employment showed that workers who had tested positive for illicit drug use at pre-employment had a 59 per cent higher absenteeism rate and had a 47 per cent higher involuntary turnover rate than those who had tested negative. A second prospective controlled study examined the association between pre-employment drug screening results and employment outcomes in 2537 postal employees[36]. Cannabis users identified at pre-employment testing had a higher turnover compared to non-users. They also had a greater risk of accidents at work, sickness absence and disciplinary hearings. The same was not found for cocaine users identified at pre-employment testing, although the risk of work-related injuries was significantly higher than that of non-drug users and they had the highest absence rates. Use of cannabis appears to be linked to unsafe risk perceptions that could have important workplace health and safety implications.

A qualitative UK study of attitudes of UK young people towards driving after smoking cannabis or drinking alcohol has found a marked difference between risk perceptions of drinking and driving and those of smoking and driving[37]. Whilst driving after drinking alcohol was seen as risky and antisocial, similar risks were not perceived with respect to smoking cannabis. This is despite evidence that smoking cannabis affects judgement and motor skills. Cannabis users have been found to have twice the normal frequency of road traffic accidents in a 6–12 month period before they are convicted for cannabis use and they have nearly as many accidents under the influence of cannabis alone as they do under the influence of alcohol[10]. The effects of cannabis may be prolonged: a single cannabis joint can cause impairment for more than ten hours. The recent downgrading of cannabis from a class B drug to a class C drug in the UK has sent out a confusing message about the safety of this drug, which will only compound the risk misconceptions about its use and workplace health and safety.

Testing for drugs is complicated by the fact that positive results may be obtained some time after the drug has been taken. Cocaine metabolites may be detected up to 72 hours later and cannabis may be detected more than two weeks after cessation of use in someone who was a daily user[10]. This may catch some job applicants out when presenting themselves for testing. Of course, other drugs can also impair performance, such as benzodiazopines or antidepressant medication. The high prevalence of psychoneurotic illness in the western world may mean that a proportion of job applicants may be taking physician-prescribed medication when they are tested at pre-employment assessment. If we are serious about promoting health and safety in the workplace then performance-based testing, in addition to biological testing may become established. This is an area that needs further development but there is evidence that performance on computerised tasks can be measured in the workplace. Serial measurements can establish baseline performance indicators that might be used to identify impairment at an early stage[38].

Recent accounts

TESTING IN THE US

At present, widespread routine drug and alcohol testing in the workplace is still a US phenomenon. By 1993, 93 per cent of companies with more than 5000 employees had a drug testing programme, although this has steadily reduced over the years to 77 per cent in 1998, to 70 per cent in 2000 and to 68 per cent in 2001[35]. This is linked to access to employee assistance programmes (EAP) which typically offer assessment, short-term counselling and referral services to employees with substance-abuse and other work-related problems[5]. Utilisation of EAPs, however, remains relatively low, and a noticeable discrepancy exists between the estimated number of substance abusers in an organisation and the number of employees who seek help for substance abuse[39]. It is reported that only 5.5 per cent of employees use EAPs and of these, approximately one quarter do so for substance-abuse problems. It has been suggested that reasons for the low uptake include lack of awareness of EAPs, lack of support for substance-abuse policies and the degree of tolerance of co-workers of employees misusing substances of abuse.

This underlines the need to address social factors in the workplace in order to control the use of drugs and alcohol. In a study of employee attitudes to workplace alcohol testing, 65 per cent of 6370 workers supported pre-employment testing, whereas 81 per cent were in favour of testing after an accident and only 49 per cent supported random testing[40]. Testing was more likely to be supported by transportation workers, compared to sales workers or service sector employees. This might reflect the history of workplace testing in transportation or an acceptance of the need for testing in an industry with a high number of safety-critical jobs. The study also found that workers classified as 'problem drinkers' were least likely to support testing, as were workers who admitted to drinking at lunch time. Thus, workplace testing should be introduced only in conjunction with initiatives to address workplace drinking cultures and emphasising the importance of rehabilitation.

TESTING IN THE UK

In the UK, workplace drug testing is limited. In a survey of 204 UK businesses only 4 per cent of companies conducted tests[41], however 10 per cent of firms are reportedly considering introducing testing within the next year■. Drug and alcohol testing in the workplace takes place, in the main, in the transportation industry and in the power/oil/gas industries. EAPs are not as well established in the UK, although companies with drug and alcohol policies do acknowledge the importance of early detection of problems to facilitate rehabilitation.

London Underground has a policy of no alcohol, no drugs, drug and alcohol testing, and support and rehabilitation if the problem is declared and treatment complied with. Alternatively, disciplinary action will be taken against employees who breach the policy or who test positive at work. Pre-employment testing is carried out for new employees recruited into safety critical jobs, whereas post-accident testing and random testing can be carried out on any employee. Treatment for substance-abuse problems is tailored to individual needs and is managed in-house, not by outsourcing to an EAP. Approximately 90 employees are referred for treatment each year following an in-depth assessment, out of over 12 000 staff, and between 69 and 79 per cent have kept their jobs in recent years.

The UK off-shore industry has also implemented drug and alcohol testing, linked to the oil industry. Although testing is not an integral part of the periodic medical assessment carried out on behalf of the UK Offshore Operators Association, it is requested by many companies. One occupational health service in the Aberdeen area performs approximately 5000 tests each year. Positive results at pre-employment testing are not infrequent, usually due to cannabis use by young workers. In most cases a positive result leads to a withdrawal of a job offer.

The armed services do not carry out biological screening of new recruits, but the recruitment interview does include questions about the recruit's history of drug and alcohol usage. Use of a class A drug will lead to a rejection. Similarly, a history indicative of a dependency problem will prevent acceptance. All service personnel are subject to random testing, once in post. Until recently, a positive result would lead to automatic dismissal. In some circumstances, today, individuals testing positive might be retained, subject to successful rehabilitation. The Royal Navy has legal powers to deal with drug users (The Navy Act).

■ *Hazards Magazine Testing Times* http://www.hazards.org/testingtimes/drugtesting.htm (Accessed 26/1/04)

Manufacturers, such as Proctor and Gamble and GKN, do not screen for drugs and alcohol in the workplace, but encourage rehabilitation. A similar approach is taken by the John Lewis Partnership, a national retailer in the UK, where referral of staff suspected of having substance-abuse problems to the in-house occupational health service is part of the company's guidelines for the management of drug abuse in the workplace.

The UK's largest employer, the National Health Service, has guidance on implementing a drug and alcohol policy that highlights key elements, such as raising awareness, recognition of problems, self-referral, treatment and rehabilitation and the role of occupational health services. The guidance states that 'random testing of staff, as a tool for managing substance misuse, is not considered an appropriate form of action for NHS employers at this time'*.

Conclusion

In conclusion, the issue of workplace testing for drug and alcohol remains controversial. As the prevalence of drug and alcohol misuse in society continues to be a cause for concern, employers are required to assess the need to introduce testing to safeguard their businesses and the public. The emergence of 'lean and efficient' firms during the last 30 years has meant that the performance of individual workers has come under the spotlight, in terms of health and safety and productivity. However, there are civil liberties issues and human rights requirements that, rightly, demand a careful consideration of the purpose and context of testing before it is implemented.

There is evidence that substance misuse is associated with some health and safety problems, sickness absence and increased labour turnover, but the evidence is not as strong as might be thought. The reason for this is, probably, because research has used rather crude measures both of alcohol and drug abuse and of workplace factors. This means that, in numerical terms, moderate alcohol abuse is likely to be more damaging than alcoholism in the workplace, because many more people moderately abuse alcohol than are alcoholics. Even moderate abuse can cause health and safety problems.

Clearly employers will wish to identify alcoholics and drug addicts and there is evidence that screening programmes tend to exclude them from the workplace. Results from the 1997 US Household Survey on Drug Abuse suggest that workplace drug testing programmes may act as a deterrent to illicit drug use. Employees who are current illicit drug users are 20 per cent less likely to work for an employer who tests 'post-accident', 50 per cent less likely if the employer drug tests 'for cause' and 25 per cent less likely if the employer tests at 'pre-employment' or 'randomly' when compared with those who do not currently use illicit drugs[42].

The recent all party group on drug misuse has concluded that there is no real consensus or clarity about what the aim of drug testing in the workplace is or should be[27]. They have recommended that testing should aim to protect the public, employees and employers and, as such, it should be one part of a workplace ethos that is intolerant of workers being at work under the influence of illicit drugs or alcohol and which promotes healthy lifestyle behaviours.

There is growing evidence that peer-group attitudes are probably the most important

---

*   *Taking Alcohol and Other Drugs out of the NHS Workplace*. Department of Health, February 2001

influences for controlling substance misuse in the workplace. Biological screening at pre-employment assessments is intrusive and must be handled sensitively and in an ethically correct manner. Such screening is likely to be more acceptable to job applicants and to other workers if it is carried out as a manifestation of a well thought out and explained workplace policy for managing drugs and alcohol. Screening of applicants for jobs involving driving, or working off-shore, can be justified based on health and safety research. However, untargeted pre-employment screening, in isolation, appears to be unproductive without a clear cost-benefit.

Thanks for assistance in the preparation of this chapter are extended to:

Dr Olivia Carlton, Chief Medical Officer, London Underground (Part of Transport for London)
Surgeon Commodore Philip Raffaelli, Royal Navy
Dr Martyn Davidson, Chief Medical Officer, John Lewis Partnership
Dr Alex Grieve, Chief Medical Officer, GKN
Dr Grant Logan, Occupational Physician, AON
Dr Paul Nicholson, Lead Occupational Physician (Europe), Proctor and Gamble.

References

1. Rantanen J, Kauppinen T, Toikkanen J, Kurppa K, Lehtinen S, Leino T. Work and Health Country Profiles: Country profiles and national surveillance indicators in occupational health and safety. *People and Work: Research report 44.* Helsinki, Finland: Finnish Institute of Occupational Health; 2001.
2. Ilmarinen J. Aging Workers. *Occupational & Environmental Medicine* 2001;**58**:546–552.
3. Malcolm M. A century of alcoholism conferences: unchanging themes. *Alcohol & Alcoholism* 1991;**26**(1):5–15.
4. Ames G. Cultural influences on alcohol policies in the workplace: A historical review. *Alcoholism* 1994;**30**(1–2):75–84.
5. Jacobs J, Zimmer L. Drug treatment and workplace testing: Politics, symbolism and organisational dilemmas. *Behavioural Sciences & the Law* 1991;**9**(3):345–360.
6. Hutcheson G, Henderson M, Davies J. *Alcohol in the Workplace: Costs and Responses.* Sheffield: Department for Education and Employment; 1995.
7. Verstraete A, Pierce A. Workplace drug testing in Europe. *Forensic Science International* 2001;**121**(1–2):2–6.
8. Pierce A, Tormey W, Cahalane O, Chong L. Pre-employment screening for drug use – current experiences in Ireland. *Journal of the Irish Colleges of Physicians and Surgeons* 1998;**27(2)**:91–93.
9. Bruno F. Drug and alcohol problems in the workplace in Italy. *Journal of Drug Issues* 1994;**24**(4):697–713.
10. Smith G, Lipsedge M. Stress, alcohol and drug abuse. In: Cox R, Edwards FC, McCallum RI, editors. *Fitness for Work, the medical aspects.* Oxford: Oxford Medical Publications; 1997. pp. 396–412.
11. Mendelsohn S, Morrison K. Testing applicants for alcohol and drug abuse. *Personnel* 1988;**65**(8):57–60.
12. Kloss DM. Pre-employment Screening and Health Surveillance. In: *Occupational Health Law.* Third edn. Oxford: Blackwell Science; 1998. pp. 89–114.
13. Polcin D. Rethinking confrontation in alcohol and drug treatment: Consideration of the clinical context. *Substance Use and Misuse* 2003;**38**(2):165–184.
14. Lawental E, McLellan A, Grissom G, Brill P, O'Brien C. Coerced treatment for substance abuse problems detected through workplace urine surveillance: Is it effective? *Journal of Substance Abuse* 1996;**8**(1):115–128.
15. Beaumont P, Allsop J. An industrial alcohol policy: The characteristics of worker success. *British Journal of Addiction* 1984;**79**(3):315–318.

16. Chick J. Substance abuse and the workplace. In: Baxter P, Adams P, Aw TC, Cockcroft A, J.M. H, editors. *Hunter's Diseases of Occupations*. 9th edn. London: Arnold; 2000. pp. 557–567.

17. Brooke D. The addicted doctor: Caring professionals. *British Journal of Psychiatry* 1995;**166**(2):149–153.

18. Kendell R. The political dimensions of the problem. In: Ghodse H, Mann S, Johnson P, editors. *Doctors and their Health*. Sutton, Surrey, UK: Reed Healthcare Publishing; 2000. pp. 15–20.

19. Alleyne B, Stuart P, Copes R. Alcohol and other drug use in occupational fatalities. *Journal of Occupational Medicine* 1991;**33**(4):496–500.

20. Hollo C, Leigh J, Nurminen M. The role of alcohol in work-related fatal accidents in Australia 1982-1984. *Occupational Medicine* 1993;**43**(1):13–17.

21. Webb G, Redman S, Hennrikus D, Kelman G, Gibberd R, Sanson-Fisher R. The relationships between high-risk and problem drinking and the occurrence of work injuries and related absences. *Journal of Studies on Alcohol* 1994;**55**(4):434–446.

22. Hoffman J, Larison C. Drug use, workplace accidents and employee turnover. *Journal of Drug Issues* 1999;**29**(2):341–364.

23. Spicer R, Miller T, Smith G. Worker substance use, workplace problems and the risk of occupational injury: a matched case-control study. *Journal of Studies on Alcohol* 2003;**64**(4):570–578.

24. Ames G, Grube J, Moore R. The relationship of drinking and hangovers to workplace problems. *Journal of Studies on Alcohol* 1997;**58**(1):37–47.

25. *Report and Recommendations on Improving Access to Occupational Health Support*. London: Occupational Health Advisory Committee, Health and Safety Commission; 2000.

26. *Guidelines on Testing for Drugs of Abuse in the Workplace*. London: Faculty of Occupational Medicine of the Royal College of Physicians; 1994.

27. All Party Parliamentary Drug Misuse Group. *Drug Testing on Trial*. London: Houses of Parliament; 2003.

28. Sgan S, Hanzlick R. The Medical Review Officer: A potential role for the Medical Examiner. *Am J Forensic Med Pathol* 2003;**24**:346–350.

29. Hartenbaum N, Martin D. Qualifications of Medical Review Officers (MROs) in regulated and nonregulated drug testing. *Journal of Occupational and Environmental Medicine* 2003;**45**(1):102–103.

30. Von Euler M, Villen T, Svensson J-O, Stahle L. Interpretation of the presence of 6-Monoacetylmorphine in the absence of Morphine-3-glucuronide in urine samples: evidence of heroin abuse. *Therapeutic Drug Monitoring* 2003;**25**:645–648.

31. Fraser A, Zamecnik J. Impact of lowering the screening and confirmation cut-off values for urine drug testing based on dilution indicators. *Therapeutic Drug Monitoring* 2003;**25**(6):723–727.

32. Hermansson U, Helander A, Huss A, Brandt L, Ronnberg S. The Alcohol Use Disorders Identification Test (AUDIT) and Carbohydrate-Deficient Transferrin (CDT) in a routine workplace health examination. *Alcohol Clin Exp Res* 2000;**24**(2):180–187.

33. Ames G, Grube J. Alcohol availability and workplace drinking: Mixed method analyses. *Journal of Studies on Alcohol* 1999;**60**(3):383–393.

34. Suff P. Underground testing. *Occupational Health Review* 2003;**104**:15–18.

35. Logan quotes: An evaluation of periodic testing for drug abuse in the oil industry: a comparison of two populations [Dissertation (MFOM)]. London; 2003.

36. Zwerling C, Ryan J, Orav E. The efficacy of preemployment drug screening of marijuana and cocaine in predicting employment outcome. *Journal of the American Medical Association* 1990;**264**(20):2639–2643.

37. Danton K, Misselke L, Bacon R, Done J. Attitudes of young people toward driving after smoking cannabis or after drinking alcohol. *Health Education Journal* 2003;**62**(1):50–60.

38. Kelly T, Foltin R, Emurian C, Fischman M. Performance-based testing for drugs of abuse: Dose and time profiles of marijuana, amphetamine, alcohol and diazepam. *Journal of Analytical Toxicology* 1993;**17**(5):264–272.

39. Reynolds G, Lehman W. Levels of Substance Use and Willingness to Use the Employee Assistance Program. *The Journal of Behavioral Health Services & Research* 2003;**30**(2):238–248.

40. Howland J, Mangione T, Lee M, Bell N, Levine S. Employee attitudes toward work-site alcohol testing. *J Occup Environ Med* 1996;**38**(10):1041–1046.

41. Trinh T, Ilett, P. Most UK employers are open-minded about drug and alcohol testing at work. *Mori Polls & Surveys* 2003. http://www.mori.com/polls/2003/drugscape.shtml

42. Substance Abuse and Mental Health Services Administration (SAMHSA). *Summary of Findings from the 1997 National Household Survey on Drug Abuse*. 1998. www.samhsa.gov.

15 Ethical, Legal and Practical Aspects of Testing

William Cheng and John Henry

Ethics is literally 'the right way of acting or behaving'. It is based on principles which almost all societies consider to be valid. These principles embrace the rights of human beings to respect for their human dignity and this, for example, includes their rights to life, health and bodily integrity. It also includes their right to know the truth, and their right to their property and possessions. At the same time, people also have duties and obligations; rights have their limits often demanding that the rights of others be respected. In the words of an American politician, 'My right to swing my fist stops where your nose begins.' The duties include respect for the autonomy and integrity of the individual, respecting their freedom and privacy, and obtaining informed consent for anything that might breach these. Ethics differs from civil laws, which are drawn up by public consent, and are intended to enable the proper functioning of society. The laws established by a society should take ethical principles into account. Sometimes governments make laws which do not respect the ethical principles that should underlie human behaviour; in some cases an individual may feel bound in conscience to disobey a law that they believe to be unjust.

Drug use and drug testing both have ethical dimensions, and each is also (like virtually all other aspects of human activity) regulated by the laws of the country. There are many arguments – legal and ethical – for and against drug use (or misuse) and drug testing in the work environment. Here we deal with the ethical aspects of drug testing. Many ethical issues lead to a polarisation of opinion which is often based on subjective reactions rather than on a clearly thought out approach which dissects the issues involved and attempts to determine a correct course of action, applying principles of fairness to all parties concerned.

Drug testing in the workplace is certainly an issue that leads to a wide range of opinions. To some extent this depends on the type of workplace involved. Very few people disagree with the concept of testing airline pilots for use of alcohol or illicit substances – nobody wants to fly in a plane whose pilot is drunk or 'stoned'. Similarly, there is now a wide acceptance of drug testing in the police and armed forces, prisons, public transport, nuclear power stations and other particularly sensitive areas. Thus, public safety is a major concern, and any right that an individual may claim to indulge in an intoxicating substance is overridden by the harm to others that might ensue. Here we examine this and other ethical and legal issues surrounding workplace testing for drug use. All organisations must acknowledge the substantial probability that substance abuse and dependency has touched their workforce. The question is not whether to respond to the issue of substance abuse, but rather, what form the response will take. It must be a prudent, well-considered response that properly evaluates the moral, ethical, legal and human resource management ramifications. Perhaps with this chapter we can help employers and managers who are concerned about their liabilities and responsibilities to find common ground with employees and job applicants who strongly defend their right to lead their own lives without undue interference from their employer.

Why should an employer introduce workplace testing?

Numerous factors are thought to motivate the establishment of substance-abuse programmes and initiatives[1, 2, 3]. The following are among the motives frequently cited:

- a concern about the well-being of employees and the promotion of the common good;
- a belief that, in the long run, firms will save money by assisting workers;
- a wish to improve productivity and profitability;
- pressures to comply with legal regulations and mandates;
- concerns about legal liabilities;
- 'public relations' – a desire to promote the corporate image;
- safety and security concerns.

Ethical and practical arguments in favour of testing

In recent years, bodies such as the Institute of Personnel and Development and Alcohol Concern have highlighted the extent of alcohol and drug problems among employees and emphasised their damaging effects, both on the work produced and on the physical well-being of staff. It is claimed that persons who tested positively for drugs and alcohol at the workplace have a higher level of absenteeism, have levels of productivity 10 to 60 per cent lower and are involved in significantly more accidents than non-users. It has been estimated that alcohol misuse alone costs the UK industry up to £2 billion a year. Employees whose performance, behaviour or attendance at work is affected by alcohol or drugs risk being dismissed on the grounds of misconduct or incapability. Let us examine some of the issues involved.

PREVENTION

An argument in favour of drug testing is that it will identify employees with drug and alcohol problems and encourage them to seek assistance before their condition deteriorates. By using the threat of job loss as the 'stick' and assurances of continued employment as the 'carrot', it is believed that drug users will be motivated to seek help rather than be dismissed. Testing programmes can be used to identify employees already using drugs and/or alcohol

---

1   McClellan K; Miller RE; EAPs in transition: purpose and scope of services. *Employee Assistance Quarterly* (Binghampton, New York) 3:3/4:25–42, 1988.
2   Scanlon WF; *Alcoholism and Drug Abuse in the Workplace*. 2nd ed. New York, Praeger, 1991.
3   Spicer J; Owen P; Levine D; *Evaluating Employee Assistance Programmes*. Center City, Minnesota, Hazelden, 1983.

in a way that could threaten their health, in order to facilitate their recovery, and this could be viewed as a preventative measure. By promoting drug-free values and norms, the testing programme will improve the quality of working life through higher employee morale. By demonstrating a commitment to a drug-free work environment, the organisation will foster public trust and improve its corporate image. Workplace drug testing has been considered a tool in reducing substance use and may thus be considered a public health measure.

PRODUCTIVITY

Drug and alcohol misuse can affect the productivity and hence the profitability of an organisation. Drug use can lead to a higher incidence of mistakes and accidents, increased absenteeism, additional workloads for colleagues affecting team morale and employee relations, poorer quality work, adverse effects on the organisation's image and customer relations, loss of workplace harmony and even theft.

Drug screening will generally lead to increased organisational productivity and lower overall costs. Reducing and ultimately eliminating drug use in the workforce should lead to better attendance, with a corresponding increase in productivity and cost savings through retaining experienced workers.

DETERRENCE

Pre-employment screening implies that the organisation is endeavouring to deter substance abuse through selective hiring practices, in effect, a 'deterrence by avoidance' strategy. Deterrence involves retributive discipline as part of an overall eradication programme. The contracts of known abusers are terminated. The knowledge (or fear) of possible detection being followed by dismissal is likely to deter future substance abuse on the part of other, perhaps like-minded, employees. In this context, the non-user is in the same setting to testing as the non-drinking driver who is stopped at a police checkpoint, the honest traveller who has to go through a metal detector in an airport or the honest taxpayer who is audited. The only way to ensure the safety of the entire organisation is to subject everyone to a test without exception, because otherwise the prevention system is liable to failure. Once it is seen within the workforce that an employee is 'getting away with it', colleagues have the choice of denouncing the individual (which is putting an unfair burden on them) or of staying quiet and being disgruntled – and perhaps even covering up for drug-induced absences or errors among their work colleagues.

Ethical and practical arguments opposing testing

Opponents of drug and alcohol testing feel that the goal of ensuring a drug-free and alcohol-free workplace is achieved at too high a social cost and that the testing process constitutes an unwarranted invasion of the privacy of the individual. Many opponents of drug and alcohol testing in the workplace also wish to resist an employer's plans to introduce or implement a policy of workplace testing because they are against it on the grounds of freedom of the individual workers to do what they wish. However, since there are also strong grounds in favour of testing, the arguments put forward are not simply based on libertarian views but also focus on valid technical and practical issues. Many of the points raised serve to demonstrate clearly evident weaknesses in the procedures proposed or implemented, and can ultimately lead to a fairer testing system being introduced.

THE INABILITY TO DEMONSTRATE IMPAIRMENT

A drug screen can detect the presence of drugs or alcohol, but particularly in the case of drugs, it cannot show impairment or allow any inferences to be made about whether the individual is a safety threat[4, 5]. Neither does a positive drug or alcohol test mean that the individual is a chronic user or is drug or alcohol dependent. Urine drug tests are only capable of revealing prior consumption of a substance. This may have occurred while the employee was off duty. Urine drug screening is therefore of limited use because it cannot distinguish between drug use, drug abuse and drug dependency, nor does it reveal how an individual behaves or performs. It is also incapable of proving that any impairment that has been demonstrated was due to a substance found on testing. It merely indicates that the person has used an unknown amount of drugs at some point in the recent past, generally ranging from hours to weeks.

With the exception of alcohol, drug use or presence on testing has not been linked reliably with behavioural impairment. The US National Institute on Drug Abuse acknowledges that positive results of a urine screen cannot be used to prove intoxication or impaired performance[6].

INACCURACY OF DRUG TESTING

The relatively cheap mass screening devices cannot differentiate between certain common cold remedies and drugs of abuse[6] ('false positives'). A pilot study by the National Institute on Drug Abuse (NIDA) reported a false positive rate of between one and two per cent[7]. While this figure seems low, it becomes quite significant in the context of mass urine testing involving thousands of employees. The injustice of taking action against an employee with a testing system that has even a low false-positive rate is clearly apparent. According to accepted statistical theory, the problem of false positives is exacerbated when applied to the testing of randomly selected workers among whom the prevalence of drug use is relatively low.

On the other hand, if testing were limited to individuals for whom there is probable cause to suspect drug impairment, the prevalence of drug use within such a pool, if appropriately selected, would be far greater than that for the general population, and the incidence of false positives would be lower.

All urine drug tests employ cut-off levels below which drug traces will be reported as negative. Cut-offs levels are necessary, firstly because at some point, it becomes increasingly difficult to distinguish between drug metabolites and products endogenously produced by

---

4   Ontario Law Reform Commission; *Report on Drug and Alcohol Testing in the Workplace*. Ottawa, 1992.

5   Beyerstein B; Beyerstein D; Jackson D; *Drug Testing in the Workplace*. Position paper of the British Columbia Civil Liberties Association, 1989.

6   Morgan; Problems of Mass Urine Screening for Misused Drugs, 16J. *Psychoactive Drugs* **305**, 305–317 (1984).

7   Davis; Hawks; Blanke; Assessment of Laboratory Quality in Urine Drug Testing, *JAMA* **260** 1749–1752 (1988).

the body, and secondly to minimise the possibility of detecting, for example, secondary inhalation of cannabis smoke or ingestion of food containing poppy seeds. Therefore, drug testing will also produce 'false negatives' – that is, urine containing traces of drug below a predetermined threshold level that will be reported as negative when they are in fact positive – whether that positive is due to illicit drug use or to some other innocent reason.

LIMITATIONS OF TEST PROCEDURES AND METHODS

Drug and alcohol screening procedures cannot detect causes of worker impairment due to drugs not tested for (such as prescription medications) or non-drug causes (such as fatigue, stress, domestic problems, low morale and organic disease), nor does it address other employment practices (such as extended or rotating shifts, or similar practices which could lead to serious safety problems).

The opponents of drug and alcohol screening argue that it can be counter-productive because too often drug tests are seen by employers as a panacea for perceived workplace safety and productivity problems, to such an extent that they become a substitute for effective performance evaluations and close supervision, and delude employers into false complacency. Focusing energy on drug testing risks diverting attention and resources from more prevalent and serious problems in workplace safety.

UNFAIRNESS OF BLANKET TESTING

Random drug testing on a blanket basis challenges the notion of due process. If testing is seen as a form of search, it would not be a power available to the police under the UK Police and Criminal Evidence Act 1984, without individualised reasonable suspicion. The testing of presumably innocent people is probably justified by the argument that 'if you are innocent then what have you got to fear?' It is the same notion that underpins such apparent violations of personal privacy as identity cards, closed circuit television in public places, DNA testing and other intrusive policy measures. In the 'suspect community', the idea that an individual is innocent until proved guilty has now become a thing of the past.

INVASION OF PRIVACY

In the late nineteenth century, Samuel Warren and Louis Brandeis first articulated the concept of a distinct 'right to privacy', prohibiting unreasonable intrusions into the lives of private individuals. This protection extends beyond the tangible, physical intrusions traditionally prohibited. It does not cause damage to an individual's relations with the community; rather, the damage is personal or spiritual in nature and may have no material consequences. The common law secures to each individual the right of determining, ordinarily, to what extent their thoughts, sentiments and emotions shall be communicated to others. It is concerned with protecting both the sanctity of an individual's private space (security) and preserving their ability to control the communication of private information about themself to others (similar to the Fourth Amendment in the US Constitution). Loss of control over what information is disclosed, and to whom, threatens the psychological integrity of the individual.

The provision of a urine sample for analysis is basically a 'search' of an individual that, conducted without consent, would be considered an assault or trespass. The process thus constitutes an unwarranted invasion of privacy. It can be argued that requiring an employee either to submit to a urinalysis or to be disciplined with a threat of dismissal infringes on civil liberties[5]. An employee who is to be tested may be required to urinate while being observed in order to ensure the origin of the sample and to prevent tampering with or replacement of the sample. Opponents of drug testing argue, and proponents admit, that this is a highly intrusive and potentially degrading and embarrassing procedure, no matter how courteously and clinically conducted[8, 9].

Drug and alcohol screening invades six distinct privacy domains:

- The testing process cannot show whether employees are impaired in their ability to perform their contracted duties, which is all that the employer is justified in knowing.
- To prevent sample tampering, urine collection needs to be witnessed, which generally involves exposure of the human anatomy.
- Body fluid is taken by an employer's representative, not by one's own physician.
- The compelled disclosure of intimate medical information (to prevent misdiagnosis by the laboratory), by revealing all medications taken recently and thereby giving clues to the nature of any underlying medical conditions (which the employer in general has no right to know).
- Drug screening is tantamount to surveillance of off-the-job conduct, since when using sensitive testing methods the inhalation of cannabis can produce a positive urine test for a month or more, while cocaine metabolites may be excreted for several days. In each case, these tests will remain positive long after any psychoactive effect has worn off. Also, it is frequently argued that the passive inhalation of cannabis smoke can produce a positive urine test result. However, in practice, the cut-offs are set to exclude passive consumption and previous use going back more than 24–48 hours (unless it has been very heavy).
- There is a possibility of unwanted disclosure or dissemination of test results, due to inadequate safeguards of confidentiality.

At issue in the dispute over drug testing is nothing less than whether workers may be subjected to 'police state' tactics in the workplace, whereby their bodies may be seized and ransacked through the compelled extraction and analysis of body fluids in order to determine not on-the-job impairment or drug use, but prior exposure to drugs which could have occurred days or weeks before the test, while the worker was off duty[10].

Privacy advocates acknowledge that employers have a right to protect their property, but contend that '...since the values, needs and intelligence of people do not change when they enter the workplace, there is no reason why the rights and responsibilities they enjoy as citizens should be withheld from them in their role as workers'[11]. However, it can also be

---

8   Coombs CJ; RH Coombs; The impact of drug testing on the morale and wellbeing of mandatory participants. *International Journal of the Addictions* (New York) **26(9)**981–992, 1991.

9   Heshizer B; Muczyk J; Drug testing at the workplace: balancing individual, organisational and societal rights. *Labour Law Journal* (Chicago) **39**:342–357, 1988.

10   Chen E; Kim P; True J; Common law privacy: a limit on an employer's power to test for drugs. *George Mason University Law Review* (Arlington, Virginia), **12:4**, 1990.

11   Information and Privacy Commissioner of Ontario. *Workplace Privacy, A Consultation Paper.* Toronto, 1992.

argued that the responsibility of a private individual walking along a public road to remain free of intoxicating substances is markedly different from that of a crane driver on a building site.

IMPLICATIONS RELATING TO DISCRIMINATION IN THE WORKPLACE

The issues of fairness and discrimination relate to society as a whole and to the individual being tested. For society, the question is whether it is right to refuse or dismiss a person who tested positive to a drug or alcohol without offering them the opportunity of being counselled or helped[5]. For the individual, a positive test creates a perception of being a 'problem employee', even though positive tests do not establish the existence of dependency. If an organisation is determined to engage in pre-employment testing, then perhaps a more equitable approach would be to have a policy where screening occurs only after an employment offer is made, and to provide for counselling and rehabilitation, as opposed to simply not hiring the person who tests positive[12].

Workplace testing may be used as a subtle form of discrimination to intimidate employees. In the absence of an objective, an appropriate definition of what constitutes evidence of impairment or of the criteria used to decide who to test and under what circumstances to test, workers may be tested arbitrarily or maliciously, for example, due to their involvement in union activity or in disclosing workplace safety problems. Written policies about testing should be promulgated prior to implementing testing programmes, and should be applied uniformly and consistently to all employees.

Discrimination on the grounds of sex, national origin, disability, age and so on is prohibited in many jurisdictions. To establish a violation of the Act, a discriminatory purpose need not be proved. It is conceivable that a policy of mandatory drug testing might be used as a tool to facilitate the utilisation of discriminatory practices, however illegal, depending upon the penalties adopted by a specific organisation in the event that a positive result has been obtained or that a person has refused to be tested.

Random drug screening might not be applied in a 'random' manner if the goal is to discriminate surreptitiously. Selective use of drug testing procedures could be used to deny or terminate employment of, for instance, persons of a certain race or national origin, or persons of a certain age group, if the penalty for drug use is dismissal from or denial of employment. Adverse impact discrimination is the application of prima facie neutral policies or practices that have 'an adverse effect on minority group members as compared to majority group members'[13]. Research has shown that most consumers of illicit drugs are in the 18 to 29 age group. Drug testing could thus have an adverse effect on persons in that age group, such as termination of employment or non-recruitment of a significant proportion of persons in that age group.

As a result of workplace testing, employees and applicants who do not have drug or alcohol problems testing may be mistakenly identified as substance abusers. To guard against inaccuracies resulting from systematic errors, it is essential that all initial positive screening tests be confirmed by an independent test based upon a different analytical principle – for example, conclusive identification of a drug by gas chromatography-mass spectrometry (GC-MS). False positives can be avoided by limiting testing to situations where

---

12   Toronto-Dominion Bank; *Alcoholism and Substance Abuse Policy*. Toronto, 1990.
13   Petney W; *Discrimination and the Law*. Toronto, Richard de Boo Publishers, 1990.

there is independent evidence suggesting impairment, allowing individuals who test positive an opportunity to explain or dispute positive tests, and informing applicants in advance about testing. Advance notice of the testing programme, including information about substances that can be detected and warning that some substances are detectable for prolonged periods after use, provides a safeguard for applicants who do not have substance-abuse problems, while detecting applicants who are dependent on alcohol or drugs or who are unable to refrain from use.

Workplace testing may detect medically prescribed drug use unrelated to an employee's job performance and thereby lead to discrimination against employees with medical problems. Laboratories should be instructed to test only for alcohol and specified drugs. Results of testing should be reported only to an independent physician. It would be the responsibility of the physician to discuss positive tests with the individual tested and to determine whether use of a drug was prescribed by a physician for a medical condition and whether drug use or the medical condition could interfere with the ability of the individual to perform the job safely. Only after making such a determination would the physician notify the employer that the individual did or did not meet the medical standards for the job (in the case of applicants) or was or was not likely to have been impaired by the detected substance (in the case of employee testing).

Although drug testing samples are only supposed to be used to test for the presence of illegal substances, they might also be used to test for pregnancy, thus leading to potential discrimination against women employees. The presence of medication to combat diseases and disabilities, including AIDS, if so desired by an employer for some reason, might also be discovered during the testing procedures. The result could be employment decisions that discriminate against the persons being tested. However, such an unwarranted violation of the agreed grounds for testing is clearly unethical, since it involves dishonesty, and (although no such case has yet occurred) would be likely to lead to a successful challenge in the courts.

Potential problems resulting from workplace testing

The arguments given against workplace testing for alcohol and drugs mean that employers need to be aware of the difficulties presented and need to address them in an open and fair fashion. Workplace testing may lead to abandonment of more effective and less problematic approaches – for example, investigation to determine whether other factors may have led to an accident occurring at work. Regardless of whether or not the employee was impaired, safety hazards in the workplace may have contributed to the accident. Another bias that needs to be addressed is that workplace drug testing programmes may concentrate on illicit drugs and divert attention from alcohol abuse, the latter being the most abused substance at work causing impaired safety.

There is a possible danger that workplace testing programmes may result in the creation of a pool of unemployable individuals. Although facilitating treatment of impaired individuals is (or should be) a major motivation of workplace testing programmes, workplace testing may lead to a loss of employment or rejection of applicants rather than support and treatment. If the individuals who test positive do not receive treatment or if their early failure to pass the urine test creates a record that prevents subsequent employment, one positive test may lead to permanent unemployment. In order to prevent this unwanted consequence, employers who decided to use workplace testing have an obligation to inform employees or applicants who test positive about the existence of treatment facilities in the community. Test results should be treated with the utmost confidentiality, and disclosure of test results to individuals outside the testing business should be avoided. Finally, in order to avoid making individuals who have occasionally tested positive permanent outcasts, employers should allow these individuals to return to work or reapply without prejudice after a defined period of time or after the completion of a course of treatment.

Consent and confidentiality

Any constraint on individual freedom must be justifiable and must also be imposed with the consent of those involved. Potential employees need to be told that the company operates a testing policy at least before they are appointed to a post, and the procedures need to be made clear in advance. In this way, they are giving consent to the stated policy once they accept their appointment.

Drug or alcohol testing involves an invasion of privacy and requires that any results be subject to strict confidentiality. This imposes a burden on those involved in recording or assessing results, and anyone who may have access to them. Any breach of this confidentiality should be met by the appropriate sanctions within the company.

Differences between drug and alcohol testing

The results of breath, urine or blood tests used to detect alcohol impairment are accepted at face value, whereas a positive drug urinalysis screen requires a second confirmatory test. This is largely a matter of the long time that alcohol tests have been available, but it also reflects the difference between tests on drivers leading to a fine or an endorsement, while workplace drug tests may lead to the end of an individual's career. A breath sample can accurately record alcohol consumption as well as providing a generally accepted measure of the likely degree of impairment[4]. The literature is full of controversy contesting the accuracy of drug urinalysis tests[5, 14, 15].

The legal nature of alcohol consumption and the social acceptance of alcohol distinguish it from drug testing. A large part of the difference lies in the illegality and 'morality' aspects of drug consumption or possession. Alcohol is a legally permitted substance, and so policy makers are not concerned about its presence; the issue is how much the person tested is above an established threshold impairment level.

A positive urine drug test result may reflect off-duty use that may indicate previous abuse with no current impairment of function, but it may also be that the employee's work performance is impaired at the time of the test, and the amount of drug in the body may be sufficient to render the employee dysfunctional. Unlike the breathalyser test for alcohol, urine drug tests are incapable of measuring the level of drugs currently in the employee's

---

14 Sonnenstuhl W. et al.; Employee assistance and drug testing: fairness and injustice in the workplace. *Nova Law Review* (Fort Lauderdale, Florida) **11(3)**:709–731, 1987.

15 Privacy Commissioner of Canada; *Drug Testing and Privacy*. Ottawa, Supply & Services Canada, pp.1-78, 1990.

bloodstream. For example, there is no scientific proof that marijuana or cocaine continue to impair beyond twenty-four hours after their use, yet the former may produce a positive test up to three days after consumption, and much longer than this if a sensitive test with a low cut-off is used.

Issues relating to testing during employment

Testing during the course of an individual's employment has a number of differences to testing employees before they commence employment, and requires special approaches. The main issue revolves around the need to demonstrate 'due diligence' concerning drug and alcohol testing, so that the employer is seen to be using methods which are fair and just, and the employees are satisfied that they are being decently and justly treated.

DUTY TO INVOLVE EMPLOYEES IN THE PROCESS

If in-employment (as opposed to pre-employment) screening is being considered, the employer needs to secure the agreement of the workforce to a specific testing policy, otherwise the organisation may face practical difficulties, for example with employees refusing to provide specimens, and disciplinary action taken in such circumstances would run the risk of unfairness. The most effective way to gain workplace support for a testing policy would be to involve a committee of employee representatives in devising the policy.

Individual disciplinary rules rarely form part of employees' contracts of employment. As Lord Justice Roskill put it in Secretary of State for Employment v ASLEF and others (No. 2), 'Rules are usually merely instructions given by the employer in accordance with its general legal right to give reasonable instructions to its employees.' In Dryden[16], the UK Employment Appeal Tribunal (EAT) emphasised that 'an employer is entitled to make rules for the conduct of employees in their place of work, as he is entitled to give lawful orders, within the scope of the contract'. Even where the disciplinary rules are expressly incorporated into the contract of employment, there is likely to be some provision for the rules to be changed unilaterally by the employer from time to time. It will therefore usually be possible to put any changes to the disciplinary rules into effect without the need for the employees' consent. The changes will need to be brought to the employees' attention, however, not only to ensure that they affect the employees' behaviour, but also to avoid accusations and findings in court of unfair dismissal[17, 18].

Where contractual changes are regarded as necessary, the employer will be able to bring them into effect immediately for new recruits. On the other hand, new terms can be introduced for existing employees only if they give consent, either individually or as a body. If consent is not forthcoming, the only lawful way of introducing new terms is for the employer to dismiss, with the appropriate length of notice, and offer its employees new contracts on the revised terms. An employer that takes this path must act reasonably if it is to avoid findings of unfair dismissal. It must, for example, inform and consult with employees on the need for the new terms and make clear that a failure to consent to them will result in dismissal. Employers may argue that bargaining with employees over the right to test for drug and alcohol is not mandatory, because it is a means of ensuring a safe working environment. Even though this may be true, an employer (in the United States legal system) may only act unilaterally where the parties do not agree after good faith bargaining[19]. Arbitrators have upheld testing where it was based simply on a rule which was imposed unilaterally[20].

REASONABLE SUSPICION

In some workplaces, testing is carried out on suspicion of intoxication, or following an incident that may have been caused by intoxication. In Terry[21], the US Supreme Court reduced the minimum standard for a reasonable search from 'probable cause' to 'reasonable suspicion'. In Jones v McKenzie[22], the appellee challenged a mandatory drug testing programme initiated by the District of Columbia School System for employees in its Transportation Branch. The court applied the balancing test and concluded that such a test, administered by a school system, is not unreasonable where:

• the purpose is to ensure the physical safety of young school children;
• the testing is conducted as part of a routine medical examination;
• the test has a nexus to the employer's legitimate concern about safety.

A policy based on 'reasonable suspicion' is fundamentally deficient, because it leaves the selection of employees for drug and alcohol screening to the 'unbridled discretion' of their supervisors[23]. It vests in medically unqualified lay persons, who are susceptible to overt or subconscious bias, the unchecked power to determine who will be tested and when. The employee has a right to assurances that urine testing for drugs or alcohol does not become a new management tool to deal with inadequate performance that could be due to fatigue, stress or overwork.

The US Arbitrator in Springfield Mass Transit District upheld a rule permitting the employer to administer random breathalyser tests to a bus driver who was known to abuse alcohol. The arbitrator refused to limit testing to times that the employee was suspected of being intoxicated, emphasising that the public interest in safety outweighed the individual's interest in concealing information about drug or alcohol abuse.

To eliminate alcohol and drug use at the racetrack, the US Racing Commission had implemented regulations authorising the use of daily breath and random urine tests on jockeys, trainers, officials and grooms. This was challenged by the jockeys (Shoemaker v Handel[24]) but failed. The court stated that the government has a legitimate purpose by providing statistical evidence of drug and alcohol use by jockeys to indicate that there is a high probability that testing would uncover or deter such use and that the intrusion into privacy is reasonable due to the potential for accidents caused by drug and alcohol use to

19   NLRB v American National Ins. Co., 343 US 395, 401-04 (1952).
20   Alameda-Contra Costa Transit Dist., 80-1 Lab. Arb. Awards (CCH) 3264, 3265, 3275 (1979)
       (Randall, Arb.).
21   Terry v Ohio, 392 US 1 (1968).
22   Jones v McKenzie, 833 F.2d 335, 338 (D.C. Cir. 1987).
23   Delware v Prouse, 440 US 648, 661 (1979).
24   Shoemaker v Handel 619 F. Supp. 1089 (D.N.J. 1985).

occur at a racetrack. It was justified by the licensing requirement and also by the need to protect the public from organised crime. It was emphasised that a jockey has a lower expectation of privacy, due to the notoriety and public attention attributed to being a sports personality.

NOTICE

An employer is required to notify employees of the criteria that are used to establish a drug or alcohol violation. In one well-publicised case, the US arbitrator refused to permit the dismissal of an employee for positive breathalyser results where the employer had not set any standards to determine whether the employees were intoxicated[25].

TESTING PROCEDURES

The procedures must comply with reasonable and specific standards (for example, conducted properly by trained personnel) for implementation. Failing to meet these requirements may constitute an unreasonable search and seizure[24]. Random testing has been extremely successful in reducing the number of workplace accidents. Signs of drug use are often very difficult to detect because no single physical symptom provides definitive evidence that an individual is abusing drugs. Ironically, courts generally have permitted testing without suspicion of drug and alcohol use after an accident has occurred. The value of random testing is that it is pre-emptive – it has the ability to uncover a problem before it becomes serious enough to impair an employee's performance, while at the same time, employees who do not use any substances should have nothing to fear from any testing carried out.

EQUAL IMPLEMENTATION AND EQUAL PROTECTION

Employers who fail to implement uniform practice may open themselves to charges of discrimination. Any testing policy has to be applied consistently to all employees[24]. Managers, sales staff, office workers and shop floor operatives within a large organisation all need to be exposed to the same level playing field. However, a similar organisation may operate a markedly different policy applying to its workforce: this is not a matter of an uneven playing field but of different playing fields.

Accuracy of testing and accusations of unfair dismissal

A major problem with drug screening is the issue of accuracy – an employee could be dismissed following a false-positive test result (leading to a stigma of drug-related reasons for dismissal) and the employer faces the possibility of unfair dismissal claims. Where rules exist which prohibit the use of drugs at work, the dismissal of an employee for drug-related offences will invariably be fair. However, even in the absence of such rules, testing of the case in the courts will usually result in a declaration that the dismissal was fair. Employees are expected to realise that drug-influenced behaviour leading to criminal conduct is

---

25   Northrop Worldwide Services, Inc., 64 Lab. Arb. (BNA) 742, 749 (1975) (Goodstein, Arb.).

forbidden[26]. Nevertheless, as with alcohol and misconduct dismissals, employers will be expected to carry out a proper and accurate investigation.

Employers must provide employees with an opportunity to challenge the results of a drug and alcohol test[24]. The employer is required to preserve a breath, blood or urine sample to allow independent testing by the accused employee[20, 27]. The employer must not violate any of the employees' common-law rights based on contract or tort. Wrongful dismissal or discharging an employee for using sick leave to receive drug or alcohol rehabilitation treatment is actionable.

In order to avoid a finding of unfair dismissal, an employer must show that there was a reason for dismissal which fell within one of the categories listed in Section 98 of the UK Employment Rights Act 1996 (ERA). These categories include:

- the employee's capability or qualifications;
- the employee's conduct;
- the fact that the continued employment of the employee would have involved a contravention of some statutory duty or restriction;
- 'some other substantial reason of a kind such as to justify the dismissal of an employee holding the position which the employee held'.

IDENTIFYING THE ISSUE

Employers have traditionally regarded the consumption of intoxicating drugs as an act of misconduct, to be dealt with under disciplinary procedures like any other misbehaviour in the workplace. However, there is a clear distinction to be made between those employees who use illicit drugs on an occasional basis, where disturbed conduct is the issue, and those who take drugs for some underlying medical reason such as drug dependency or depression, where the employee's capability may be the problem (rather than an effect of the drugs), as in other cases of ill-health. There is an increasing trend towards treating long-term alcoholism and, to a lesser extent, dependence on illegal drugs as serious illnesses which are therefore covered by the organisation's sickness policy.

Many employers have adopted specific policies for dealing with alcohol- and drug-related problems at work, including permitting time off for medical treatment. ACAS, in their advisory handbook 'Discipline at Work', suggests that employers should consider introducing measures to help employees who are suffering from the effects of alcohol or drug abuse. The Employment Appeal Tribunal's (EAT) unfair dismissal decision in Strathclyde Regional Council[28] is generally taken as establishing that misconduct or poor performance caused by alcoholism should be treated as an illness and that the employers should have obtained independent medical advice. If an employee fails to undergo treatment, dismissal may be fair[29, 30]. Although the company's alcohol policy was sympathetic, employees had no contractual right to insist that it was applied. The employer was not obliged to follow its alcohol policy in all cases. In some cases, the nature of the

---

26   Anderson v Oak Motor Works Ltd. (1982).
27   Banks v Federal Aviation Administration, 687 F.2d 92, 93 (5th Cir. 1982).
28   Strathclyde Regional Council v Syme EAT 233/79.
29   Carter v Plevshire Ltd.COIT 1190/108.
30   McDowall v Seaforth Maritime Ltd 22.8.86 (S) EAT 458/86.

employee's job (for example safety-sensitive) and the danger of relapse may make dismissal a reasonable response[31].

Tribunals have recognised that employers can reach the point where they are entitled to say that 'enough is enough'[32]. In London Borough of Tower Hamlets v Bull[33], the EAT stressed that, whilst ordinary principles of fairness require an employer to investigate an employee's medical condition in most cases before dismissal on grounds of ill-health, there is no absolute obligation for an employer to consult the employee's general practitioner. Case law has shown that the procedure which tribunals consider a reasonable employer would adopt in cases of misconduct is quite different to that which they expect to see applied in ill-health cases.

Consulting the employee is important in ill-health cases[34]. An employee who has a drug-related illness may reveal that he or she has been using drugs in response to pressures stemming from the work environment. The employer may have contributed by providing inadequate training, support or supervision for the employee. Responsible employers should take reasonable steps to try to remedy the position before considering dismissal. The possibility of alternative employment[35] should be considered, if practicable. Drinking or drug taking, either on or off duty, may be a potentially fair reason for dismissal under Section 57(2) of Employment Protection (Consolidated) Act, on grounds of either capability or conduct.

It is clear from the decisions in Morse v Wiltshire County Council (CSR Vol 22, p11) and Clark[36] (CSR Vol 22, p.27) that an employer's duty to make reasonable adjustments in cases of disability applies equally to dismissals.

Among the factors considered by arbitrators in deciding such cases are:

- the clarity of the employer's rules;
- the consistency of rule enforcement[37];
- the type of industry (for example danger to public or co-workers);
- any history of prior warnings;
- whether the employer carried out an adequate investigation or not;
- the employee's length of employment and work history;
- any other mitigating circumstances that may exist.

MITIGATING CIRCUMSTANCES/FACTORS

Employers should investigate any mitigating circumstances put forward by employees in the event of alcohol- or drug-related misconduct. In Chamberlain Vinyl Products Ltd[38], the employee was suffering from recurrent depression and was on medication. The EAT has also criticised an employer for failing to investigate the matters raised in mitigation[39]. In a case

---

31   Welch v British Railways Board – Scotrail EAT 668/92.
32   Evans v Bass North Ltd EAT 715/86.
33   London Borough of Tower Hamlets v Bull EAT 153/91.
34   East Lindsey District Council v Daubney [1977] IRLR 181.
35   P v Nottinghamshire County Council [1992] IRLR 362.
36   Clark v TDG Ltd (trading as Novacold) [1995] 25th March 1999, per Mummery LJ at page 2, D and F of transcript.
37   Paul v East Surrey District Health Authority 1995 IRLR 305.
38   Chamberlain Vinyl Products Ltd v Patel EAT 796/94.
39   Craggie and Eilliamson v Weetabix Ltd COIT 2068/104.

involving Thorn Security Ltd[40], the tribunal took into account an employee's working conditions as a relevant factor. In this case, it was found that he would have been unfit for duty even if he had been sober, because of the long hours he was required to work. EAT upheld the tribunal's finding of unfair dismissal.

POSSESSION OF ALCOHOL AND DRUGS AT WORK

There may be an absolute prohibition on the possession of alcohol or drugs where safety considerations are paramount. Where workplaces (for example distillers) afford easy access to alcohol and drugs, such rules should not be applied rigidly[41]. In this case, the EAT upheld the tribunal's decision that the dismissal was unfair because the breach was trivial. If an employee is in possession of soft drugs on company premises and there is no specific rule, dismissal may not be a reasonable response[42]. The tribunal decided that the dismissal was unfair because the employee was not distributing or smoking the cannabis at work and off-duty use did not affect the performance of her job. If the employee had been caught in possession of a hard drug, the dismissal might well have been held to be fair.

DRINK-DRIVING CONVICTIONS

A driving ban is a potentially fair reason for dismissal under Section 98(2)(d) of the ERA and under Section 57(2)(d) EP(C) Act, which covers the situation in which a banned employee cannot continue their job without contravention of 'a duty or restriction imposed by or under an enactment'. The dismissal of an employee in this situation may, nevertheless, be unfair in some circumstances, if it is possible for them to continue to carry out the work despite the driving disqualification – for example, if driving only formed a small part of their job and could have been covered by fellow employees[43]; or if they could continue to carry out their duties by arranging someone to drive them (on occasion using public transport)[44]. Where a dismissal in these circumstances is found to be unfair, compensation is likely to be reduced to reflect the employee's contributory conduct[45, 46]. In the case of Watts[18], dismissal was unfair because there had been earlier instances where the employer had not dismissed senior employees for a driving ban. The alternative arrangements (travel by public transport) suggested by the disqualified employee in John Liddington Ltd[47] were not sufficient to make it viable to retain him as an employee. The industrial tribunal upheld that his dismissal was unfair, but this was reversed by the EAT on the basis that the employer is entitled to take account of the commercial impact and had acted reasonably in all the circumstances.

CONCEALING DRUG DEPENDENCY ON RECRUITMENT

People with a drug problem may be tempted to conceal their condition when applying for

---

40   Thorn Security Ltd v Agyei EAT 50/92.
41   Scottish Grain Distillers Ltd v McNee EAT 34/82.
42   Moyes v Payless DIY Ltd COIT 1712/242.
43   Toase v Milk Marketing Board COIT 1165/7.
44   Stone v Polygon Retailing Ltd COIT Case No. 28367/94.
45   Nairne v Highland & Islands Fire Brigade 1989 IRLR 366.
46   Summers v Marshall of Cambridge Aerospace Ltd COIT 2977/164.
47   John Liddington Ltd v Blackett 14.6.94 EAT 504/92.

a job. If the employer subsequently discovers the employee's condition, it may consider dismissing the employee. In O'Brien[48], the EAT accepted that it may be fair to dismiss an employee who has a medical condition which they concealed from the employer at the time of recruitment, and which the employer reasonably believes makes the employee unsuitable for the job which they hold because the employee's condition poses a risk to health and safety or affects their ability to do the job. A job applicant is under no obligation to disclose any criminal conviction for a drug-related offence if the conviction is 'spent' under the terms of the Rehabilitation of Offenders Act 1974. In Walton[49], the industrial tribunal decided that the dismissal was fair because the employee deliberately concealed his drug addiction at the time of recruitment; and secondly, the employer's decision that it could not employ a drug addict was a reasonable one. This was upheld by the EAT.

GROUP DISMISSALS

Where a number of employees are suspected of drinking or taking drugs on the employer's premises but it is not possible to identify the individual perpetrators, the employer may in certain circumstances be justified in dismissing each member of the group. The criteria governing such dismissals are set out in Parr[50]. In Evans[51], the EAT upheld the tribunal's finding that the dismissals were fair, stressing that it was inevitable in a group dismissal case that innocent employees might lose their jobs.

OFF-DUTY DRUG-RELATED CONDUCT

Another frequent issue is whether, and under what circumstances, employees may be disciplined for drug-related conduct occurring away from company premises while employees are on their own time. It is a widely accepted principle of arbitral law that what employees do on their own time is their own business and is not an appropriate subject of disciplinary action, unless the conduct could reasonably be said to:

- affect the company's business, reputation[52] or product;
- render the employee unable to perform properly the duties of the job;
- affect other employees' morale or willingness to work with the employee[53] (for example conviction for a drug-related offence might undermine the relationship of trust and confidence[54]).

The ACAS Code of Practice on disciplinary procedures states that criminal offences committed away from the workplace should not be treated as automatic reasons for dismissal. Some arbitrators have recognised that off-duty drug-related conduct, especially

---

48   O'Brien v Prudential Assurance Co Ltd [1979] IRLR 140.
49   Walton v TAC Construction Materials Ltd [1981] IRLR 357.
50   Parr v Whitbread PLC t/a Threshers Wine Merchants 1990 IRLR 39.
51   Evans and others v Dista Products Ltd EAT 1227/94.
52   H B Taylor v McArdle EAT 573/84.
53   Mathewson v RB Wilson Dental Laboratory Ltd [1988] IRLR 512
     Sandhu v British Airways PLC COIT 2948/193
     Stuart-Hutcheson v Brent Walker Group PLC 15.2.94 EAT 303/93
     Thomson v Alloa Manor Co Ltd [1983] IRLR 403.
54   Booth v Southampton Airport Ltd COIT 1276/230.

where selling is involved, may justify disciplinary action[55]. Usually, however, an employee's arrest or conviction for off-duty possession or use of drugs has not been considered just cause for dismissal. The employer should consider whether the offence renders the individual unsuitable for the type of work they carry out or unacceptable to other employees.

It is unlikely that any dismissal in such circumstances will be fair, unless:

- the employee is involved in a critical role in a safety-sensitive industry;
- vulnerable groups may be affected by the employee and a responsible attitude towards the misuse of drugs is essential (such as in healthcare or education);
- the employee has, through their actions, brought the employer's name into disrepute;
- other employees refuse to work with that individual.

Wanting to protect the privacy of off-duty employees, an arbitrator in Weirton Steel Division[56] refused to permit an employer to dismiss three steelworkers although drug tests showed traces of cannabis and cocaine in the employees' urine. The US arbitrator recognised that urine tests may provide a positive reading long after use, and the employees claimed that they had used the drugs while off duty. Because the employer had not observed any adverse physical or mental effects on the employees' job performance, the arbitrator declined to find that the positive test results established that the employees were under the influence.

In Texas Utilities Generating Co.[57], a company security officer found a cannabis cigarette in an employee's car. Although the employee was driving on company property, he was not driving as an employee nor during working hours. The US arbitrator ruled that the employee had no obligation to submit to a drug test and the employer had no right to test if the employee smoked cannabis away from the company property on his own time.

In City of Palm Bay v Bauman[58], a Florida District Court of Appeals held that Palm Bay could require police officers and fire-fighters to undergo testing when it appeared that they had been using drugs or alcohol, whether such use was on or off the job. Medical evidence shows that drug use has long-term mental, physical and psychological effects. The Court emphasised that police and fire-fighters must be unimpaired to ensure the safety of the general public, as well as the employees themselves. Testing these employees for off-duty use would not be an impermissible invasion of privacy. Where an employee performs a job that affects public safety, the employer may be able to prohibit off-duty drug and alcohol use.

The fact that the employee may have consumed the drugs during off-duty hours does not matter; what is important is that the drug is still present in the body, the active ingredient of the drug could inhibit the employee's ability to perform safely. Justification comes from the assertion that impairment is not always physically evident. Flight simulator studies have demonstrated that pilots who inhaled cannabis 24 hours previously, and who otherwise were well rested, still deviated significantly from the runway in landing tests[59].

---

55   Martin-Marietta Aerospace, Baltimore Div., 81 Lab. Arb. 695 (1983) (Aronin Arb.)
      Group W Cable, Inc., 80 Lab Arb. 205 (1983) (Chandler, Arb.)
56   Weirton Steel Division 81-1 Lab. Arb. Awards (CCH) 3931, 3933-34 (1981) (Kates, Arb.)
57   Texas Utilities Generating Co., 84-1 Lab. Arb. Awards (CCH) 3112, 3117 (1983) (Edes, Arb.)
58   City of Palm Bay v Bauman 475 So. 2d 1322 (Fla Dist. Ct. App. 1985).
59   Bensinger PB; Drug testing in the workplace. *American Academy of Political and Social Science Annals*; **Vol. 498**. Beverley Hills, California, Sage Publications, 1988.

There is a need for standards of behaviour that limit the privacy of employees such as airline pilots, train drivers, truck drivers and construction workers, by constraining their freedom because they could cause risk to others. This clearly is a more serious and more important issue than reduced productivity of an individual worker because of drug- or alcohol-related impairment.

Proposed course of action for employers

Drug and alcohol screening of employees is not as common in the UK as it is in the US, where legislative developments in the 1980s led to the widespread implementation of screening programmes by employers. In recent years, following the Transport and Works Act 1992, some UK companies (such as British Rail and London Underground) have introduced drug and alcohol screening in the workplace.

Employees have individual rights and civil liberties, including rights to privacy and confidentiality. The balance is going to shift depending upon the individual work and the nature of the particular job. In safety-sensitive areas where there is significant risk either to co-workers or the public, the balance shifts toward a more aggressive approach by the employer.

The large majority of workers who are not drug users seem to support the prospect of ridding their working lives of the influence of the drug culture and by and large seem willing to sacrifice a certain degree of personal privacy to achieve this goal. Unions seem to be recognising that it is consistent with a commitment to fair representation to recognise that drug use among members cannot be condoned and they do support the use of fair and reasonable detection methods.

The UK Health and Safety Executive (HSE) Guidance suggests that a model policy should cover the following:

- why and to whom it is being applied;
- what constitutes drug and alcohol misuse;
- the date that testing will commence;
- the drugs to be tested for;
- how employees are expected to behave;
- reassurance for employees;
- that absence for treatment will be regarded as normal sickness;
- that drug and alcohol problems will be treated in strict confidence;
- that help is available, and encouragement will be given to seek it voluntarily;
- information about the effects of alcohol and drugs;
- the disciplinary action that will be taken if the result is positive;
- what constitutes gross misconduct.

CONSIDERATIONS IN DEVELOPING A DRUG AND ALCOHOL TESTING PROGRAMME

The organisation wishing to introduce a drug or alcohol testing policy will need to address a number of issues from the start. These include:

- when to test (pre-employment, testing on suspicion, random testing);
- who to test (to cover the fairness and non-discrimination issue);
- what to test (dealing with the invasiveness and impairment issues);
- where to test (to establish credibility);
- how to test (the reliability issue).

In assessing whether or not a proposed testing procedure is reasonable and should be implemented, the following questions are relevant:

- Is there clear and demonstrable evidence that drug and alcohol use is a problem at the workplace?
- Is there a significant issue of public safety?
- Does the testing programme minimise the infringement of employee privacy rights?
- Are no other less intrusive functional tests available that would determine the ability to perform essential duties?
- Is testing being uniformly applied to the workforce?
- Are tests administered by qualified medical personnel?
- Has employee consent been requested? (However, failure to consent to such testing, assuming that the testing is legally justifiable, may be a cause for employee discipline.)
- Will drug and alcohol screening determine the ability to carry out the essential requirements of the work?
- Are samples sent to accredited independent laboratories for analysis?
- Do the procedures adopted ensure or seek to maximise test reliability? Drug tests are estimated to be at least 98 per cent accurate, and, if confirmed by follow-up tests, the results are considered virtually 100 per cent accurate.
- Does the testing regime minimise or eliminate the hazard of sample tampering ('chain of custody')?
- Are those employees that tested positive to drug and alcohol being 'accommodated'?
- Is there an employee assistance programme?

SCHOOLS – A SPECIAL CASE?

There is evidence, particularly from the US, that random drug testing of pupils leads to a marked reduction in drug misuse and an improvement in academic performance within a school. It can also support pupils by reducing peer pressure to use drugs. However, people attending schools are minors. Any procedure imposed on young people should normally be carried out only with the consent (explicit or implicit) of their parents. If a school wishes to introduce a testing procedure on its pupils, it should ensure that all parents are informed and their consent is obtained. Once a procedure is in place, the parents of potential pupils can decide whether they wish their children to attend such an institution.

Conclusion

The goals of workplace strategies to reduce and prevent substance use-related difficulties are multiple and complex, and the different groups involved tend to have different standards by which they judge the value of any alcohol and drug abuse management strategy. For example, although interests will overlap, government representatives may be most concerned about how workplace testing programmes affect the overall drug use in the community. Management personnel may be more interested in reduced costs and increased productivity. Worker groups may place relatively greater emphasis on the protection of worker rights, guarantees of confidentiality and assurances of workplace safety.

While the legal, moral and ethical issues are the same, no single country has a universally applicable approach to drug and alcohol testing. One must attempt to balance organisational or societal collective concerns, such as productivity, safety, control and deterrence, with concerns related to individual rights, such as privacy, confidentiality and discrimination. Employers must simultaneously engage in three difficult and delicate balancing acts. Firstly, they must select investigative techniques that will be effective and reliable without alienating the workforce or violating employees' privacy rights. Secondly, in deciding how to deal with identified abusers, they must walk the fine line between rehabilitation and discipline. Thirdly, they must weigh the need for discipline against the risks of costly litigation or arbitration. However, balancing those conflicting concerns may have negative consequences, since it may result in a subjective environment, open to abuse and worker–management confrontation. While it is not possible to standardise all the legal, moral and ethical aspects of the drug and alcohol screening issue, it seems that codifying certain elements would be one way to create a more objective approach.

All workplace initiatives that respond to alcohol-related and drug-related problems are based on at least four inter-related assumptions:

- Substance use poses serious difficulties in the workplace.
- The particular response that is implemented will resolve those difficulties.
- The benefits gained by implementing an initiative outweigh the costs of the initiative (for example industrial relations and financial).
- The response is consistent with ethical and legal standards.

Drug testing in itself is not the solution. It is one of the identification tools. Education toward prevention and rehabilitation provides the real solution. This is the most cost-effective and the most humanitarian means of solving the drug and alcohol abuse problem.

Education of managers and employees is imperative. Managers should be taught to spot the signs of alcoholism and drug dependency and to confront a dependent employee appropriately. All employees should be taught the symptoms of alcoholism and drug addiction so that they might identify it in themselves. 'Denial' is frequently part of the addiction. Recognising that a problem exists can be the first step toward rehabilitation. Recruiting and training new employees is expensive.

The aim of alcohol education strategies is to provide information on a range of relevant issues, including the dangers associated with excessive consumption, what constitutes sensible drinking, and the costs of alcohol abuse, as well as to make employees aware of the existence of company procedures (such as employee assistance programmes) designed to deal sympathetically and confidentially with problem drinkers. Education programmes can play a valuable role in minimising collusion amongst the workforce by persuading employees that covering up for a colleague is not in that person's long-term interests.

In its booklet *The Problem Drinker at Work*, the HSE provides guidance on formulating a workplace alcohol policy and suggests that such a policy might be referred to in the employer's statement of general health and safety policy required under Section 2(3) of the HASAW Act 1974.

The majority of workplace drug and alcohol policies consist of two main components:

- prevention of drug and alcohol misuse, including education initiatives;
- operational procedures designed to identify, assess, assist and ultimately return to productive work employees with drug and alcohol problems, without recourse to disciplinary procedures.

The employer should ensure that all employees are given appropriate background information and a copy of the drug and alcohol policy, agreed with the trade union involved, during their induction period and reinforced by in-house training seminars.

Effective implementation of a policy relies on a number of factors:

- commitment from senior managers;
- an on-going education programme;
- training for managers, occupational health staff and trade union representatives;
- ensuring that the provisions of the policy are well known and understood (especially relating to confidentiality);
- adopting a fair and consistent approach for all employees, regardless of seniority or status.

Some of the main problems experienced in implementation include:

- lack of early identification of problem employees;
- failure to persuade employees that the policy is there to help them and that cooperation will not result in disciplinary action being taken;
- difficulties in persuading managers that, once a problem employee has been identified, something constructive can be done;
- difficulties in encouraging a problem employee to seek help;
- collusion.

No one can claim that a pre-employment or regular test was unexpected, and this weighs in favour of the conclusion that such tests do not infringe on personal privacy. Random urine tests given when an employer has no basis for suspecting a particular employee of being under the influence of drugs are intrusive. They allow the employer to pry into their employees' personal lives for evidence of deviant, as opposed to dysfunctional, behaviour. It is an assault on personal integrity and a violation of the right of privacy. Only where there is a reasonable basis for suspecting a particular employee of being under the influence of drugs should the need to conduct an unannounced urine test be held to outweigh the intrusion on privacy.

If an applicant knew that they were going to be tested as a part of the assessment procedure and still tested positive for drugs or alcohol, then an employer can assume that that person may have a problem. Inability to refrain from using drugs or alcohol for a short time prior to the interview could be a strong indication of dependency.

Drug testing can be used effectively in 'probable cause' where an employee is suspected to be affected by substance abuse which threatens the safety of others.

Urine tests involve no puncturing of the skin. It is intrusive because it does involve a compulsory taking of body fluids and a disclosure of physiological information. The personal affront caused can be minimised by maintaining an intimate testing environment.

To avoid unnecessary invasion of privacy, the voiding of a specimen need not be directly monitored, but can be done indirectly (for example by measuring the urine temperature, pH and specific gravity). The chain of custody of the specimen should be carefully monitored and documented for the employer's credibility. The specimen should only be tested for the substances mentioned and nothing else.

Future considerations

There should be a definition of risk. Consideration should be given to the question of whether risk should be limited to physical injuries or whether it should encompass the risk to the profitability of the organisation, including factors such as company reputation and customer trust.

In examining a possible codification of workplace impairment, consideration should be given to the question of whether impairment should be job-specific or at a set threshold level for all occupational groups. It is easy to imagine justifiable policies that require airline crews to abstain from alcohol consumption for a specified period before going on duty; however, if a financial officer has 'one too many' the night before and then makes an error in judgement, there could be serious consequences. Should there be policies to cover such situations?

The impact of the testing procedure (sample collection) on self-esteem needs addressing. Humane guidelines should be established that balance rehabilitation efforts against disciplinary measures, while protecting the privacy and safety of substance abusers, their co-workers and the public at large. Factors to be considered in deciding whether a drug and alcohol testing process illegally invades a person's privacy include:

- the nature of the test
- the conditions under which it is performed
- its justification
- whether less intrusive alternatives are available.

This privacy right is not absolute – the US Court ruled that a State may compel disclosure of otherwise private information when its interest in that information outweighs the individual's interest in non-disclosure. It appears that courts and arbitrators may allow testing on a random basis when the interest in public safety outweighs privacy rights.

The way forward

If it is well designed and executed, and protects and respects the interests of society at large as well as those of both employer and employee, workplace testing may well need to be implemented in some shape or form, depending on the nature of the work involved. There are many pitfalls in any testing system and clear safeguards need to be in place so that in particular the rights of employees should not be usurped. In some cases it may be on entry to a company, with subsequent random testing of a sample of employees at intervals, while in others it may be that testing takes place when there are reasonable grounds for suspicion of impairment due to drug use. At the same time, the employer who introduces a test system incurs an added responsibility for employee welfare. Implementation of a drug and alcohol system imposes on a company the responsibility to provide support and counselling facilities for employees found to test positive.

The defect of not being able to demonstrate impairment with a urine sample for illicit drugs is a serious one. In future, there may well be machines which can test for impairment; they are currently being piloted and may fulfil a role. This would then lead to a further round of debate about urine testing. For the present, however, blood, urine or breath tests of alcohol are accepted as evidence of impairment, while urine testing for drugs is unlikely to be superseded in the foreseeable future. Principles of fairness need to be invoked in the application of every testing programme.

16 *Employee Assistance Programs*

Jill Bachman, Andy Siegle and Elizabeth Pace

Introduction

The purpose of this chapter is to describe the function and value of employee assistance programs (EAPs). An EAP is a worksite program designed to help employees with any number of problems that could affect their work – stress, relationship issues, financial worries and substance abuse for example. In order to be consistent with the theme of this book, this chapter will intentionally focus upon drug and alcohol problems, even though EAPs deal just as much or more with other problems not related to drugs or alcohol. A hypothetical manufacturing company is described to illustrate relevant content, and there are three case studies toward the end of the chapter. Information about two employee assistance associations and other references are included at the conclusion.

St Charles Manufacturing Company

The St Charles Manufacturing Company, established in 1972, assembles parts for aircraft engines. The St Charles workforce of 300 people is comprised mostly of young, single, entry-level employees. St Charles does business with commercial aircraft makers, both foreign and domestic. St Charles is a financially successful company, and most quarters have yielded a profit. But over the last six months, three disturbing trends have developed together: a 15 percent increase in employee turnover, now at 27 percent, a 20 percent increase in absenteeism and a 10 percent increase in the number of on-the-job accidents.

Patrick Gooch, who supervises 20 employees, has been concerned about two individuals whose job performance has deteriorated over the past three months. Mark is a forklift operator. Patrick has noted Mark's issues: tardiness, absenteeism (especially on Mondays), decreasing productivity and occasionally falling asleep on the job. Most recently, Mark was involved in a workplace accident. While operating a forklift, Mark dropped a pallet on a coworker, breaking his leg in two places. At the time of the accident, Mark's blood alcohol level registered .06, which is in violation of St Charles company policy. What should Patrick do?

Patrick has also been aware of Sarah's declining job performance. Sarah used to have the highest productivity and quality ratings in Patrick's work group. But over the last three months, Sarah's performance has declined. Over this same period of time, Patrick observed that Sarah 'has not been herself'. Sarah often seemed extremely melancholy and withdrawn.

Whenever Patrick asked Sarah 'What's going on?' the only response that he'd received from Sarah was 'Nothing – I'm fine.' Sarah has a feeling that that her job is in jeopardy.

Patrick and a few of his manager colleagues have been talking about some of the common employee issues they have encountered recently. They are all concerned about turnover. Replacement costs are estimated at one-third of an employee's wages, and with increasing competition for their outside contracts, St Charles can't afford to 'throw money away' simply to hire new employees. They have heard a rumour that some of the employees have started meeting away from work to discuss certain issues they are planning to bring to St Charles' administration. Patrick and his manager group know they must figure out what's behind the turnover and how to halt that disturbing trend.

What should the St Charles Manufacturing Company do about these problems? What can the managers do to reduce turnover? Where can Mark and Sarah go to get help for their respective issues? Some supervisors might inform them of the services of their EAP. Still others might ignore the problems, hoping that they would work themselves out in time. Other supervisors might feel obligated to deal with the employee's personal issues on their own. If you were a supervisor at St Charles, what would you do?

The workplace is a useful place to intervene

The reality is that a majority of substance abusers are employed, either full or part time. It is estimated that 70 percent of all illicit drug users or heavy drinkers are employed full time. It is also estimated that 1 in 10 employees abuse drugs or alcohol (SAMHSA 1997[1], 1999[2], 2001[3]).

The workplace is an ideal place to intervene because jobs and livelihoods are powerful motivators. Most employed individuals want to retain their jobs. Wages provide the resources to pay the rent/mortgage, operate vehicles, save for the future, educate children, purchase health insurance and take a holiday. For many people, jobs and income are also tied to feelings of power and self-worth. If a troubled employee doesn't get the help they need and job performance continues to decline, they will most likely be terminated. Faced with the prospect of losing a job, many employees will agree, even if reluctantly, to deal with their problems in order to retain their employment.

Employees with a drug or alcohol problem have a much better chance of positive outcomes if the problems are identified and addressed early. The longer a substance-abuse disorder/behavior continues, the harder and more expensive it is to treat. Cancer and addiction are similar in some respects. If treated early, successful outcomes can be achieved. If treated in its late stages, after the condition has taken hold or metastasized, outcomes may be extremely poor. Early problem identification and appropriate treatment can lead to healthier outcomes for individuals as well as the businesses that employ them.

Employee assistance (EA) and employee assistance programs (EAP)

According to the Employee Assistance Professionals Association (2004)[4]:

> employee assistance (EA) is the work organization's resource that utilizes specific core

technologies to enhance employee and workplace effectiveness through prevention, identification, and resolution of personal and productivity issues. An employee assistance program (EAP) is a worksite-based program designed to assist (1) work organizations in addressing productivity issues, and (2) 'employee clients' in identifying and resolving personal concerns, including, but not limited to, health, marital, family, financial, alcohol, drug, legal, emotional, stress, or other personal issues that may affect job performance.

In other words, an EAP has two clients – the organization, and the individuals who work there.

PROGRAM TYPE

There are two major types of EAPs, internal and external. An internal EAP is actually employed by the company it serves. EAP staff is typically housed within or very near the main work location/s, and often report to human resources or a chief operating officer, though other reporting structures also occur. An external EAP contracts with a company to provide service, but is not employed by the company. The external EAP is more likely to maintain office space off site.

There are pros and cons to both structures. The internal EAP may have greater opportunity to be involved in the company's overall direction and day-to-day management decisions. There may be a greater tendency to seek EAP support and involvement with organizational issues. On the other hand the appearance of neutrality and protection of confidentiality may be issues for employees if the EAP is an internal one. If not properly managed, this climate may discourage employees from seeking EA services.

Another EAP type is the labor assistance program, also called member assistance program or peer assistance program, which relies heavily upon peer referral to resources and aid within a unionized environment. The expectations of this program are typically included as part of the collective bargaining agreement.

CONFIDENTIALITY

This is one of the most important hallmarks of an EAP. Whether the program is external, internal or union, employees are guaranteed that information about themselves will be kept confidential, consistent with applicable laws governing privacy of information. If information needs to be shared with someone else, for example another health care provider, the employee must consent to release that information. For an external EAP, program fees are often negotiated on a per capita basis, prior to any utilization. This then eliminates any billing that could identify an employee to his company. Confidentiality is a necessary prerequisite to making sure that any employee (line worker, CEO or manager) sees the EAP as a safe resource for any problem.

REFERRALS

Employees may refer themselves to the EAP for assistance, or managers or policy may require that a contact with the EAP be made. Another common term for employee referral is self-referral, or informal referral. An informal referral may also result from a suggestion from a colleague, or even a manager who is concerned about the employee, but not requiring the EAP session for performance improvement. The vast majority of referrals to an EAP are self-referrals.

Other terms for a required referral are mandatory referral, work performance referral or formal referral. A formal referral is an action taken by the company, requiring the employee to see the EAP or face the prospect of losing their job. There is usually an element of urgency about this type of referral, and the employee's job performance in specifically identified areas must improve, or they face discipline or termination.

In a formal referral, the person making the referral informs the EAP that this referral has been made, and why. When the employee meets with the EA provider, a consent to release information is obtained, and the provider communicates limited information with the referral source. Whether or not the employee keeps the appointment, and whether or not they comply with recommendations is usually the extent of information revealed. The particulars of the employee's problem, history, possible diagnosis, treatment detail and so on are not the kinds of information typically released to the manager. And, even though the employee has met with the EA provider and is following recommendations, if the work performance improvement required by the employer is not forthcoming, the employer is not required to continue to tolerate work performance that is unacceptable.

History of employee assistance programs

Though the term 'employee assistance program' did not come into usage until the early 1970s, modern EAPs have their roots in the occupational alcoholism programs of the 1940s. These programs developed not long after Alcoholics Anonymous (AA) first demonstrated that support groups could help individuals recover from alcoholism. At a time when companies were more paternal and Americans were much more likely to spend their entire careers working for a single employer, the success of AA proved to employers that they could preserve their investments in long-term employees through support of occupational alcoholism programs. These programs recognized that concerns about job loss, even more than loss of family and friends, could break through denial.

Early occupational alcoholism programs were mostly staffed by men in recovery who encouraged workers with alcohol problems to attend AA meetings. They expected supervisors to diagnose alcoholism, a task that many were reluctant and unqualified to perform. As the programs pushed to identify alcohol problems earlier in the continuum, they acquired an evangelical flavor that alienated some employers and workers who felt that questions about off-the-job drinking were an invasion of privacy.[5]

Why have an EAP?

According to the UK Chapter of EAPA (2004):[6]

> Organisations continue to face unprecedented pressures and demands from increasing competition, heavier workloads and longer hours, all of which have to be dealt with at a personal level. It is inevitable that these continuous pressures will cause problems both for every organisation and many individuals.

In this climate EAPs help individuals, managers and organisations to:

- cope with work-related and personal problems and challenges that impact on performance at work;
- improve productivity and workplace efficiency;
- decrease work-related accidents;
- lessen absenteeism and staff turnover;
- promote workplace co-operation;
- manage the risk of unexpected events;
- position the organisation as a caring employer;
- recruit and retain staff;
- reduce grievances;
- assist in addiction problems;
- improve staff morale and motivation;
- provide a management tool for performance analysis and improvement;
- demonstrate a caring attitude to employees;
- assist line managers in identifying and resolving staff problems.

In short, EAPs represent a proven, cost-effective solution to many of the people problems employers face today. The UK EAPA recommends that all organisations consider seriously how a relevant form of EAP can be introduced into their organisation.

Even though the benefits of an EAP are significant, it is important to emphasize that the EAP is not 'a benefit' to the employees of an organization, as health insurance might be a benefit. An EAP is a management tool to aid the organization with problems that may seriously affect productivity and, ultimately, survival.

How do today's EAP's work?

In order to assist organizations, EA practice is founded on the following 'core technology' (Roman and Blum, 1988).[7] As EA has evolved, some programs provide additional services to add value for their clients, but the core set of seven services constitutes fundamental EAP practice. Any programme that claims to provide an EAP service should include all the following components:

- consultation with, training of and assistance to work organization leadership (managers, supervisors and union stewards) seeking to manage the troubled employee, enhance the work environment and improve employee job performance; outreach/education of employees/dependents about availability of employee assistance services;
- confidential and timely problem identification/assessment services for employee clients with personal concerns that may affect job performance;
- use of constructive confrontation, motivation and short-term intervention with employee clients to address problems that affect job performance;
- referral of employee clients for diagnosis, treatment and assistance, plus case monitoring and follow-up services, as well as to organizations and insurers;

- assistance to work organizations in managing provider contracts, and in forming and auditing relations with service providers, managed care organizations, insurers and other third-party payers;
- assistance to work organizations to support employee health benefits covering medical/behavioral problems, including but not limited to: alcoholism, drug abuse and mental/emotional disorders;
- identification of the effects of employee assistance services on the work organization and individual job performance.

STIGMA – A MAJOR THREAT TO THE WORKPLACE

Before any program or effort can reduce the negative impact of alcohol and drugs in the workplace, stigma must first be acknowledged and dealt with. Stigma is defined as 'a sign of social unacceptability'[8]. Many behaviors in our modern society are stigmatized. The stigma of getting help for substance abuse problems or mental health concerns is very much present today (Bennett and Lehman 2003)[9], and prevents many people from actually seeking help at all. In terms of substance abuse disorders, stigma is the most frequently cited reason for not coming to treatment earlier (Copeland, 97)[10].

For those readers who believe that the stigma associated with substance-abuse treatment and/or counseling for any personal problem no longer exists, consider the various political races where a worthy candidate is 'discounted and discredited' for admitting that they received counseling in the past. What biases are operating here?

How does stigma manifest itself in the workforce? Will a fellow employee be labeled and ostracized for seeking substance abuse treatment or will they be encouraged and supported by their coworkers for 'doing the right thing'? It depends on how enlightened the workforce is.

This concept of employee enlightenment relates directly to the notion of workplace culture. What are the drinking norms in a particular work group? According to the International Labour Organization[11] 3–5 percent of the workforce is alcohol dependent and more than 25 percent consume enough to be at risk of alcohol dependence in the future.

St Charles could expect that approximately 60 employees might bring problem behaviors related to alcohol to work as shown in Table 16.1. When other problems such as illegal drugs, prescription drug misuse/abuse and emotional problems are included, a significant number of employees could be affecting the workplace. If St Charles has an

Table 16.1   St Charles employees' alcohol use patterns

Type of drinker	General population estimate (%)	St Charles Manufacturing Company (No. of employees)
Abstinent	10	30
Responsible	70	210
Problem	15	45
Alcohol dependent	5	15

'alcohol encouraging culture' as do many types of industry, these estimates could be much higher. The culture of encouragement, which may be manifested in the stigma against getting help, can provide many challenges for a modern business.

The three main stigmas that operate in the workplace are the stigma of being labeled a drug or alcohol abuser, the stigma of 'getting help' for a mental health or substance abuse concern and the stigma against abstinence in work settings where the drinking culture is strong. For many persons, the stigma of admitting that they are misusing a drug is too much to bear. If an employee thinks they might have a substance misuse problem, rationalization and minimization might take several forms. How many times have you heard 'I might drink a little too much, but doesn't everyone once in a while?' 'I'm not an alcoholic, I only drink beer.' 'I might take some prescription pain killers like oxycontin every four to six hours but at least I've never used needles.' 'I only drink on the weekend.' Without this societal stigma, employees could freely acknowledge, 'My relationship with my drug of choice has become extremely unhealthy and problematic. I'm scared because I don't know how to "get out". I need help.'

USING THE EAP TO REDUCE STIGMA

How does an EAP help to minimize the effects of stigma? An EA provider doesn't have to label someone in order to offer help. A visit to the EAP can be a self-referral or a friendly supervisor suggestion. A formal referral is based on company policy and/or job performance, not a presumptive label. Any individual, including a member of the administrative team, can make an appointment simply to 'talk things over'. Unlike a visit to a physician's office, there is no insurance billing code based on pathology or problems to address and fix.

The EA provider can also address the concept of stigma at the organizational level. In meetings or educational sessions with managers, they can help to identify the norms that may be operating to encourage drinking, drug use or other risky behaviors. Identifying the norms is the first step to questioning their effect and developing approaches to substitute other, healthier norms for the unhealthy ones. The EA provider can offer information that relates to physical, social and emotional health, not moral judgment. Focusing on responsible drinking, or how to know if drinking is causing a health problem are approaches less likely to increase stigma.

Stigma is an extremely powerful force in the workplace and can prevent the process of getting help. And when people don't get the help they need, problems generally worsen. Employers should work hard to combat stigma by creating an atmosphere where getting help (for anything that could negatively affect one's life or work) is highly encouraged. Asking for help should be considered a strength and not a weakness.

USING THE EAP TO INTERVENE WITH ALCOHOL AND DRUG PROBLEMS

Since the EAP is a worksite program with two clients – the organization and the individual – and misuse of drugs and alcohol has a significant negative effect on the workplace, an EAP is perfectly positioned to be involved with prevention, intervention and treatment of problems related to substance misuse. Drinking too much alcohol is a pattern that occurs at the individual level, and can be reinforced at the organizational level. For example consider a company where all the assembly-line workers go out for drinks together two or three times during the week. Are they using alcohol to cope with personal stressors, work stressors or an unhealthy work climate? Are they doing this as a form of socializing? Are the workers who do not join them avoided and ridiculed during work hours? Whatever the reasons, this is an example of a work culture that reinforces an individual problem.

Why is an EAP preferable to a simple referral to a counselor or therapist? There are two important reasons. First, since the EAP, be it internal or external, is knowledgeable about the business and the people involved, the EAP has an understanding about the work culture, which is a significant issue in managing drug and alcohol problems. Second, because an EAP functions at the organizational level as well as the individual one, the EAP can be instrumental in four important activities of the organization – policy development, policy implementation, supervisor education and employee education.

The organization's written policy about drugs in the workplace provides the overall structure, sets the tone, defines expected standards and describes how problems will be handled. The policy should contain information stating the conditions under which drug testing (if used) will be conducted, what the organization's response will be when an employee has a positive drug test, under what circumstances an employee might lose their position, and what appeal mechanisms exist. These decisions can have a significant effect on the company, and lots of thought should go into the policy development. The EAP can function as a consultant to the administrative team making the policy decisions. The EAP can share information with the group about problems that bring employees to the EAP for individual problem solving, and what resources exist for drug testing, for example. Although the EAP is not in a position to implement the policy directly with the employees, the consulting role that the EAP plays makes it desirable to include EA providers in the initial policy discussions.

Once the policy has been developed and a date set for implementation, the EAP can continue to support the organization by assisting with education. This education can take several forms – educating employees about the company's policy, their role in it and the role of the EAP, educating supervisors and managers about their responsibilities in implementing the policy, and educating the employee community about substance misuse. In addition, EAPs can also educate employees about conditions that may lead to substance misuse such as stress, dysfunctional communication, conflict within the work group and healthy responses to all these issues, helping the individual to make a positive contribution at the organizational level.

Supervisor training is a crucial component for effective, fair and consistent organizational response. Among their many necessary skills, supervisors need to be able to recognize signs of employee distress, communicate in a caring yet professional manner to make a good referral, understand how to respond to behavioral problems, request that an employee submit to a drug test, make a formal referral to the EAP or terminate an employee subject to the conditions of the policy. One of the most pressing questions of supervisors is that of identification – 'How do I know that John Smith is using illegal drugs?' Information provided during supervisor training focuses upon the employee's work performance, not on identifying an exact cause for a suspected impairment. Although supervisors are trained to recognize signs that someone may have been using drugs or alcohol, they are not trained to make a diagnosis. In other words, it really doesn't matter why the employee's performance is questionable, it matters that someone notices it and takes action. Supervisors need education and reinforcement to perform these roles that are sometimes difficult.

Let's take a closer look at the EAP's role in prevention, intervention and treatment of drug and alcohol problems.

Prevention

The EAP is a resource for many issues which may cause disruption in the employee's life and create negative effects on the workplace. A failed drug test is one example. EA is considered preventive when it helps the employee avoid the use of alcohol, or decrease their use of alcohol to cope with a problem.

At the organizational level, EAP education about substance misuse, wellness, stress management and other similar topics is designed to help people make healthier choices and take care of themselves. Other approaches at the organizational level include implementing workplace wellness programs such as Team Awareness. Team Awareness, developed in the US, is a workplace wellness program aimed at increasing the use of the EAP by employees, and modifying the workplace culture to increase employees' peer referral, understanding and ownership of policy and increasing wellness norms[12].

Intervention

Self- or formal referral of an employee to the EAP due to a problem with drugs or alcohol is considered to be intervention at the individual level. The focus of the sessions is on the substance misuse/abuse, and the measure of effectiveness is whether or not the employee's work performance improves.

Organizational intervention may take various shapes. One type of intervention is working with the employee's manager and colleagues to ease the transition back to the workplace, if the employee has had to be away for treatment or a medical leave. The following example illustrates another type of organizational intervention.

> Acme Teleservices Company had its annual holiday party at a nice hotel away from the worksite. At the event, alcohol was available without question to anyone who had a ticket to attend. Many of Acme's employees are under the legal drinking age. Two employees were involved in a vehicle accident returning home after the party, one underage and one older. The underage employee was driving. The second employee was killed. The accident also killed a pregnant nurse driving home after her evening shift at the hospital.
>
> Acme's administrator informed the EAP manager of the accident the following morning. The EA provider was able to intervene and provide support to the company in several ways. Crisis debriefing sessions were scheduled for staff around the clock. Individual follow-up intervention occurred for three employees who were having symptoms of stress disorder and anxiety. The EAP manager initiated an immediate policy review to identify places where changes were necessary to prevent a similar accident, then presented that information to the company the next day. (If the EAP had identified policy weaknesses before such a tragedy occurred, that work would be considered preventive.)

Treatment

EA sessions are not considered to be treatment. EA providers may be involved in facilitating treatment for drugs, alcohol or other mental health concerns by providing referral information, encouraging a referral, assisting a family or work group with an intervention for a troubled employee. Another role for the EA provider is in treatment monitoring. How is the employee doing during treatment? Is the employee compliant? Is the referral a positive one? Does it seem to be effective? Are the employee and their family satisfied with the referral?

If an employee has had to be off work for any length of time for treatment, the EA provider can maintain communication with the employee while they are away, if appropriate. When the employee is ready to return to work, the provider may organize a meeting with the employee, the manager, the HR representative, a family member and a union representative if applicable, to discuss and determine the conditions and expectations for a successful return to work.

St Charles' case studies

Mark

According to St Charles Policy and Procedures Manual, the supervisor made a mandatory referral to the EAP. Mark attended his scheduled appointment. A thorough assessment and evaluation was completed over a two-hour period. Both the EA provider as well as Mark came to the conclusion that he was drinking more than he intended to at least three nights a week. Mark was never alcohol dependent, but he was beginning to misuse it (it contributed to a workplace accident). Mark also disclosed that on a few lunch breaks, he and some fellow employees have had a 'few' pints at the local pub. St Charles policy states that employees in safety-sensitive positions may not have a positive blood alcohol level.

After the 'diagnosis' of alcohol misuse/abuse (not dependence), the EA provider presented Mark with one of two options: complete abstinence or a controlled drinking regime. Mark decided to pursue the controlled drinking regime.

Upon Mark's second visit to the EAP, he and his counselor agreed to the following controlled drinking plan:

- to consume no more that twelve units per week (1 unit = 1 twelve oz beer/lager/ale no more than 5 per cent alcohol, a 1 oz shot of hard liquor, or 4 oz of wine);
- to never consume more than four units in one sitting/drinking period (getting up and changing seats doesn't count as a second sitting);
- to never drink and drive;
- to abstain from all alcoholic beverages during work hours;
- to keep a 'drinking log' that states when and where he consumed his alcoholic drinks as well as his mood states at the time of consumption.

Mark returned to the EA provider for follow-up visits over the next three months. After three months Mark was doing extremely well. He moderated his alcohol drinking (off site) and was abstinent (on site). Mark had become an alert, efficient, and safe employee. Mark enjoyed feeling fully present at the job site. He was rarely late for work and had actually become a role model to new employees in his work unit.

Sarah

Sarah knew that she had not been herself lately. She also knew that her job performance was slipping. Wanting to get some help, she called the EAP and made a voluntary appointment. She saw an EA provider two days later and a comprehensive assessment was completed. Sarah knew that these visits to the EAP were confidential and off the record. She told her counselor that her mother passed away a few months ago and that she was still grieving. She didn't want anyone at St Charles to know that she was having trouble. 'They all think I'm too soft, and can't take any pressure.'

Sarah attended two sessions with her EA provider. Following these sessions, and with Sarah's agreement, the EA provider referred her to an experienced therapist who specialized in grief and loss issues. Sarah saw this specialist twice a month for the next three months. The EA provider made monthly check-in telephone calls just to see how Sarah was doing. Sarah always appreciated these calls.

After three months Sarah was getting back to her normal self again. Her productivity level was high. And slowly but surely, Sarah was again an engaging and energetic employee – a real asset to her organization! She reached out for help and received it.

Organization

Patrick Gooch, supervisor at St Charles, contacted the EAP and asked the EAP manager to join him, two other managers and the HR Director to discuss 'turnover'. As the meeting unfolded, the EAP manager shared some general perceptions with the group about the work stress some of her clients had expressed. As the group discussed it further, and the HR manager brought up other examples, they began to think there were more serious issues. The group wondered if the quality of manager orientation and training could be a big part of the problem. There were a few newer managers who had been brought in at a time when the training department was in significant turmoil. There were also rumors that two of the managers were particularly lenient when it came to employee discipline, contrasted with one senior manager who was very harsh.

The team decided they needed more information. The HR manager offered to develop an anonymous employee survey about general managerial practices. The EAP manager discouraged the focus just on managers, and recommended instead that they ask the employees what they believed to be the main reasons for turnover. She also suggested that they add two line workers to the 'turnover team' to help increase buy-in to the survey process.

As the team continued to meet over the next few months, they began to uncover broader issues they wanted to address. Following are some of the changes they made as a result of the work of the turnover group.

> The training director worked with the managers to create an orientation checklist for new managers, and gave it to all current managers to update and identify areas that might have been overlooked.

> The EAP manager created a series of lunchtime meetings to which managers could bring their most difficult employee problems for group discussion and problem solving. Use of and referral to the EAP were always stressed in these sessions.

> The manager group decided to shift their focus from recruitment to retention. They developed a specific plan to address several strategies including an awards program and mentoring employees into advancement positions.

Use of the EAP at the organizational level is an area that needs to be stressed for its value. The EAP brings a knowledgeable, yet more objective point of view to the table. Not simply representing the concerns of troubled employees, but respecting the business concerns about productivity and survival, this role is a crucial one to assist in organizational change efforts. If a business can avoid operating from a position of fear ('We don't want an outsider to see our problems') and adopt one of using every available resource to help in today's competitive environment, it will demonstrate a valuable organizational message – getting help is a sign of strength, not a weakness.

References

1   Substance Abuse and Mental Health Services Administration. (1997) *Guidelines and Benchmarks for Prevention Programming: Implementation Guide*. DHHS Publication NO. (SMA) 95-3033. Rockville, MD.

2   Substance Abuse and Mental Health Services Administration. (1999) *Worker Drug Use and Workplace Policies and Programs: Results from the National Household Survey on Drug Abuse* (NHSDA). Rockville, MD.

3   Substance Abuse and Mental Health Services Administration. (2001) *Summary of Findings from the 2000 National Household Survey on Drug Abuse* (Office of Applied Studies, NHSDA Series H13, DHHS Publication No. SMA 01-3549). Rockville, MD.

4   www.eapassn.org

5   'EAPs: Workplace Opportunities for Intervening in Alcohol Problems' accessed at www.ensuringsolutions.org/pages/primer/primer5/primer5.html, on Feb 2, 2004. Ensuring Solutions to Alcohol Problems website, George Washington University.

6   www.eapa.org.uk

7   Roman, P. and Blum, T. (1988) 'The Core Technology of Employee Assistance Programs,' *The ALMACAN*, August, pp. 17–22.

8   Encarta World English Dictionary, 2004, accessed at www.encarta.msn.com/dictionary on Feb 2, 2004.

9   Bennett, J. and Lehman, W. (2003) *Preventing Workplace Substance Abuse: Beyond Drug Testing to Wellness*. American Psychological Association, Washington, DC.

10   Copeland, J. (1997) 'A qualitative study of barriers to formal treatment among women who self-managed change in addictive behaviors'. *Journal of Substance Abuse Treatment*, **14**, 183–190.

11   Institute on Alcohol Studies Fact sheet. (2/20/2003) 'Alcohol and the Workplace', accessed at www.ias.org.uk/factsheets/wokplace.pdf on Feb 2, 2004.

12   For more information about Team Awareness, visit the website at www.organizationalwellness.com

Organizations devoted to employee assistance

- EAPA: Established in 1971, the Employee Assistance Professionals Association is the world's oldest and largest membership organization for employee assistance professionals, with approximately 6200 members in the United States and more than 30 other countries. EAPA hosts an annual conference, publishes a journal for the employee assistance profession, and offers training and other resources to enhance the professionalism of its members and the industry. The UK Employee Assistance Professionals Association is a chapter of EAPA.

- EASNA: The Employee Assistance Society of North America is an association for employee assistance program (EAP) professionals and organizations dedicated to the professionalism and growth of the employee assistance field. EASNA's EAP Accreditation program, membership services, and professional training opportunities promote high and fair standards of employee assistance practices.

17 *Employment Law*

Gillian Howard

Introduction

Employment legislation, medical ethics and drug protocols are some of the issues that govern the way employers are permitted to deal with drugs in their workplace. Not only are there common law duties[1] on employers to take reasonable steps to safeguard their staff and others from reasonably foreseeable risks of injury but there is also a wealth of employment protection legislation and EU directives.

The English legal system is based on the common law but has been much extended by statute law made by Parliament and by EU directives[2].

Employers must now also have regard to the individual's right to respect for privacy under Article 8 of the Human Rights Act 1998 where it could be argued that a policy that tests for drugs used in an employee's private time breaches their right to respect for privacy (see later).

Employer also have rights and obligations under the Data Protection Act 1998 to obtain, use and disclose medical data including test results from drug tests in accordance with the Act and Code of Practice (see later).

Dismissals for drug taking or drug abuse are prescribed by the 'unfair dismissal' legislation and both statute and case law govern this (see later).

Employers also have clear duties under the Health and Safety at Work Act 1974 (HASWA) to maintain a safe workplace and employees have corresponding duties to take reasonable care for their own and others' health and safety and so on. This Act imposes criminal liability[3] on employers (and directors) who can be fined and/or sent to prison for serious

---

1   The English legal system was largely based on judge-made law (law developed through decisions of the judges when cases came before them, called common law). Scotland has its own system of law quite different from the rest of Great Britain. Even after Parliament in the seventeenth century started to create statute law through Acts of Parliament, the development of case law still remains an important source of law. A statement of law made by a judge in a case can become binding on later judges by way of a doctrine called 'stare decisis' – stand by what has previously been decided – if the decision has been made by a judge in a sufficiently senior court (usually Court of Appeal or House of Lords) and the pronouncement forms part of the ratio decidendi (the reasoning behind the decision). Obiter dicta (sayings by the way) do not have the same force and are not strictly necessary for the legal basis for the decision and are only of persuasive authority. The ratio decidendi will compromise the legal principles and rules which are necessary to solve the problem before the court. In Scotland the legal system is based on Roman Dutch law and is different both in the area of civil and criminal law. However as far as the employment protection legislation regime is concerned, Scotland applies the same as England and Wales, although the procedure in employment tribunals is in some respects different.

2   Directives normally need domestic legislation to become effective.

3   Section 35 of the Act yet to be implemented will allow individuals injured as a result of breaches of the Act to sue in the civil courts for damages for personal injuries.

breaches of the Act. Further the Health and Safety Executive has powers to issue enforcement notices including improvement notices and prohibitions notices.

According to a survey of 1800 personnel professionals[4] 18 per cent reported drug-taking incidents at their workplace. One major drug-testing organisation[5] has reported that between 10 per cent to 15 per cent of drug tests test positive for drugs, cannabis being the most common.

Drugs and drugs money has also been cited in the Court of Appeal[6] in the case of Bank of Credit and Commerce International SA v Ali and Others (No.3) where the employees have claimed stigma damages in respect of their dismissals from the bank because of the appalling practices of the Bank that have become public, rendering the employees (albeit innocent) unemployable. One of the allegations made in this case was that certain employees were required to assist in money laundering where the money had come from known drug dealers.

Even the infamous email has been used to detect drug abusers. In the case of Miseroy v Barclaycard[7], Hilary Miseroy was dismissed for dealing drugs on the premises and sending offensive emails, detected when a full-scale investigation was launched into the 900 personal emails found in his sent box, containing offensive language and evidence of his boasting about his drug deals.

Main legal considerations for employers

The main legal issues for employers can be summarised in this way. Employers have a duty to uphold the law both criminal and civil. At common law (both civil and criminal) this means guarding against reasonably foreseeable risks of injury.

Under the Health and Safety at Work Act 1974 (HASWA) there are several legal duties imposed on employers relating to their own and other people's employees who may be working on the employer's premises.

HASWA is an enabling Act, which allows the Secretary of State to pass more detailed Regulations under the Act. There have been numerous Regulations including: Control of Substances Hazardous to Health Regulations 2002 (COSHH), which require employers to control exposure to hazardous substances to protect both employees and others who may

---

4   Chartered Institute of Personnel and Development.
5   City Medical Services.
6   BICC v Ali; Malik and others [2002] IRLR 460 where it was alleged that the fraudulent activities were not isolated, but systematic over a very long period of years. They took on a life of their own. They formed, or related to, part of the Bank's banking activities. The wrongdoing included payments of bribes and kickbacks (to employees of the Bank, officers of other banks and public officials), the preparation of false records (including the recording of sham and fictitious transactions) and the creation of fictitious (forged) documentation; the unlawful purchase of its own shares; money laundering (including the laundering of drug money); defalcations; and the preparation and filing of false annual accounts vastly overstating assets and understating liabilities. Even today the liquidators cannot say what is the full extent of the frauds. The sums involved in the frauds were massive, running into billions of dollars. Such was the Bank's wrongdoing that, when the house of cards collapsed, the insolvency of the Bank ran into billions of pounds, causing huge losses to customers. The fraudulent activities were recorded principally in the Cayman Islands and in other offshore locations, but were orchestrated, and sometimes conducted, from London.
7   Miseroy v Barclaycard – unreported tribunal decision.

be exposed from their work activities; Management of Health and Safety at Work Regulations 1992; Display Screen Equipment Regulations 1992 and so on.

Section 2(1) of HASWA imposes a general duty to 'ensure so far as is reasonably practicable, the health, safety and welfare at work of all his employees'.

Section 2(2) imposes five more detailed duties which are all prescribed with the words 'so far as is reasonably practicable':

- to provide and maintain safe plant and systems of work;
- to ensure safe use, handling, transport and storage of articles and substances;
- to provide information, instruction, supervision and training;
- to ensure a safe place of work;
- to ensure a safe working environment.

The scope of these duties extending as they do to other people's employees working on the employer's premises can be seen in the cases of R v Swan Hunter Shipyards and Telemeter Installations Ltd[8]. In both these cases the courts held that in order to protect their own workers, the main employer in each case (Swan Hunter Shiprepairers and Associated Octel) had a duty to give information and instruction to other people's employees who came to work on the employer's premises.

So drugs policies should include a section on visitors and contractors. Those individuals should be given appropriate sections of the drugs policy and there should be a requirement that such individuals read and accept the rules and policy, so that they do not endanger themselves or others.

Employers can also be held guilty under the criminal law for allowing illegal substances onto their premises, that is those drugs forbidden under the Misuse of Drugs Act 1971[9] for example: Class A drugs such as ecstasy, heroin and cocaine; Class B such as amphetamines and barbiturates (cannabis became a Class C drug in July 2003); and Class C such as various types of prescription drugs including sleeping pills and most benzodiazepines (tranquillisers) as well as anabolic steroids.

Diligent employers should include in any policies and notices clear instructions that no illicit substances may be brought onto site, nor stored, nor carried on anyone's person, nor used whilst at work, nor dealt in at work. Strange herb-like smells or paraphernalia associated with drug taking should be investigated with vigour and the culprits dealt with.

Employers may forget that the influence of prescribed or over-the-counter medication (OTC drugs) can be just as harmful and potentially far more common than the taking of illicit substances. Accidents or injuries caused by employees under the influence of this type of drug can potentially lead to prosecutions under the health and

---

8   R v Swan Hunter Shipbuilders Ltd and Telemeter Installations Ltd [1981] IRLR 403 and R v Associated Octel Ltd [1997] IRLR 123.

9   Sweet v Parsley [1970] AC 132. The Magistrates Court (upheld in the Divisional Court) had convicted Miss Sweet, a teacher and owner of a farmhouse outside Oxford, rooms of which she let to students. Following a police raid, cannabis was found in the students' rooms. Under the Dangerous Drugs Act 1965 (s.5(b)) Miss Sweet was found guilty of being concerned in the management of premises which were being used for the purposes of smoking cannabis. The House of Lords overturned her conviction and held that since she had no knowledge (mens rea) of what the students had been doing and she had no control over her tenants, the offence for which she was charged did not impose strict liability and her conviction was quashed. ('Strict liability' offences impose criminal liability irrespective of the knowledge of the accused.)

safety legislation. Some employers have a policy of testing for drugs pre-employment and during employment.

There are some interesting legal issues concerning the processing of that data under the Data Protection Act 1998: the legal position of an employee who refuses to undergo a drugs test; the correct protocol for drugs testing; the issue of informed consent; what an employee/job applicant should be told about the actual tests to be performed; the fairness of a dismissal under employment protection legislation; whether an employer has the right to carry our secret surveillance to investigate whether drug misuse is taking place at work; whether drug misuse outside work can ever be grounds for a fair dismissal or fair grounds for rejection for a job; whether the standards of at-work and outside-work behaviour are higher for professionals such as teachers and doctors!

Duty to recruit reasonably competent employees

Employers have a common law duty to recruit competent, healthy and safe workers. This means conducting a competent recruitment process, which may include drug testing for certain highly safety critical posts.

The courts have made it clear that where employees are recruited into positions of trust, employers must make reasonably careful enquiries as to the competency and trustworthiness of the employee to be recruited, otherwise the employer can be held vicariously liable not only for the negligent acts of that employee but also their criminal acts. Whilst this is rare, it is possible.

In Nahhas v Piers House Management (Cheyne Walk) Ltd (1984) 270 Estates Gazette 328, a porter was recruited to look after the block of flats in Cheyne Walk, Chelsea, in London. His employers had not undertaken even the barest of checks such as asking for references from previous employers. Had they done so they would have found that he had had over 20 previous convictions for theft and burglary. He had been entrusted with the keys to a flat by the tenant, Miss Nahhas. He entered her flat and stole over £30 000 worth of her jewellery. She sued the porter's employers for negligence and won.

The employers were held to be liable for the financial loss suffered as a result of the criminal acts of that porter because they had been negligent in recruiting a 'professional thief' and had breached the duty to protect the residents' flats.

The implications here are clear. If an employee or contractor works in a safety-critical job, employers should consider the use of drug and alcohol testing both pre-recruitment and during employment.

Asking the right questions

It is important that employers ask the right questions, which are relevant to the post being applied for. So questions on a pre-employment medical questionnaire could include questions such as:

- Have you or are you currently taking or using any illegal substances for recreational or medical reasons? If Yes please give details.
- Are you currently taking any medication either prescribed or over the counter? If Yes please give details.

Employers who may worry that refusing to employ someone with a drug addiction (even smokers) could be successfully sued, need not worry. Whilst drug addiction is a 'disability' under the definition under the Disability Discrimination Act 1995[10], the 1996 Regulations exclude from the scope of its protection any addiction to illicit substances. Employers are therefore free to refuse to recruit any job applicant who admits to or is found to be addicted to illicit substances (or who smokes tobacco!).

Lying in law is treated differently from not offering information when not specifically requested to do so. In the latter case, unless the circumstances are so obvious, there is no legal requirement for a job candidate to volunteer information to questions not asked. In Walton's case (see below) the Employment Appeal Tribunal held obiter dicta that 'it could not be said that there is any duty on the employee in the ordinary case, though there may be exceptions, to volunteer information about himself otherwise than in response to a direct question'.

However, deliberately lying about a drug addiction when specifically asked about such matters has been held as a fair reason for dismissal (some other substantial reason for dismissal) once the employer found out about it, even if this is over a year from the date of recruitment.

In Walton v TAC Materials Ltd[11] Mr Walton was dismissed after working for the company for 13$^1/_2$ months when it was discovered that he was a heroin addict. Before being employed he had been asked questions about his health and had had a medical inspection by a company nurse. In response to the question 'Give details of serious illnesses and accidents' he had answered 'None'. And when asked 'Give details of all accidents, operations or illnesses' he did not disclose that he was then injecting himself with heroin.

Shortly after his employment started, Mr Walton of his own initiative began treatment for heroin addiction at a local hospital. Under treatment he was taken off intravenous heroin and had substituted methadone taken orally. When the Company found out, they sought the advice of the company doctor who said that he could not advise them to retain a drug addict in employment. He was summarily dismissed without notice or pay in lieu.

An industrial tribunal (since 1998 called employment tribunal) held that the dismissal was reasonable in the circumstances, firstly because by not admitting his addiction to heroin, Mr Walton had obtained the employment by deception, and secondly because it was entirely reasonable for the respondents to postulate that they would not employ anyone who was a drug addict.

Mr Walton appealed to the employment appeal tribunal. The EAT held that the industrial tribunal had not erred in law in holding that the employer had acted reasonably in dismissing the appellant after they discovered that he was a heroin addict in accordance with their policy not to employ anyone who was addicted to drugs. In this case, the industrial tribunal were entitled to find that the employer's policy of not employing drug addicts was entirely reasonable and that a dismissal in accordance with that policy could be rightly found fair.

Employers would be wise to include specific questions about drug addiction and drug taking if these questions are relevant to the employment.

---

10   Disability Discrimination Act 1995 defines a disability as a physical or mental impairment which is long term and has an adverse and substantial effect upon the normal day-to-day activities of that individual. However the Disability Discrimination (Meaning of Disability) Regulations 1996, Regulation 3 specifically excludes from the scope of the Act any addiction to alcohol, nicotine or any other substance (other than addiction to a prescribed medication).

11   [1981] IRLR 357.

Drug testing

Under the Transport and Works Act 1992, it is a criminal offence for specified people to work on the railways and tramways whilst 'over the limit' or 'unfit' through alcohol or drugs.

The employer will also be liable unless it can be shown that they have exercised 'all due diligence' to prevent the commission of the offence. In practice this means that those employers must carry out routine, 'for cause' and random alcohol and drug-testing – and they do.

The protocol for drug testing is well recognised and well publicised and it is not something that has a place in this chapter. Suffice it to say that the Faculty of Occupational Medicine has published a very useful guide on the medical and ethical issues of drug testing in the workplace[12].

Informed consent

It is essential that informed consent of the individual is obtained before any drug testing is administered. This means that the consent must be 'informed', that is the individual told the purpose for the which the testing will be done, the nature of the tests that will be carried out and what will happen to the results. The individual should also give their consent in writing in order for it to be explicit and for there to be a clear and unequivocal record. Further, the consent must be freely given. This means giving the individual a real choice whether or not to consent with no penalty arising from withholding consent.

The ethics of drug testing are very well set out in the Faculty of Occupational Medicine's guidance on testing for drugs (see above and at footnote 10).

The importance of the individual being told the complete information – the truth – was highlighted in the case of X v Commission of the European Communities [1995] IRLR 320[13]. This involved a man who had applied for a temporary post of typist. He had undergone a medical examination but refused to be screened for HIV antibodies. After giving blood and undergoing the medical and disclosing his medical records, the medical officer ordered blood tests in order to determine the T4 and T8 lymphocyte counts. When these were below the normal ratio, the medical officer concluded that Mr X was suffering from a significant immuno deficiency constituting a case of full-blown AIDS. He was thus rejected on the grounds of his physical condition. His doctor was informed.

Mr X complained to the Court of First Instance that he had without his consent been subjected to an AIDS test and sought an annulment that he was unfit for work and damages for the non-material damage that he had suffered. The ECJ held that:

> *The Court of First Instance had incorrectly held that, in view of the abnormalities found in the medical examination of the appellant as part of his application for a temporary post...the Commission's medical officer was entitled to request that a T4/T8 lymphocyte*

---

12   *Guidelines on testing for drugs of abuse in the workplace*, published by the Faculty of Occupational Medicine, 6 St Andrew's Place, Regents Park, London NW1 4LB. This is being updated in 2005.

13   IRLR is the citation for *Industrial Relations Law Reports* published by LexisNexis, Butterworths, 2 Addiscombe Road, Croydon, Surrey, CR9 5AF, telephone 020 8402 1800.

count be carried out, notwithstanding that the appellant had expressly refused to undergo an HIV test. The manner in which the appellant had been medically examined and declared physically unfit constituted an infringement of his right to respect for his private life as guaranteed by Article 8 of the European Convention on Human Rights.

The right to respect for private life, embodied in Article 8 and deriving from the common constitutional traditions of the Member States is one of the fundamental rights protected by the legal order of the Community. It includes in particular a person's right to keep his state of health secret.

Although the pre-employment medical examination serves a legitimate interest of the Community Institutions and if the person concerned, after being properly informed, withholds his consent to a test which the medical officer considers necessary in order to evaluate his suitability for the post for which he has applied, the institutions cannot be obliged to take the risk of recruiting him, nevertheless that interest does not justify the carrying out of a test against the will of the person concerned.

The right to respect for private life requires that a person's refusal to undergo a test be respected in its entirety.

In the present case since the appellant expressly refused to undergo an AIDS screening test, that right precluded the administration from carrying out any test liable to point to or establish the existence of that illness in respect of which he had refused disclosure.

Yet it was apparent that the lymphocyte count in question had provided the medical officer with sufficient information to conclude that the candidate might be carrying the AIDS virus.

The Court of First Instance had wrongly considered that there was an obligation to respect a refusal by the person concerned only in relation to the specific test for AIDS and that any other test could be carried out which might merely point to the possible presence of the AIDS virus.

Therefore the decision of the Court of First Instance would be annulled to the extent to which it held that the medical officer was entitled to request a lymphocyte count, as would the decision of the Commission informing the appellant that he did not satisfy the conditions as to physical fitness for recruitment.

The appellant's claim for compensation for non-material damage suffered by him had correctly been dismissed by the Court of First Instance on the ground that the correct administrative procedure under the Staff Regulations had not been followed in relation to it.

An example of a medical consent form for drugs testing is shown overleaf:

MEDICAL CONSENT FORM – DRUG TESTING

I,... certify that I have given a specimen of my urine to the collector and that the specimen is in the bottles each marked with a reference number identical to the one on this form. The bottles were sealed in my presence with the labels which carry my signature and the reference number.

I give my informed consent for the specimen that I have donated to be tested by **[ADD DRUG SCREEN COMPANY]** for the drugs and their metabolites requested and for the results of the analysis to be reported to **[NAME OHP OR OH NURSE]**. I also authorise **DRUG SCREEN COMPANY** to validate that the sample that I have provided has not been tampered with in any way.

I accept that this testing conforms with the Company's Drugs and Alcohol Policy, a copy of which has been given to me and which I have read.

I hereby disclose any prescribed drugs or OTC drugs that I an currently taking and will if required bring them to this office for inspection:
....
....
....
....
DONOR SIGNATURE..DATE............................

Data protection issues

If employers (or their occupational health departments) wish to keep, use or disclose at any time records of drug tests, they must comply with the requirements of the Data Protection Act 1998 and the Code of Practice, Part 4, on 'Information on Workers' Health', paragraph 3.5.

For example the Code recommends that employers should have clear policies and terms in the contract regarding drugs and alcohol testing and should ensure that all their workers and job candidates know and understand the rules in advance. Testing for drugs should only be done where it is necessary to do so and can be justified such as in safety-critical jobs. It is recommended that Drug Testing should only be done after a decision has been made to offer the job. In order to satisfy Principle 1 of Schedule 1 of the Act – that data must be obtained fairly and lawfully – the individual must be told exactly what the tests will test for. So if a T cell count is to be done to test for the presence of HIV, the individual must be told in advance. No covert testing should be done.

Part 4 of the Code of Practice will be essential reading for all occupational health physicians, HR directors and directors who either currently or will in the future undertake drug testing.

---

14   The Information Commissioner in the Code of Practice (part 4) on Data Protection Act 1998 'Information on Workers' Health' sets out clear guidance at paragraph 3.5 about the legal issues regarding the testing of drugs.

Refusing drugs test at recruitment

If a job applicant refuses to undergo a drugs test at recruitment, then it would appear that they would have no legal redress if the employer refused to continue with the recruitment process. There appears to be little or no debate about consent being freely given at recruitment because the individual at that stage has a real choice whether or not to consent, without any duress or threat[15].

However, there may be an issue if the drugs test is undertaken only when a job offer has been made. In this case the threat to the individual is that the job offer will be withdrawn if consent is not given. The employer is here coming close if he has not gone over the line in obtaining 'freely given' consent. This will be an issue under the Data Protection Act 1998 in respect of the employer being able to 'process' this data as it is regarded as 'sensitive data' (information on a worker's physical or mental health) under Section 2 of the Data Protection Act 1998[16].

Employers should take note that merely testing for drugs at recruitment is normally not sufficient. 'For cause' testing during employment is commonly undertaken by employers who test for drugs. This is because a drugs screen at recruitment may not detect any illicit drugs at that particular time either because the individual has ceased taking the drugs sufficiently far in advance of the test for no traces to be revealed or they may start taking drugs after the employment has started.

One large organisation which currently undertakes drugs testing was informed by a local addiction clinic that individuals attending the clinic were asking how long they should refrain from taking cannabis, before applying for a job as they would be requested to take a drugs test in order the test to show negative. The answer was about two weeks! Some employers have adopted the testing of hair as a means of drug testing as traces of the drug remain present in hair for considerably longer than in urine.

Testing for prescribed medication

The testing protocol must contain clear guidelines to the laboratory testing the samples as to the spectrum of drugs for which the testing is required.

Eating a Jordan's poppy seed bar will produce a positive drugs test depending how the spectrum has been set.

Similarly it will be very important to explain to any individual about to undergo the drugs test that they should declare on the medical consent form what prescribed or OTC medicines they are taking so that these can be excluded from the test. The consent form above seeks information about prescribed or OTC medicines/drugs.

It may be rare but some individuals may be taking hormone drugs for medical reasons,

15 The Code of Practice (Part 4) concludes on page 13 that at the pre-recruitment stage valid consent can be obtained because individuals in the open market will usually have a free choice whether or not to apply for a particular job and even if consent to a drugs test is a condition of employment, this will not prevent the consent being freely given.

16 Section 2 and Schedule 3 of the Data Protection Act 1998 set very clear requirements for the processing of sensitive data. One such condition is that the worker's 'explicit' consent is obtained – defined as expressly given after being informed and freely given. Sensitive data includes in Section 2(e) data relating to the physical or mental health or condition.

for example if they are undergoing a sex change. Prior to the Sex Discrimination (Gender Reassignment) Regulations 1999, it was not unlawful for employers to discriminate against male-to-female or female-to-male transsexuals in employment. So a male-to-female transsexual who was taking female hormones was, prior to these Regulations, held not to have been unlawfully discriminated against, for, amongst other things, being banned from taking hormone drugs which were part of their treatment[17].

Now under the 1999 Regulations it would be regarded as an act of discrimination to treat a transsexual less favourably including refusing to allow them to take their hormone drugs.

If employers wish to ban the taking of certain prescribed medications for employees doing certain kinds of jobs, they must take care not to offend the 1999 Regulations. And employers must therefore be careful in vetting both the medication disclosed as being taken and the tests that they are asking the laboratory to perform in order to ensure that this kind of discrimination does not occur.

Drug-testing policy and term in the contract

As a start, it is essential that an employer has a drug-testing policy and a term both in the application form and in the contract making it clear what the policy is on drug testing both pre- and post-employment.

A simple term on the application form may read like this:

It is this company's policy to test for drugs and alcohol both prior to offering a job and during employment. We test for illicit substances and in order to perform appropriate screening we need to have disclosed all prescribed and over-the-counter medications that you are taking.

Anyone found to have a positive test result for any illicit substances or non-disclosed prescribed or OTC medication will not be offered a position in this company and will not be considered for any job within the following 12 months.

You have the right to refuse to take the drugs test (which requires a specimen of urine) and in such a case we will not continue with the recruitment process.

No negative or adverse inference will be drawn and no record of your refusal will be kept or disclosed.

A term in the contract may read something like this:

The Company has a well-publicised drugs and alcohol policy which includes a drugs and alcohol testing policy.

The Company reserves the right to test for drugs and/or alcohol at any time during your employment and to have the test results released to an HR manager and your line manager. Such tests will only be required where there are reasonable grounds for

---

17   Lynsay Watson v British Transport Police.

belief that drugs or alcohol may be involved in an incident, accident, sickness absence issue or any other relevant matter. Any refusal to undergo the tests and/or give consent for the test results to be released to the Company will lead to disciplinary action which could include dismissal with or without notice.

However anyone who *before* undergoing testing admits the taking of drugs or alcohol and is able to show some convincing evidence of an alcohol or drug-addiction problem may be leniently treated on this one occasion and may be referred for counselling and treatment in the first instance.

Case law on drug taking, drug addiction and dismissal

EMPLOYMENT PROTECTION

Unfair dismissal protection is granted to employees with at least one year's continuous service[18] in the Employment Rights Act 1996[19], which provides for five fair reasons for dismissal and that employers satisfy the test of acting reasonably laid down in Section 98(4) of the 1996 Act.

ACAS CODE OF PRACTICE

The ACAS Code of Practice[20] recommends that workers know what standards of conduct and performance are expected of them. The Employment Rights Act 1996[21] requires employers to provide written information for their employees about certain aspects of their disciplinary rules and procedures. Managers should also know and be able to apply the rules and the procedures they are required to follow.

In particular the Code of Practice recommends the following:

- When drawing up disciplinary rules, the aim should be to specify clearly and concisely those that are necessary for the efficient and safe performance of work and for the maintenance of satisfactory relations within the workforce and between workers and management.
- It is unlikely that any set of disciplinary rules can cover all circumstances that may arise. However, it is usual that rules would cover issues such as misconduct, sub-standard performance (where not covered by a separate capability procedure), harassment or victimisation, misuse of company facilities including computer facilities (such as email and the Internet), poor timekeeping and unauthorised absences. The rules required will necessarily vary according to particular circumstances, such as the type of work, working

---

18 Section 108. Unless the dismissal is for an inadmissible reason such as unlawful discrimination, pregnancy, trade union membership or activities, whistleblowing etc when no service qualification is required.
19 Employment Rights Act 1996, section 98 provides for conduct, capability, redundancy, illegality and some other substantial reason as the five potentially fair reasons for dismissal.
20 The ACAS Code of Practice on Disciplinary and Grievance Procedures 2004.
21 Section 3 requires employers to give employees a note specifying any disciplinary rules applicable to them or refer them to a document containing such rules and that document must be reasonably accessible.

conditions and size and location of the workplace. Whatever set of rules is eventually drawn up they should not be so general as to be meaningless.

- Rules should be set out clearly and concisely in writing and be readily available to all workers, for example in handbooks or on company Intranet sites. Management should make every effort to ensure that all workers know and understand the rules including those whose first language is not English or who have a disability or impairment (for example the inability to read). This may best be achieved by giving every worker a copy of the rules and explaining them orally. In the case of new workers this might form part of any induction programme. It is also important that managers at all levels and worker representatives are fully conversant with the disciplinary rules and that the rules are regularly checked and updated where necessary.
- Workers should be made aware of the likely consequences of breaking disciplinary rules or failing to meet performance standards. In particular, they should be given a clear indication of the type of conduct, often referred to as gross misconduct, which may warrant summary dismissal (dismissal without notice).
- Summary is not necessarily synonymous with instant and incidents of gross misconduct will usually still need to be investigated as part of a formal procedure. Acts which constitute gross misconduct are those resulting in a serious breach of contractual terms and will be for organisations to decide in the light of their own particular circumstances. However, they might include the following:
  - bringing the employer into serious disrepute;
  - serious incapability whilst on duty brought on by alcohol or illegal drugs;
  - serious negligence which causes or might cause unacceptable loss, damage or injury;
  - serious infringement of health and safety rules.

As indicated earlier this list is not intended to be exhaustive.

RULES

The rules should be clearly spelt out and copies given to all employees with regular reminders and updates either in paper and/or electronic form.

The different rules relating to drugs can include:

- coming to work under the influence of illicit substances, addictive substances or being unfit for duty due to the taking of prescribed or OTC medications; 'addictive substances' can include glue sniffing or alcohol;
- being found in possession of illegal drugs or illicit substances;
- storing illicit substances in lockers, locker rooms or anywhere on company premises or in company vehicles;
- using illicit substances whilst at work or on company premises;
- dealing in or passing on for others' use illicit substances;
- aiding and abetting others in any of the above;
- failing to report any knowledge of or suspicion of any of the above;
- helping to cover up any of the above;
- failing to cooperate in any investigation into any of the above;

Email and intranet are useful means of disseminating and reminding employees of the company's rules and policies.

THE BURCHELL TEST

Case law such as BHS v Burchell[22] has established that an employer must satisfy a tribunal about three issues – a three-point test which must be satisfied before the tribunal will make a finding of fair dismissal. Firstly the employer must establish that they had a genuine belief in their reason for dismissal. Secondly, it must be shown that the employer had in their mind reasonable grounds upon which to sustain that belief. And, thirdly, the employer at the stage at which they formed that belief on those grounds, must have carried out as much investigation into the matter as was reasonable in all the circumstances of the case.

FAILING A DRUGS TEST

In drug-related cases, the employment tribunals appear to be unsympathetic to employees who either lie about their drug addiction in order to gain employment (Walton's case, see above) or those who flagrantly flout a policy that drug-taking is forbidden and that drug-takers will be dismissed.

In Sutherland v Sonat Offshore (UK) Inc[23], the EAT has endorsed the use of proper drug testing by employers and declared a dismissal of an employee in breach of this policy to be fair. The employer had used OMS Ltd to provide medical services and used OMS to provide drug-testing facilities and had tested the urine of one of their employees after his two-week shift off shore.

His contract of employment made it clear that possession of alcohol or narcotics whilst on a drilling unit or causing such items to be brought on to the unit or reporting for duty under the influence of an inebriated or drugged condition would be regarded as gross misconduct. In January 1991, Mr Sutherland had signed a notice that had made it clear that unauthorised possession or use of illegal substances, narcotics, alcohol or firearms was not permitted on Sonat's property as they posed a serious threat to the safety of the company's employees. Further the notice made it clear that employees agreed to the company conducting the drug testing and that any employee who refused to submit to testing would be subject to disciplinary action which could include summary dismissal.

OMS Ltd provided medical services to Sonat and conducted the drug screening.

Mr Sutherland's drug test proved positive showing the presence of cannabis and this was confirmed by further tests. Since he had obviously used the cannabis whilst off-shore, he was summarily dismissed.

He argued that traces of cannabis had been found in the specimen of one other employee but he had not been dismissed. However the traces were so small that OMS decided that they could have been attributable to passive smoking. The EAT held that the employer was entitled to rely upon the results of the test in dismissing Mr Sutherland. Although Mr Sutherland strenuously denied taking any drugs at all times, he never gave any explanation as to how the cannabis was present in his urine.

The tribunal was satisfied that the employer had conducted a thorough investigation by the use of the testing procedures which the company had set up. In a question which was so complex such as the detection of drugs, the employer was entitled to rely upon its medical advisors and the procedures which they had adopted. The company had not acted selectively in dismissing Mr Sutherland as it was 'entirely reasonable in the circumstances'

---

22   [1978] IRLR 379.
23   (S) EAT 186/93.

to dismiss Mr Sutherland. Mr Sutherland was not given any formal disciplinary hearing and even in light of this procedural flaw[24], but the EAT refused to accept that this rendered the dismissal unfair.

The EAT held the industrial tribunal was entitled to conclude that the urine sample obtained from Mr Sutherland showed the presence of cannabis to an extent which was not explicable by the persistence of traces of cannabis consumed prior to his last shift on the platform or by some means which did not involve the positive ingestion of the substance by him, such as passive smoking. That was a conclusion that Sonat was entitled to reach on the information before it.

Given the very clear terms of his contract and the importance that the company attached to the strict observance of those terms, it seemed to the EAT that this was a case in which the employer could legitimately have taken the view, from the time that the sample was confirmed as positive, that to hold a formal disciplinary hearing would serve no useful purpose.

Sonat had in fact communicated to Mr Sutherland and did give him an opportunity to offer an explanation. It had nevertheless been entitled to reject his protestation that the test result was an error. Although the EAT did not underestimate the importance of giving someone a chance, formally, to offer an explanation or defend himself, the tribunal was entitled to determine whether in the particular circumstances the failure to give such an explanation would lead to a conclusion that a dismissal was unfair.

There will be no cases from 1 October 2004 onwards where the failure to allow the employee the opportunity to explain himself will render the dismissal fair.

SAFETY-CRITICAL JOBS

Where the job involves safety-critical aspects, the employment tribunals are not sympathetic to those employees who fail drugs tests and are dismissed.

In Flockhart v Racal Services (Communications) Ltd[25], Racal also had a very strict policy on drugs which included the provision that anyone who tested positive would normally be dismissed. Miss Flockhart tested positive for drugs (cannabis). Her job entailed going trackside working as a telecommunications engineer. This meant that she would have to work on railway tracks, without safety cover, doing work which was safety critical. At her disciplinary hearing she argued that she had inhaled passive smoke from her boyfriend's reefers. When the medical evidence disproved this argument (the amount found in her bloodstream was too high), she sought to bring evidence from friends that her boyfriend must have spiked her food maliciously. She was dismissed.

The EAT held that this was a fair dismissal and approved the argument of the company's counsel that members of the public would think it odd if an employer was held to have unfairly dismissed an employee who had tested positive for drugs, particularly in an industry in which safety was critical.

---

24 From 1 October 2004 under the Employment Act 2002 a basic disciplinary procedure has to be followed. This basic procedure consists of a letter to the employee stating the nature of the alleged offence and the basis of the employer's belief that he has committed such an offence; a hearing at which the employee will have a right to be accompanied by a fellow worker or TU representative and following the hearing, written reasons as to why the decision has been made and a right of appeal if requested. Dismissal when failing to comply with this procedure will render the employer liable to pay increased compensation.

25 EAT/701/00.

In Ireland v South West Trains[26], Mr Ireland, a guard, was dismissed when he failed a drugs test. The employer had an automatic dismissals policy for staff in safety-critical jobs who failed a drugs test. He tested positive for cannabis and benzodiazepines. At his disciplinary hearing Mr Ireland argued that his food must have been spiked. He was dismissed. The EAT held that the dismissal was fair.

DRUG DEALING AS OPPOSED TO DRUG TAKING

Not surprisingly the courts take an even tougher line with allegations of drug dealing and it will very rare that an employer who dismisses for drug dealing (following a fair procedure) will be found to have unfairly dismissed that individual. Even if unfair dismissal is found on a technical or procedural point, re-instatement or re-engagement will not be an appropriate remedy for the employment tribunals to order.

In Wood Group Heavy Industrial Turbines Ltd v Crossan[27], Mr Crossan, a long-serving employee, was dismissed following allegations that he had used and dealt in drugs at his workplace. Whilst the employer's investigation was found to be inadequate[28] (the third point of the test in BHS v Burchell, see footnote 13), the employers had satisfied the tribunal that it had a genuine belief in its reasons for dismissal. In such a case an Order for re-engagement was wholly inappropriate held the employment appeal tribunal.

PROFESSIONALS AND DRUG TAKING

Professionals such as doctors and pharmacists who have access to dangerous drugs are dealt with particularly harshly by the employment tribunals when they are found to have abused drugs.

In Stentiford v Goodalls Chemists, Miss Stentiford was a trainee dispenser who, anxious about her weight, obtained prescriptions for amphetamines by deception. When her employers found out they sought the advice of their professional association, discussed her behaviour with her but took the decision to dismiss. The dismissal was found to be fair by the EAT either on the grounds of misconduct or for 'some other substantial reason' for breaching the trust and confidence between herself and her employers.

The clear implication of this decision is that scientific evidence of drug testing is to be regarded in certain circumstances as analogous to these cases. The tribunal in this case readily accepted that the procedures adopted by the testing company were 'as near-fail safe as was humanly possible'.

Doctors have been struck off for drug taking and supplying drugs. The General Medical Council (GMC)[29] has found doctors guilty of serious professional misconduct when abuse of drugs has been in issue.

Teachers who are in a position of influence over children are also dealt with harshly by the employment tribunals when drugs offences are in issue. In Norfolk County Council v

---

26   [2002] ALL ER 180.
27   [1998] IRLR 680.
28   The employer found evidence of collusion and conspiracy amongst some of the witnesses and some evidence that the witnesses were 'out to get' Mr Crossan because of unrelated incidents in another part of the factory, yet made no attempt to assess or investigate this further. Rather they preferred to use the witness statements at face value and dismiss Mr Crossan.
29   Dr Michael Thear-Graham v GMC (1999) Privy Council 14/4/99.

Bernard[30] the EAT held that a drama teacher's dismissal was fair when he was dismissed for possessing and growing cannabis following his conviction. The EAT held that the Council was correctly fearful of its reputation and credibility if it continued to employ Mr Bernard following his conviction for drugs offences.

Whilst it does not follow that it is automatically fair to dismiss a teacher following a conviction of this nature, if the facts of the case can support the argument that any reasonable employer would and could have made the same or similar decision[31], dismissal can ensue.

RANGE OF REASONABLE RESPONSES

The correct test in determining whether an employer's decision to dismiss is fair or not is the test of 'range of reasonable responses' (see footnote 31).

In Foley and Madden's cases, the Court of Appeal held that 'in cases where there is room for reasonable disagreement among reasonable employers as to whether dismissal for the particular misconduct is a reasonable or an unreasonable response, it is helpful for the tribunal to consider "the range of reasonable responses"'. In other words: would any reasonable employer have adopted the same response as this employer?

An extreme example of the tribunals' approach to drug taking can be seen in the EAT's decision in Mathewson v RB Wilson Dental Laboratories[32] where a dental lab technician responsible for polishing chrome dentures was dismissed after he had been picked up by the police at lunchtime waiting at a bus stop, in possession of cannabis. He was subsequently charged and convicted of possessing cannabis.

A Scottish industrial tribunal found by a majority that his dismissal had been fair because the employer genuinely believed that it could no longer continue to employ a skilled worker who 'used drugs', could influence the younger workers and was an admitted user of illegal drugs. The EAT sitting in Scotland found no error of law in upholding the employer's decision as reasonable given the employee's involvement in illegal drug taking, the involvement of the police, the admission that he purchased and was in possession of cannabis, the possible influence over younger members of staff and the suitability of employing someone in his position. The EAT upheld the tribunal's view that this decision fell within the range of reasonable responses that a reasonable employer might have adopted.

It is doubtful whether a similar decision would be reached in 2005, particularly given the 'downgrading' of cannabis to a Class C drug. Nevertheless it stands as good law until overturned.

CONCEALING THE IDENTITY OF WITNESSES

What does an employer do when witnesses are prepared to make statements but request anonymity as to their identity ?

In Asda Stores Ltd v Thompson and others[33] an interesting issue concerning the

---

30   [1979] IRLR 220.
31   The 'range of reasonable responses' test laid down in Post Office v Foley and HSBC Bank plc (formerly Midland Bank plc) v Madden [2000] IRLR 827.
32   [1988] IRLR 512.
33   [2002] IRLR 245.

disclosure of witness statements to the employees to be dismissed was aired in the Employment Appeal Tribunal.

In this case Mr Thompson, a manager at Asda Stores, was dismissed following allegations that he had used and supplied illegal Class A drugs (cocaine) at two company-organised events. Two other managers were also implicated and were similarly dismissed. The Company had taken evidence from various employees whose allegations had formed the basis of the decision to dismiss. The evidence had however never been shown to Mr Thompson or the other two managers who were dismissed.

At a preliminary hearing the employment tribunal ordered the employer to disclose the witness statements in their totality to the ex-employees. The employer appealed against the order, arguing that they had guaranteed confidentiality and anonymity to those witnesses.

The EAT held that the employment tribunal had been wrong to order the witness statements to be disclosed in their totality. Documents can be

> anonymised or redacted (adapted or edited) in order to conceal the identity of the witnesses and maintain the employer's promise of confidentiality to those making the statements...In investigating complaints where hard drugs are involved, it is an entirely proper procedure for an employer to give a promise of confidentiality and one which the tribunal should maintain. Nothing should be disclosed which in any way identifies the makers of any of the statements unless they specifically agree to be identified...

TRIBUNALS' ATTITUDE TO RANDOM TESTING

Whilst it may go against a strictly ethical policy on drugs testing and is not recommended practice supported by the Faculty of Occupational Medicine, random testing has not fallen foul of employment protection legislation.

The tribunals and the employment appeal tribunal have upheld the 'legality' of random drugs testing in spite of powerful arguments that this may breach Article 8 of the Human Rights Convention[34], the right to respect for privacy.

In O'Flynn v Airlinks[35] the EAT upheld an employment tribunal's ruling that the dismissal of Miss O'Flynn was fair after she failed a random drugs test. She was a customer care assistant helping manoeuvre coaches and serving hot drinks on moving coaches. Her company had a zero-tolerance drugs policy and every year randomly tested 10 per cent of its workforce. When she was selected for a random test she admitted having taken cocaine and cannabis at weekends. She tested positive and was dismissed.

The EAT considered the impact of the Human Rights Act 1998, Article 8 and whether such a zero-tolerance drugs policy was an unlawful interference with a person's private life. The EAT held that:

> So far as the company's policy rules were concerned, an employee was, on the face of things,

---

34 Human Rights Act 1998, Article 8, the right to respect for a person's privacy, family life and correspondence. The Human Rights Act 1998 is only directly applicable to public sector bodies so employees working for employers in the private sector cannot bring claims under this Act. However since the employment tribunals and courts are public bodies they are required to consider the Human Rights Act 1998 when making their decisions.

35 EAT/02/0269/01.

free in his or her own time to take as much or as little of whatever substances he or she pleased. The company's rules engaged only when, so far as is relevant, an employee tested positive at work or reported for work with drugs in his or her system or refused to take the test whilst at work. We say 'at work' as there is nothing to suggest the company had any means to test other than whilst an employee was at work and the only test of which there was evidence was one at work on a Monday morning. In what one might call true private life outside work an employee could indulge as much as he or she might wish, subject to the constraint to the criminal law, and the company's policies only bit on the employee at work.

It is thus difficult to see how the policy entrenched upon Miss O'Flynn's private life save to the limited extent of her being required to provide a sample of urine as part of an established and unopposed random screening process and save also to the extent that the company's policy and the practical effects of the testing process inescapably meant that no drugs having certain persistent detectable characteristics could be taken by employees in their private time without probably jeopardising employment...

Appendices

1 Shell International: Drug and Alcohol Policy

Michael Forbes

Introduction

The requirement for a drug and alcohol policy was highlighted to all industrial companies by the Exxon Valdez tanker disaster – this major oil spill had devastating effects on the local Alaskan fishing communities and presented Exxon with horrific financial and reputation issues to deal with.

Shell is a similar major international oil company, and managing the risks associated with drugs and alcohol consumption by its employees has been a vital activity of the HR, HSE and health divisions of the company. The work sites of the company vary from normal office situations to high risk areas such as offshore exploration and production platforms, tankers and refineries and chemical plants. The drug and alcohol policy is designed to cover all such sites, but elements of it (for example, with cause testing) are focused on the what are judged to be the safety sensitive sites. The policy is designed to be robust yet humane, and requires of the employees to be honest and to seek help if they find they are becoming addicted.

It was put together and introduced after extensive consultation and education within the company, and this paved the way for a smooth launch. Its benefits were soon seen in the UK North Sea sector, where helicopter evacuations from offshore rigs for alcohol withdrawal symptoms decreased significantly. Employees became very aware of the consequences of excess alcohol consumption, and altered their drinking habits to avoid the risk of suffering DTs on the 'dry' offshore installations.

Confidentiality is a most important aspect of the policy, especially when employees are encouraged to admit to their addiction and seek help. This can prove a delicate matter in areas where there is a strict cultural taboo and somewhat draconian laws exist governing drugs and alcohol consumption (the Middle East for example). Some of these countries call for automatic notification of such problems to the local authorities, so management of drug and alcohol cases in these areas is very difficult. Other areas, such as the Yemen or Bolivia, where the chewing of qhat or coke leaves is seen as a cultural norm, require extensive consultation and discussion with the local workforce in order to promote the benefits of introducing a proper drug and alcohol policy.

Closer to home the occupational health aspects of the incoming UK Data Protection Act are going to make companies rethink their drug and alcohol policies if these include pre employment or random testing in benign office situations. The emphasis of the new Act is on demonstrating impairment, rather than looking for unseen cases of drugs or alcohol users. This might be seen as a retrograde step, as the ever-present threat of random testing does have a preventitive effect on the workforce.

As with all fields of medicine, prevention is always better than cure, and money spent on prevention is very much more effective in cutting abuse than the huge funds that are required to put individuals through a month of detoxification therapy and the ensuing rehabilitation process.

In Shell the drug and alcohol policy is seen as a fundamental part of the conditions of employment – it is well accepted, and the occasional employee who seeks help under the scheme is expected to sign a drugs and alcohol abstinence contract as part of the rehabilitation programme. This can lead to dismissal in the case of persistent failure to meet the terms of the contract, but in our experience it provides a very real stimulus to the employee to stay off drugs of addiction.

We have to keep up with local legislation wherever we operate, and the drug and alcohol policy is a prominent part of the health and safety management of all our operations.

Following are extracts from some of the key documents concerning Shell's policy on drugs and alcohol:

Section 1 – Contracts of employment and main employment policies

APPENDIX 4 – ALCOHOL AND DRUG ABUSE POLICY STATEMENT

Purpose

The Company recognises that an employee's state of health may affect his/her ability to perform his/her job, may restrict the kind of work he/she can perform and may affect his/her future employability. The Company also recognises that alcohol and drug abuse rank as major health problems world-wide. This statement of policy is to inform employees of the Company's viewpoint on physical or behavioural disorders resulting from use of drugs or alcohol, to encourage an enlightened attitude towards these disorders and to provide guidelines for consistent handling, throughout the Company, of problems resulting from alcohol and drug use. The Company's specific rules in respect of alcoholic drinks and drugs are detailed in Section 8.22, Clauses 10 and 11. Notwithstanding these rules the following applies.

Policy

The Company will give the same consideration to employees with dependencies on alcohol and/or drugs as it does to employees having any other disease. The Company is concerned only with those situations where the use of alcohol or drugs interferes with the employee's health, safety or job performance, adversely affects the job performance of other employees or is considered to be so serious as to be detrimental to the Company's business. The Company will not intrude in the private lives of employees.

In order to achieve successful treatment and rehabilitation and a return to productive employment with minimal disruption to personal, family and social life, it is most important that problems due to dependencies on alcohol and/or drugs are recognised early. The Company will assist an employee to obtain effective treatment and an employee who conscientiously seeks such help, will not place his or her job in jeopardy by doing so. The normal Company benefits which apply to any illness will be available to such an employee. The Medical Department or Medical Adviser will assist in arranging treatment, and necessary absence from work will be regarded as sick leave.

Legal drugs

An employee may have legal access to drugs which might impair his/her work performance or create a risk of accidents. These would include alcohol and some drugs prescribed for an employee by a doctor. An employee is prohibited from work whilst his or her work performance is affected by them. Where prescribed drugs cause impairment, it is in the best interests of the employee, his/her colleagues and the Company that he/she be given sick leave.

Illegal drugs

For the purpose of this policy, illegal drugs are those drugs which cannot be obtained by legal means or drugs which are legally obtainable but which have been obtained by illegal means. This includes all forms of narcotics, stimulants, tranquillisers and hallucinogens whose sale, purchase, transfer, use or possession is prohibited or restricted. Employees are prohibited from being on or arriving at Company premises whilst under the effects of such drugs.

Screening

All prospective employees are medically examined before being accepted for permanent employment. All pre-employment medicals include testing for drug residues and evidence of alcohol abuse. These measures have been introduced to screen out prospective employees with drug or alcohol dependency problems. Employees, and particularly those working in high risk jobs, may be required from time to time to submit to a random urine drug screen. Such a procedure will form an integral part of accident or 'near-miss' investigations and may be requested by Management or the Medical Division in situations which give cause for concern.

SECTION 8.22

10. Alcoholic drinks

Inability to perform one's duties at work satisfactorily as a result of an excess of alcoholic liquor is gross misconduct and will normally lead to dismissal.

Alcohol is not normally available or consumed on Company premises during working hours up to 5 p.m.

Company celebrations, during the working day such as long service lunches or Christmas parties are not, however, subject to blanket prohibition, and there may also be exceptional business occasions at which it is appropriate to provide hospitality in the form of alcoholic drinks.

Any alcohol supplied at such Company-sponsored entertainment during the day requires the advance approval of the responsible Division Head.

Notwithstanding the foregoing the Company recognises that dependency on alcohol is an illness and will treat it as such where the employee recognises the need for help and continues in an agreed programme of treatment (see Section 1 Appendix 4). Employees with this dependency should be encouraged to discuss their problem as early as possible so that they can receive help. Medical Division can provide professional advice on treatment and rehabilitation.

11. Drugs

The possession, use and selling or trafficking of illegal drugs or legal drugs obtained illegally on Company business or premises is gross misconduct and will normally lead to dismissal.

Notwithstanding the foregoing the Company recognises that dependency on drugs or other substances is an illness and will treat it as such where the employee with that dependency recognises the need for help and continues in an agreed programme of treatment (see Section 1 Appendix 4). Employees should be encouraged to discuss their problem as early as possible so that they can receive help. Medical Division can provide professional advice on treatment and rehabilitation.

Employees should also be alert to possible side effects of prescribed drugs or medication. These may generate a condition hazardous to the individual employee and/or others. The employee should be mindful of these possibilities and advise their Line Manager accordingly; the professional advice of the Medical Division may then be sought.

Questions and answers

WHAT IS THE PURPOSE OF THE DRUG AND ALCOHOL POLICY?

Shell in the UK is committed to providing a workplace that is safe in every sense and fully productive, so that everyone can carry on their jobs and fulfill their responsibilities unhindered. That means striving to ensure, among other things, that the workplace is free from the effects of what is commonly called substance abuse: the use of illegal drugs, the misuse of legal drugs or other substances, and the abuse of alcohol.

WHO IS COVERED BY THE POLICY?

The policy applies to all employees and contractors, but with particular emphasis on those who work at or visit safety sensitive sites and/or hold safety sensitive jobs where the consequences of drugs and alcohol abuse are greatest.

BUT WHAT I DO IN MY OWN TIME?

There is a belief that what people do outside working hours is their own concern and does not affect their working lives. But drugs and alcohol can continue to affect behaviour long after consumption. The Health and Safety at Work Act stresses that it is the responsibility of all employees to take care to protect themselves and others affected by their actions. This makes it a workplace issue too.

WHAT ARE THE KEY ELEMENTS OF THE POLICY?

There are five key elements; all employees are encouraged to read them as they form part of their terms and conditions of employment.

1. Standards of behaviour

- Employees should be fit and ready to carry out their work duties at all times.
- Except where authorised for special occasions, alcohol is not permitted during working hours on any Company sites. Some sites have also been designated alcohol free at all times.
- The misuse of legal drugs is prohibited, as is the use, possession, sale or distribution of illegal drugs.

2. Education and awareness

- Raising people's awareness of the effects of substance abuse is an essential step in encouraging those who have a dependency to recognise this and seek help, before it becomes a serious problem.
- Education is extremely important. Shell has medical advisers and occupational health units with readily available information and advice; drugs and alcohol awareness booklets and videos have been produced to increase awareness on the health issues involved.

3. Rehabilitation

- Shell is keen to help employees before a drugs or alcohol dependency affects work performance. Employees who believe they have a problem are encouraged to ask their Line Manager or Medical Adviser for support and advice.
- Drugs or alcohol dependency is recognised by the Company as an ill health condition; anyone who voluntarily discloses a dependance will be given assistance.
- The medical/occupational health department is available to offer help and advice and will assist in arranging rehabilitation treatment. It is not Company policy to provide, or pay for treatment.
- Rehabilitation could typically include medical assessment, counselling, treatment and follow-up procedures. This support will usually be tailored to the individual's needs and will be designed to achieve a sustained break from dependency.
- While the employee is away from work due to rehabilitation all usual Company benefits will apply under the sickness absence policy and normal medical confidentiality will be maintained.
- Following successful rehabilitation treatment the individual will be assessed and a decision will be taken by Line Management as to whether they can return to their previous position. If this is not advisable, alternative work will be sought. Where this is not available, medical severance may be considered.
- Following the individual's return to work, regular medical assessments, periodic, unannounced testing and follow-up counselling will be required, to ensure that the break from dependency is sustained. Continued substance abuse cannot be tolerated, failure to comply with a rehabilitation programme or its follow-up, or

failure of a periodic test will be regarded as serious misconduct. Serious misconduct will normally result in dismissal.

4. Objectives measures

Additional measures beyond clear standards, education, awareness and support for individuals with a problem are required to ensure a drugs- and alcohol-free workplace. The following two aspects of the policy apply if an employee works at or visits a safety-sensitive location, or has a designated safety-sensitive job.

a. 'With cause' testing

- Undertaken where there is good reason to test for evidence of substance abuse, such as a particular incident, abnormal behaviour or appearance, or absence problems.
- Testing procedures are designed for accuracy and confidentiality and will be carried out with the individual's consent. However, the failure of an individual to consent to the 'with cause' test will be considered as serious misconduct.
- An individual is deemed to have failed the test if the presence of drugs or alcohol in the blood streams exceeds the limit set by the Company as an appropriate standard for judging impairment. For alcohol this limit is defined as 80mg% blood alcohol content, which is the same as that which would lead to prosecution under the Road Traffic Act. The cut-off levels for drugs are designed to identify levels of drug metabolites in the system which demonstrate active drug use.
- If the analysis produces a positive result, the medical adviser will discuss this with the individual to ascertain whether a legitimate medical reason exists, such as the consumption of drugs as prescribed by the doctor or bought legitimately over the counter.
- If there is no legitimate reason then a positive result will be recorded and the Line Manager and the individual will be advised accordingly. This will be treated as serious misconduct.

b. Searching

- Searches are used as a means of safeguarding the workplace from the potential risks of drugs or alcohol abuse.
- A search may be conducted where there is good reason to believe that drugs or alcohol have been brought to the workplace or are in an individual's possession. Searches might include personal effects, desks, lockers and other Company property.
- The failure of an individual to consent to a search will be considered as serious misconduct.
- The discovery of drugs or alcohol will be regarded as serious misconduct.

5. Prescribed drugs

It is worth noting that prescribed drugs or medications, taken as treatment for a health condition, can also have possible side effects or cause impaired performance. It is the employee's responsibility to advise the medical/occupational health department or their Line Manager if they are taking prescribed drugs, so that further professional advice can be sought if appropriate.

And finally…

If you have any questions on the policy talk to your Line Manager. We must all ensure that the workplace is free from the damaging effects of drugs and alcohol. Shell Companies are determined to fulfil their obligations in this respect, but we need your help to succeed.

This Factfile applies to regional employees of Shell Companies in the UK and is for general guidance only. The detailed provisions of the policies and procedures of Shell Companies in the U.K. are set out in the Personnel Policy and Practice Manual which, together with other information, is available from your Personnel/ HR Unit.

2 British Airways: Drug and Alcohol Policy

Raj Gakhal

BA News

- British Airways is reinforcing its commitment to safety by introducing drug and alcohol testing for all UK staff.
- From August, BA staff suspected of breaking the already strict rules could be tested if they are suspected of being under the influence while on duty or if drugs or alcohol could have been the cause of a workplace accident.
- A random test can be done in the first six months of employment.
- Anyone returning to work after drug or alcohol rehabilitation can also be tested randomly.
- There will be more support available for employees who may have a problem with drink or drugs. The airline is encouraging anyone who needs help to come forward before the new policy goes live in the summer.
- Testing is an addition to the airline's existing policy that states staff must not be impaired by drugs or alcohol when they are at work.
- The move follows the introduction of new UK safety legislation earlier this year that gives police the power to breathalyse on-duty flight and cabin crew and licensed aircraft engineers if they suspect legal alcohol limits have been exceeded. BA's policy covers all UK mainline staff.
- The following is taken from an article in *British Airways News* in Autumn 2004:

  Breaches of the rules are rare but even one incident is too many. For those who are in breach we will have a definitive test. Testing reinforces our absolute commitment to safety, which is our number one priority.

  There is help available for anyone who thinks they may have a problem with drugs or alcohol. BA Health Services will offer confidential support and treatment with a view to helping people back to work.

- Testing is common in many other safety-critical industries, such as the rail, chemical and nuclear sectors.
- The alcohol limit for all ground staff will be the current UK drink drive limit of 80mg of alcohol per 100ml of blood.
- The use of controlled drugs is prohibited for all staff.
- A breathalyser will be used to test for alcohol and a urine sample for drugs.

- The Railways and Safety Transport Act, which became law in 2003, sets a tighter alcohol limit for flying staff of 20mg of alcohol per 100ml of blood, which is virtually zero. It makes it a criminal offence for flying staff and licensed engineers to be over the limits when they are working.
- Anyone can raise a concern about a possible breach of the rules with a manager who can then decide if it is appropriate to initiate a test.
- A positive test – or refusal to take a test – would result in disciplinary action and could lead to dismissal from the airline.
- The tests will be carried out by an external company, which has facilitates to test in the UK and in some locations overseas.
- All BA staff must comply with local laws governing drugs and alcohol when they are outside the UK. The airline's strict rules for flight crew governing alcohol consumption before duty remain, as do all regulatory requirements covering flying staff and licensed engineers.

Questions and answers

WHY IS DRUG AND ALCOHOL TESTING BEING INTRODUCED?

Strengthening our drug and alcohol policy to include testing demonstrates our over-riding commitment to the highest safety standards, in the air and on the ground.

Breaches of the rule are rare but even one incident is too many.

Testing is commonplace in other safety-critical sectors, such as the rail, chemical and nuclear industries. Some US carriers have had testing policies for some time.

Testing is an addition to our existing policy but for those in breach there is now a definitive test.

ARE FLYING STAFF AND LICENSED AIRCRAFT ENGINEERS COVERED BY BA'S POLICY?

Yes, they are covered by BA's policy and current legal or regulatory requirements.

BA's policy is in addition to the Railways and Transport Safety Act 2003 that makes it a criminal offence for flight crew, cabin crew, licensed aircraft engineers and air traffic controllers to be over prescribed alcohol limits at work.

The law was introduced in 2003 and gives police the power to conduct tests if they believe the limit has been exceeded.

WHY ARE OFFICE-BASED STAFF INCLUDED IN THE POLICY?

We have a strong safety culture and we believe it is right for us to have a common approach to drugs and alcohol for all our staff.

We have had a drug and alcohol policy for some time that states no employee should be at work if they are impaired by drugs or by alcohol. Testing is an addition to this policy and, again, all employees are included.

The policy also sets out the support British Airways will offer to employees who need help with drug or alcohol problems. This is available to all staff.

HOW WILL I KNOW IF I AM OVER THE LIMIT?

The revised policy sets the alcohol limit for ground and office staff at 80mg of alcohol per 100ml of blood – this is the same as the current UK drink drive limit. Flight Crew and Cabin Crew must not exceed 20mg of alcohol per 100ml of blood.

Flying staff and licensed engineers must also adhere to legal requirements under the Railways and Transport Safety Act 2003 and all existing airline and regulatory requirements governing the use of alcohol before and during duty.

The Department for Transport advice on the UK drink drive limit states:

> 'There is no failsafe guide as to how much you can drink and stay under the limit. The amount and type of alcoholic drink and your weight, sex, age and metabolism will all play their part. The quantity of alcohol in a half-pint of beer is approximately the same as in a pub measure of port/sherry or a small glass of wine.

> But:

> * Many beers and wines are stronger than average.
> * Drinks poured at home are usually more generous than pub measures.
> * Cocktails and alco-pops are very strong; their high alcoholic content is often masked by the taste of fruit juice.'

WHO IS COVERED BY BA'S POLICY?

The drug and alcohol policy covers all British Airways UK mainline staff when they are on duty in the UK or overseas.

In addition, all staff must comply with local laws governing drug and alcohol consumption when they are outside the UK. These local laws may be more stringent than the BA policy. This includes submitting to a test if required to do so by the relevant authority.

Flying staff and licensed engineers must continue to adhere to all existing airline and regulatory or legislative requirements.

Index